unlocking

the
business
environment

John Brinkman Liverpool Hope University

Ilva Navarro Bateman Liverpool Hope University

Donna Harper Liverpool Hope University

Caroline Hodgson University of Lincoln

HODDER
EDUCATION
AN HACHETTE UK COMPANY

First published in Great Britain in 2010 by
Hodder Education, An Hachette UK Company,
338 Euston Road, London NW1 3BH

Hachette UK's policy is to use papers that are natural, renewable and
recyclable products and made from wood grown in sustainable forests.
The logging and manufacturing processes are expected to conform to the
environmental regulations of the country of origin.

The advice and information in this book are believed to be true and
accurate at the date of going to press, but neither the author[s] nor the publisher
can accept any legal responsibility or liability for any errors or omissions.

British Library Cataloguing in Publication Data
A catalogue record for this book is available from the British Library

Library of Congress Cataloging-in-Publication Data
A catalog record for this book is available from the Library of Congress

ISBN: 978 0 340 94207 9

1 2 3 4 5 6 7 8 9 10

Typeset in 10/13pt ITC Stone Sans by Servis Filmsetting Ltd, Stockport, Cheshire
Printed in Great Britain for Hodder Education, an Hachette UK Company,
338 Euston Road, London, NW1 3BH by The MPG Books Group, Bodmin and King's Lynn

What do you think about this book? Or any other Hodder Education title?
Please send your comments to educationenquiries@hodder.com

www.hoddereducation.com

Contents

Features Guide

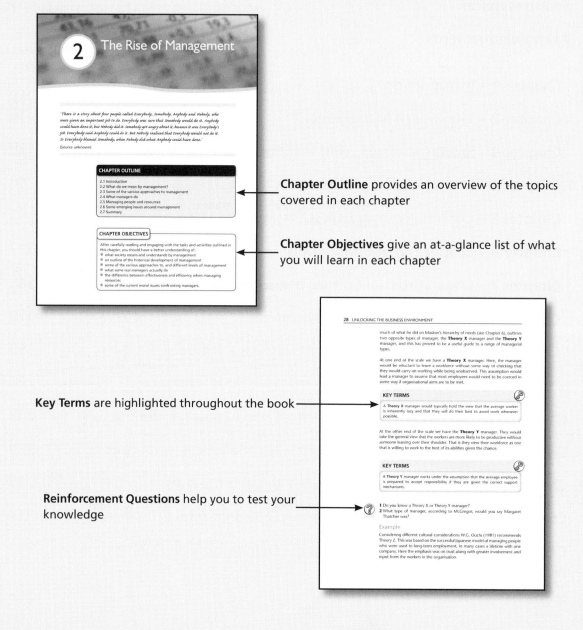

Chapter Outline provides an overview of the topics covered in each chapter

Chapter Objectives give an at-a-glance list of what you will learn in each chapter

Key Terms are highlighted throughout the book

Reinforcement Questions help you to test your knowledge

Artworks and photographs illustrate each chapter and help to explain key ideas and concepts

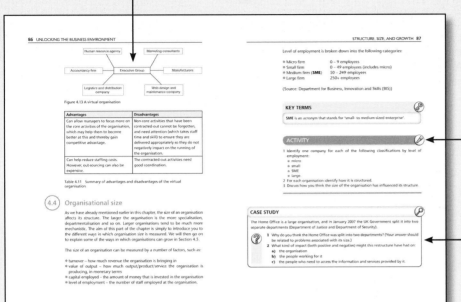

Activities provide more practical tasks to reinforce your learning

Case Study boxes include real-life examples to put your learning in context

Reflective Questions suggest ideas for further discussion and consideration

Recommended Reading helps you to explore topics in greater detail

Useful Websites allow you to access more information online

References provide full details of the sources used in each chapter

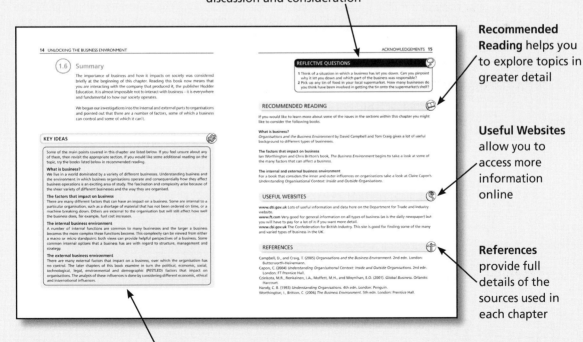

Key Ideas tables summarise the important points from each chapter

Acknowledgements

The authors and publishers would like to thank the following for use of copyrighted material in this volume:

Figure 1.1 © AGStockUSA/Alamy; Figure 1.2 Dan Kitwood/Getty Images; Figure 1.3 © Chris Mattison/Alamy; Figure 2.1 Peter Macdiarmid/Getty Images; Figure 2.2 Matthew Peters/Manchester United/Getty Images; Figure 2.4 © David Pearson/Alamy; Figure 3.3 Eden, C. and Ackerman, F. (1998) Making Strategy: The journey of strategic management. London: Sage; Figure 4.1 © Bart Pro/Alamy; Figure 4.3 © purestockX. com; Figure 6.1 © Sandro Vannini/Corbis; Figure 6.4 © Bruce Petty, reproduced with permission; Figure 6.5 Cate Gillon/Getty Images; Figure 7.1 © Glowimages RM/Alamy; Figure 7.3 © Rodger Tamblyn/Alamy; Figure 8.2 © Vasiliki Varvaki / iStockphoto.com; Figure 8.4 © kristian sekulic/ iStockphoto.com; Figure 8.5 © EschCollection Prime/ Alamy; Figure 9.1 © StephenBarnes Northern Ireland Politics/Alamy; Figure 9.2 © ni press photos/Alamy; Figure 9.3 © Jon Arnold Images Ltd/Alamy; Figure 9.4 © Shen Hong/XinHua/Xinhua Press/Corbis; Figure 10.1 Alex Wong/Getty Images; Figure 10.2 © Christophe Karaba/epa/Corbis; Figure 11.1 © webphotographeer / iStockphoto. com; Figure 11.2 Crown copyright material is reproduced with the permission of the Controller of HMSO; Figure 11.4 Crown copyright material is reproduced with the permission of the Controller of HMSO; Figure 11.5 Crown copyright material is reproduced with the permission of the Controller of HMSO; Figure 11.6 Crown copyright material is reproduced with the permission of the Controller of HMSO; Figure 12.1a Mary Evans Picture Library; Figure 12.1b Keystone/Getty Images; Figure 12.1c © Andresr/ iStockphoto.com; Figure 12.2 © Toshiyuki Aizawa/Reuters/Corbis; Figure 12.3 Haruyoshi Yamaguchi/Bloomberg/Getty Images; Figure 13.2 Alastair Grant/AFP/ Getty Images; Figure 13.3 ©vgstudio – Fotolia.com; Figure 13.4 © Andrew Holbrooke/ Corbis; Figure 14.1 © Geoff Caddick/epa/Corbis; Figure 14.2 © Nuno Andre Ferreira/ epa/Corbis; Figure 14.4 © Mark Baigent/Alamy; Figure 15.1 Crown copyright material is reproduced with the permission of the Controller of HMSO; Figure 15.2 Crown copyright material is reproduced with the permission of the Controller of HMSO; Figure 15.3 Gareth Fuller/PA Archive/Press Association Images; Figure 15.4 Crown copyright material is reproduced with the permission of the Controller of HMSO; Figure 15.5 Crown copyright material is reproduced with the permission of the Controller of HMSO; Figure 15.6 © ICP/Alamy; Figure 15.7 Crown copyright material is reproduced with the permission of the Controller of HMSO; Figure 15.8 Crown copyright material is reproduced with the permission of the Controller of HMSO.

Case study on pages 183–85 © The Times 2004/nisyndication.com; Table 11.1 on page 246 reproduced under the terms of the Click-Use Licence; Table 11.2 on page 250 Crown copyright material is reproduced with the permission of the Controller of HMSO; Table 15.1 Crown copyright material is reproduced with the permission of the Controller of HMSO; Table 15.2 on page 351 Crown copyright material is reproduced with the permission of the Controller of HMSO

Every effort has been made to trace and acknowledge the ownership of copyright. The publishers will be glad to make suitable arrangements with any copyright holder whom it has not been possible to contact.

1 Introduction

CHAPTER OUTLINE

1.1 What is business?
1.2 The factors that impact on business
1.3 The internal business environment
1.4 The external business environment
1.5 How it all fits together
1.6 Summary

CHAPTER OBJECTIVES

After carefully reading and engaging with the tasks and activities outlined in this chapter, you should have a better understanding of:
- the impact that business has on society
- the fact that there are internal and external factors that affect how businesses operate
- the difference between descriptive, prescriptive and a critique
- the concepts of macro and micro analysis
- the coverage of each of the different chapters in the book.

1.1 What is business?

Look around you. Ignore living things. Can you see anything that has not been produced by business? Business is life, everything we have has been produced by a business: the clothes we wear, the road we walk on, the iPod we listen to our music on, the chocolate we eat, the book you are reading now, the chair you sit in, the canvas you paint on, the show you watch, etc. We live in a world dominated by business, from the giant conglomerate that can have a bigger financial base than some small countries, to the sole trader who may be reliant on one day's trading to simply survive to the next day.

Understanding business and the environment in which organisations operate and consequentially how they affect business operations is both fascinating and complex. Indeed this very complexity is what makes business such an exciting area of study. You will get much more out of your studies if, as in the opening quotation, you chew over and digest some of the ideas presented here, rather than simply reading through the text.

The fascination and complexity arise simply because of the sheer variety of different businesses and the way they are organised. This book explains and analyses business environments – **internal** and **external** – in a systematic and comprehensive manner but for now we will content ourselves with looking at a few different businesses.

KEY TERMS

A business can have many factors that affect how it operates. We refer to the factors that are contained within the business as the **internal environment** in which the business operates. There are also many factors that are external to an organisation but nonetheless have an impact on the business. We refer to these as the **external environment**.

For many people business means a large profit-making organisation, such as Tesco or British Petroleum (better known as BP), which have a variety of different internal departments, e.g. Finance, Human Resources and Marketing. However, this is only a small subset of the differing types of **organisations** that exist. In fact, the majority of UK businesses are classified as small (less than 10 employees) profit-making enterprises.

It should be clear by now that business is vital for the economy, and hence welfare, of us all. Getting it right is important as we increasingly face a

Figure 1.1 An industrial scene

KEY TERMS

Organisations are sets of people who are coordinated in order for them to achieve common goals.

One of the largest organisations in the world is the National Health Service, more usually referred to simply as the NHS, which is a large non-profit making business.

Given the rich variety of differing businesses it will be useful to have a working definition of what we mean when we use the term **business**.

By **business** we mean the organised effort that is required to produce services and goods that are required by society. Note that this includes profit- and non-profit concerns and ranges from a one-person business to a large business organisation.

world of limited resources. We are not prepared any more as a society to run a business at any cost, and many people are very concerned about environmental issues.

This concern for the environment is becoming more important for the success of business. This is one of a number of themes that run throughout the book, along with ethical issues, an international dimension and **critique of theory**.

KEY TERMS

A **critique of theory** is when we analyse, as opposed to simply accepting, the facts around a particular issue.

As an example of critiquing a recognised theory, imagine that you have been told that two hours per night is the optimum time for your revision when learning a new topic. However, how do you know that this is the best way for you? It could be that four hours per night is better, or perhaps only 30 minutes. By experimenting with different times, places, etc. you may come up with an alternative theory. You could also investigate what is known scientifically about revision. Then you would have some evidence to challenge the idea that two hours per night is the optimum time. Arguing that two hours was too long without any evidence would not be a critique, instead, it would be a **subjective** opinion.

KEY TERMS

We say something is **subjective** when it is based more on personal opinions rather than hard facts. If we can manage to strip away our opinions and concentrate on what we know about something, rather than what we think we may know, then we say we are taking an **objective** view.

Businesses are under increasing pressure from different groups such as environmental and consumer groups to behave in a way that considers the consequences of their actions. The simplicity of working to the profit ideal alone is no longer accepted fully throughout society. Added to this, the impact of globalisation on all businesses of all sizes throughout the UK has introduced new challenges to the way in which businesses operate.

As well as explaining and analysing the business environments, we will attempt to demonstrate the complexity of the issues involved by offering a critique of theory and considering the pros and cons (i.e. the advantages and disadvantages) of arguments presented. To this end we will offer a range of further reading at the end of each chapter should you wish to delve deeper into a particular topic area that may have caught your interest. You will have noticed the quotation by Francis Bacon at the start of the chapter. This is a book that is best chewed over and digested.

The factors that impact on business

There are numerous different parts and processes that organisations require as they seek to conduct their business. Most of us will never actually engage with many of them although we may well hear about them (The Bank of England raising the base rate, for example). We may not even be aware of some of the different functions of organisations (you probably went through your last school without a thought about the school's finance officer) and some we know of but only have limited contact with (e.g. the finance department of a business you work for would supply details of your pay).

Each of the various parts of a business have internal factors that they need to take account of – this is the subject of the next section (1.3) and up to the end of Chapter 7. The factors that are external to a business form the subject of Section 1.4, and from Chapter 8 onwards.

CASE STUDY

Toyota, the Japanese car company, is viewed by many business experts as the ideal automobile company. This is not simply because of the quality of its cars but more because of the way they have become, from relatively humble beginnings, a car company that competes on even terms with two of the biggest automobile rivals, the Ford Motor Company and General Motors (GM). In fact, Ford and GM are two of many organisations that have tried to replicate Toyota's 'lean manufacturing' method.

Lean manufacturing has helped Toyota to develop products more quickly than its competitors. In 2006 they could build a new car in 29 hours, while GM took 33 hours. At the same time, Toyota has maintained its reputation for the quality of their car build.

Using lean manufacturing was a decision that Toyota took with regard to its own operation. Hence this is something they have control over, and so is part of their internal environment. However, even though Toyota are leaders in their field they need to be aware of the external environment and how it may affect them. An example of this is the increasing price of fuel that may affect future car sales.

Other threats from the external environment to Toyota's success could be a rise in car tax, inability to source the materials needed to build its cars (steel prices rising substantially for example). The internal environment may be affected by a new technology introduced that does not function properly, changes in the management structure, or perhaps an internal union dispute.

1.3) The internal business environment

A number of internal functions are common to many businesses. The larger a business becomes the more complex these functions become. For example, a small firm of 20 employees may have one accountant, whereas a larger firm may have a whole department dedicated to dealing with its finances. Chapter 4, *Structure, Size and Growth* deals with this in more detail.

This book will often take a **macro** view of an organisation when looking at the internal and external environment and then focus on the **micro** view as we look in more detail at different parts of a business.

KEY TERMS

Macro is a term used when we are trying to get an overview of what is going on, as this chapter is doing for this book (sometimes referred to as 'the bigger picture'). A **micro** view is when we home in on the detail. For example, watching a horse race from the stands we would have a good view of the race (a macro view) but would not see the details of any individual horse. However, if we looked through a pair of binoculars at a particular horse (a micro view) we would see the horse in detail but probably miss what else was happening in the race.

Many big organisations have complex internal structures. However, most started out as small concerns. Chapter 4 illustrates this point with a look at Cadbury's, the large multinational chocolate company. In Chapter 4 you are introduced to the various ways in which businesses choose to organise themselves. There are a number of ways and each has advantages and disadvantages. The chapter expands on a number of these themes.

Our macro view of an organisation is broken down into the various internal functions that make a business what it is (our micro view of each part). We consider different sizes of organisations, the various structures used, the stakeholders, the strategies employed, how organisations communicate internally, cultural differences, motivation, and management and leadership issues.

Of course, businesses need organising and in most organisations this role falls to the manager. We take a closer look at the role of the manager and how it has evolved in Chapter 2, *The Rise of Management*. Management is about making the best use of available resources to meet an organisations requirement. This is in fact a good place to start our look at the internal organisation. Someone needs to organise the business activities, no matter what they are or how many people they employ.

The word 'management' raises an interesting issue: is there a difference between leadership and management? We consider this in Chapter 6, *Leadership and Motivation*. As we shall see there is not as much clarity about leadership as there is about management.

We should make it clear here that this book describes business in general and so it is not **prescriptive**. If we felt that we could write the definitive management book that resolved all management issues then we would write it and retire! There are many books that make that claim. Unfortunately, most managers are still seeking out such a book. In fact, the German philosopher Karl Marx (1818–1883) famously made the comment that philosophers have so far only interpreted the world, the real achievement should be to change it!

KEY TERMS

We say something is **prescriptive** when it is offering advice on what you should do. The term 'descriptive' simply describes a situation without suggesting what could be done to improve it. Most of us can easily describe what is wrong, not as many can also prescribe a solution.

However, we do now know quite a lot about the role of the manager, which has not changed much over the last century. Research shows that it comes down to planning, organising, commanding, coordinating and control (See Chapter 2, Table 2.2).

Why the manager is planning, organising, commanding, coordinating and controlling is of course dependent on the objectives that the organisation is endeavouring to achieve. This is the subject of Chapter 3, *Strategy, Mission and Stakeholders*.

REFLECTIVE QUESTIONS

We often criticise an organisation for having no strategy. But do you have a personal strategy? That is, do you know where you want to be in the next two years, five years or ten years? Stop and reflect now on where and what you would like to be in ten years' time and check that what you are doing now, and in the next few years, will help you to reach that goal.

Clearly, businesses operate in structures that they hope will best suit their needs. As a business grows they often need to change an established structure to better match the organisation's requirements. The size of a business and how it is structured is the subject of Chapter 4, *Structure, Size, and Growth*.

CASE STUDY

In 2008 the British Airport Authority (BAA) opened up a new terminal, Terminal 5, at Heathrow Airport. This new terminal, which can handle an additional 30 million passengers a year, raises the total number of passengers passing through Heathrow each year to 90 million. This is a big increase in the size and structure for any airport but Heathrow is used to such changes. In 1946 Heathrow had only one terminal, which was an army surplus tent, and passengers made the short walk to the plane!

Figure 1.2 The Queen opening Terminal 5

The larger an organisation becomes the more difficult it is to ensure that all the parts of the organisation are working well together. One vital component of this is how the various units keep in touch with each other. This is the subject of Chapter 5, *Communicating Across Functions*.

One part of an organisation may be doing very well, but a lack of communication across departments may mean that the organisation suffers. Imagine that a production department has produced 15,000 components in a month instead of its usual 12,000. They may feel that this is quite an achievement. However, if the marketing and sales departments were not expecting this increase they would find it very difficult to sell the components. This in turn could lead to lack of storage space in the warehouse and cause other problems (for example, it may affect the amount of raw materials that could be ordered). It is vital that departments communicate effectively with each other across the organisation.

Chapter 7, *Organisational Culture and Change*, considers the effects that culture can have on an organisation. It begins by considering some of the cultural differences that make organisations unique and then assesses a number of reasons why organisations must always experience change and the difficulties associated with implementing change.

For many UK motorists the Jaguar car is seen as a symbol of British car expertise. However, although the cars are built in the UK the owners are not a UK company. In 2007, the company was sold to the American Ford Motor organisation. To the Jaguar car workers the change to becoming a Ford employee meant that they had to get used to the way that Ford operated, and they had to cope with a cultural change in their working patterns.

There was another culture change for Jaguar employees in 2008 when Ford sold Jaguar to the Indian automobile giant Tata Motors.

 ## 1.4 The external business environment

There are many factors that impact on a business over which the organisation has no control. Increases in fuel charges are a good example; another could be a shortage of a vital component that is no longer available.

Chapters 9 to 15 look at the external macro environment in which organisations operate. These chapters examine in turn the political, economic, social, technological, legal, environmental and demographic (PESTLED) factors that impact on organisations. The analysis of these influences is done at two levels. The first level considers the effect on organisations of current and future key economic influences. The second level considers how ethical and international dimensions now affect all businesses.

The very size and diversity of the external environment in which businesses operate ensures that we need to consider separately the particular segment of industry in which they do business. We refer to this as the operating environment and it is the subject of Chapter 8, *The External Micro Environment*.

For example, the large automobile industry interacts with a number of different suppliers, markets and countries. However, each car company's micro environment, their particular suppliers, markets and the countries in which they do business, is unique to them.

The first of the PESTLED factors, the political influences, is the subject of Chapter 9, *The Macro Environment – Political Influences.* Here we introduce a number of different examples that help to illustrate how businesses are influenced by the political environment in which they operate.

For businesses that operate on a global scale interesting ethical dilemmas can arise. What is viewed as unethical in the UK (offering and receiving bribes for example) is seen as normal practice in some countries.

Example

In June 2007, *The Guardian* newspaper reported that the UK company BAE Systems had paid Prince Bandar of Saudi Arabia more than one billion pounds in order to secure Britain's biggest ever arms contract. It also reported that this was done with the full knowledge of the Ministry of Defence.

The macro view of the environment is continued in Chapter 10, *The Macro Environment – Economic Influences*, by looking at what society means when we refer to the economy. A healthy and growing economy is one in which most businesses like to operate. There is more demand for goods and services from organisations and generally governments have more money to spend as the amount they are collecting in taxes rises.

Economic considerations are of course vital to any business. Organisations have to make choices, as do governments, about how they allocate the limited resources available to them. For many businesses this can mean success or failure. For example, you may be in business in a Barrow-in-Furness shipyard to supply submarines to the British Navy. A downturn in the UK economy would mean that the Chancellor of the Exchequer has less revenue from taxes to pay for all the submarines that were due to be built. This would not only affect the submarine building ship yard but also all the suppliers to that ship yard. Hence many businesses would be affected by something they had little control over.

People and organisations are heavily influenced by the conditions and attitudes that prevail at certain times. We refer to this as the socio-cultural environment. It has an effect on business, which is the subject of Chapter 11, *The Macro Environment – Socio-cultural Influences*. We take a closer look here at the trends and fashions that impact on businesses.

Example

Before the public knew about the harm to health caused by smoking and secondary smoking, smoking was very fashionable. However, in the UK smoking has now been banned in all enclosed spaces, something that would have been unthinkable only a few years ago. This changing trend has obviously meant that the tobacco industry has had to adapt its business to take account of the socio-cultural environment in which it operates.

Chapter 12, *The Macro Environment – Technological Influences* takes a close look at what we mean by technology and the influence this has had on business. Students often think that 'technology' refers to digital information technology, with computers and other electronic advances being the prime focus. But technology is to do with products and processes. For example, 200 years ago the world-famous waterfront at Liverpool was approximately 200 metres further back. The Liver Building was built on what was a wider river Mersey estuary. This was at the forefront of technological change and achievement at the time.

Figure 1.3 The Liver Building

The chapter also focuses on other areas of technological change such as the industrial revolution and the influences that technology has today on employment and the environment.

When Ken Livingstone, who was at the time the Mayor of London, introduced the congestion charge in inner London it was his legal authority as an elected representative that enabled him to act. There was significant opposition to this from many businesses who felt that they would be disadvantaged compared to other businesses outside the congestion zone, as those businesses would not incur this additional cost. An understanding of some of the legal issues that necessarily influence a business is the subject of Chapter 13, *The Macro Environment – Legal Influences*.

Not all legislation is negative for businesses. In London for example there is now a new business in collecting the congestion charge. Similarly, government laws and targets for refuse collection and recycling have provided opportunities for recycling and refuse sorting businesses.

Other legislation is concerned with the rights of employees and employers. It would be difficult, although not impossible, for an employee to be sacked for being off ill for a few days. If you are frequently late for work, however, an employer has the legal right to dismiss you. In fact, as an employee you take up a contract in law with your employer and this contract has requirements in law that both parties must adhere to.

Legislation has been introduced to encourage recycling of many products. Increasingly, automobile manufacturers state in their promotional material that they are concerned about the environment and that the action they are taking to support this claim. For example, cars may be made with recyclable parts. Chapter 14, *The Macro Environment – Environmental Influences* takes a closer look at how businesses have had to adapt to the changes required of them by widespread environmental concerns.

By including this chapter as a key external influence we are taking a slightly different approach from many textbooks, which would include a discussion of the environment as part of the more traditional socio-cultural analysis (the 'S' in PEST). We have chosen not to include it in Chapter 11, *The Macro Environment – Socio-cultural Influences* as the environment has become such a key feature of any macro environmental analysis.

The chapter raises and considers a number of interesting questions. What exactly do we mean by the terms environment, global warming and sustainable development?

Example

Issues around sustainability and ethical behaviour are not always clear cut. With regard to industrial globalisation, India recognises that it has a competitive advantage in labour costs that it would like to sustain. Indian officials, in denouncing attempts to impose trade sanctions, refer to 'their great advantage in trade: cheap labour.' (Czinkota, 2001, p. 91).

This competitive advantage however is not viewed in quite the same light by the Fair Trade movement. They see the imposition of trade sanctions as a way of eliminating child labour, used extensively in India, and imposing global anti-sweatshop standards.

The fact that India has access to a vast supply of cheap labour is part of the demographic environment in which many Indian businesses find themselves. For all organisations the age, amount and skills of the local population are an important part of the environment which will impact on their operation. Chapter 15, *The Macro Environment – Demographic Influences* considers this in more detail.

It is not just the type and availability of employees that demographic trends influence but also the type of market that is available to the organisation. For example, a large national clothing retailer who targets a teenage clientele would not be as eager to open up a store in a town with a predominately ageing and retired population.

For governments who are considering new hospitals, prisons or airport expansions, examining current demographic trends is essential. It is not always possible to extrapolate accurately from current trends – often, demographic change has happened and organisations have responded appropriately. For example, many Catholic churches began to offer mass in Polish in response to the large influx of working Polish catholic families into the UK.

 ## 1.5 How it all fits together

You should by now be beginning to understand some of the many issues that can affect a business and the forthcoming chapters look at a number of these issues in detail. As we stated at the start of this chapter, not only is business everywhere around us, but the types, varieties, structures and size of a business can vary enormously. Businesses must identify the key influences that affect them, given their particular circumstances. In studying business, however, it is important that you are aware of and can start to assess some of the options available to organisations.

1.6 ## Summary

The importance of business and how it impacts on society was considered briefly at the beginning of this chapter. Reading this book now means that you are interacting with the company that produced it, the publisher Hodder Education. It is almost impossible not to interact with business – it is everywhere and fundamental to how our society operates.

We began our investigations into the internal and external parts to organisations and pointed out that there are a number of factors, some of which a business can control and some of which it can't.

KEY IDEAS

Some of the main points covered in this chapter are listed below. If you feel unsure about any of them, then revisit the appropriate section. If you would like some additional reading on the topic, try the books listed below in recommended reading.

What is business?
We live in a world dominated by a variety of different businesses. Understanding business and the environment in which business organisations operate and consequentially how they affect business operations is an exciting area of study. The fascination and complexity arise because of the sheer variety of different businesses and the way they are organised.

The factors that impact on business
There are many different factors that can have an impact on a business. Some are internal to a particular organisation, such as a shortage of material that has not been ordered on time, or a machine breaking down. Others are external to the organisation but will still affect how well the business does, for example, fuel cost increases.

The internal business environment
A number of internal functions are common to many businesses and the larger a business becomes the more complex these functions become. This complexity can be viewed from either a macro or micro standpoint: both views can provide helpful perspectives of a business. Some common internal options that a business has are with regard to structure, management and strategy.

The external business environment
There are many external factors that impact on a business, over which the organisation has no control. The later chapters of this book examine in turn the political, economic, social, technological, legal, environmental and demographic (PESTLED) factors that impact on organisations. The analysis of these influences is done by considering different economic, ethical and international influences.

REFLECTIVE QUESTIONS

1 Think of a situation in which a business has let you down. Can you pinpoint why it let you down and which part of the business was responsible?
2 Pick up any tin of food in your local supermarket. How many businesses do you think have been involved in getting the tin onto the supermarket's shelf?

RECOMMENDED READING

If you would like to learn more about some of the issues in the sections within this chapter you might like to consider the following books.

What is business?
Organisations and the Business Environment by David Campbell and Tom Craig gives a lot of useful background to different types of businesses.

The factors that impact on business
Ian Worthington and Chris Britton's book, *The Business Environment* begins to take a look at some of the many factors that can affect a business.

The internal and external business environment
For a book that considers the inner and outer influences on organisations take a look at Claire Capon's *Understanding Organisational Context: Inside and Outside Organisations*.

USEFUL WEBSITES

www.dti.gov.uk Lots of useful information and data here on the Department for Trade and Industry website.
www.ft.com Very good for general information on all types of business (as is the daily newspaper) but you will have to pay for a lot of it if you want more detail.
www.cbi.gov.uk The Confederation for British Industry. This site is good for finding some of the many and varied types of business in the UK.

REFERENCES

Campbell, D., and Craig, T. (2005) *Organisations and the Business Environment.* 2nd edn. London: Butterworth-Heinemann.
Capon, C. (2004) *Understanding Organisational Context: Inside and Outside Organisations.* 2nd edn. London: FT Prentice Hall.
Czinkota, M.R., Ronkainen, I.A., Moffett, M.H., and Moynihan, E.O. (2001). *Global Business.* Orlando: Harcourt.
Handy, C. B. (1993) *Understanding Organisations.* 4th edn. London: Penguin.
Worthington, I., Britton, C. (2006) *The Business Environment.* 5th edn. London: Prentice Hall.

2 The Rise of Management

'There is a story about four people called Everybody, Somebody, Anybody and Nobody, who were given an important job to do. Everybody was sure that Somebody would do it. Anybody could have done it, but Nobody did it. Somebody got angry about it, because it was Everybody's job. Everybody said Anybody could do it. But Nobody realised that Everybody would not do it. So Everybody blamed Somebody, when Nobody did what Anybody could have done.'

(Source unknown)

CHAPTER OUTLINE

CHAPTER OBJECTIVES

After carefully reading and engaging with the tasks and activities outlined in this chapter, you should have a better understanding of:

- what society means and understands by management
- an outline of the historical development of management
- some of the various approaches to, and different levels of management
- what some real managers actually do
- the difference between effectiveness and efficiency when managing resources
- some of the current moral issues confronting managers.

2.1 Introduction

The quotation at the start of this chapter shows how important it is to organise people when a task needs doing. Managers need to be good organisers of people. They should not vaguely leave the responsibility of getting things done to *Somebody*, because if they do then *Nobody* will take responsibility. In addition to managing people, managers must also ensure that best use is made of the resources available to them. Managing people and resources is the role of a **manager**.

Sadly, we all have experience of bad as well as good managers and often find it difficult to understand a particular manager's course of action. The difficulty with management is that there are no easy answers to many of the issues that influence a manager's decisions. If there were then we would all be employed in companies that were well managed (as in the example of Tesco's, below). This chapter aims to introduce you to some of the complexities involved in management and give you an understanding of the historical development of management ideas.

KEY TERMS

A **manager** can be described simply as someone who gets things done through other people. As we shall see later however, this is easier said than done.

CASE STUDY

In 2006 Tesco was again the winner of Management Today's award of Most Admired Company. The award is judged over nine categories with Tesco coming top in three of them; Quality of Management, Financial Soundness and Value as a Long-term Investment. Sir Terry Leahy, CEO of Tesco, is a manager who has risen through the ranks at the company and is more interested in steadily managing his company's performance than personal grandeur. However it is not just the CEO who is recognised as a good manager, but the fact that there is also good management throughout the company.

First though, we should stop and consider if society even needs managers. We have been able as a society to survive for all but the last two hundred years without management as the profession we now know it. But we now have management at all levels of organisations and in all types of organisations: top management, middle managers, front-line managers, supervisors, project leaders, plant managers and bar managers. In fact it is hard to avoid management! So why has it become so important now?

Figure 2.1 Terry Leahy

One reason, mainly following the **industrial revolution**, is that owners no longer work directly in the organisation and rely on managers to manage the company. Somebody needs to coordinate and control the workforce on behalf of the owners.

KEY TERMS

The **industrial revolution**, which began in the late eighteenth century, saw major changes in Britain. By the mid-nineteenth century the revolution had spread to Europe and North America. By the 1950s it had become a global phenomenon. The main source of wealth and employment changed from one based around agriculture to one in which greater productivity was achieved through new technology, with steam-powered machines leading to a rapid rise in the establishment and use of factories.

The industrial revolution changed the nature of work for workers who had in the main been used to working at home at time that best suited them. Organisations now needed to get people to work in one location and at the same time, something that hitherto workers had not been used to. Hence the introduction of bells, whistles, formal rules and regulations.

CASE STUDY

The Factory Rules for the US company Amasa Whitney (Adams, 1950) consisted of 16 clearly laid out rules for the work force in July 1830. A flavour of some of the rules is given below:

FIRST: The mill will be put into operation 10 minutes before sunrise at all seasons of the year. The gate will be shut 10 minutes past sunset from 20th March to the 20th September . . .

SECOND: It will be required of every person employed, that they be in the room in which they are employed, at the time mentioned above . . .

THIRD: Hands are not allowed to leave the factory in working hours . . .

.

.

.

SIXTEENTH: The hands will leave the factory so that the doors may be fastened within 10 minutes from the time of leaving off work.

So managers were needed to enforce rules and regulations and also control the overall operation for the owner. As organisations grew more managers were needed at different levels and how to make best use of the managers themselves became more important.

We also recognise a manager in our society as a step above a non-manager. For example if you worked in a bar, would you rather be a bar person or the bar manager? The very word manager now carries with it some status. For this reason some organisations are happy to call people managers when they have nobody to manage. An accountant, who is the sole accountant of a small company who does not manage any staff would often be called the accounts manager rather than simply the accountant.

2.2 What do we mean by management?

Although there must have been **management** skills around for thousands of years (constructing pyramids, controlling armies, maintaining empires, etc.) the term is a relatively recent one. It was a French engineer, Henri Fayol (1841–1925), who was one of the first to identify specific core management tasks. He laid out the 14 principles of management, shown in Table 2.1, in an attempt to generalise the manager's responsibilities.

Fayol recognised the significance of being able to identify certain aspects of the manager's role that would be of help in recruitment and training. But he also recognised that his list may have to be adapted to particular situations and to the differing levels of management required in organisations.

Principle	Meaning	Example (Building a House)
Division of work	Divide up the work.	One person laying bricks, another plastering walls, etc.
Authority	Managers have the right to give orders and accept the responsibility that goes with it.	You accept that if you ask for a wall to be built it will be. But you will take responsibility if you ask for it to be built in the wrong spot.
Discipline	Clear agreements between the firm and its employers, with appropriate sanctions.	Builders expect payment for work done and would expect some contractual conditions.
Unity of Command	Only one line manager.	Each person needs to know who is directing their particular task.
Unity of Direction	There should only be one plan, so direction is clear.	There is only one building plan and schedule.
Subordination of Individual Interest to General Interest	The aims of the organisation are more important than individual aims.	One builder can't redesign a room because it would be easier to build.
Remuneration	Pay should be fair and encouraging for the particular role within the organisation.	We would be unable to get builders without paying the current rates.
Centralisation	This will always be present to some degree but is dependent on the context.	The same house plans might be used on a number of different sites but building workers could be sourced locally.
Scalar Chain	The hierarchy of the organisation.	The Architect would normally pass on instructions to the Site Manager who would pass them on in turn.
Order	All resources should be 'where it (or they) should be'.	Bricks with the bricklayer, roof tiles with the roofers, etc.
Equity	Kindliness and justice should be applied to all employees.	Tea breaks of the same length for all the various trades, skilled and unskilled.

Principle	Meaning	Example (Building a House)
Stability of Tenure of Personnel	Time and support are needed to enable employees to settle into their new job.	A new employee would be shown where material was, explained safety procedures, etc. (induction).
Initiative	All employees should be encouraged to display initiative.	The electrician would be allowed to determine the optimum time to lay cables.
Esprit de Corps	Teamwork – which means here people helping willingly.	Plumber helping the joiner to fit a heavy object.

Table 2.1   The Principles of Management – Henri Fayol

KEY TERMS

Management was not the original word used by Fayol. Writing in French, he referred to it as 'administration', a term used in the widely recognised management qualification the MBA, which means Master of Business Administration, one of the few academic qualifications recognised around the world.

Of course Fayol's view is one of many and, as with many ideas on management, was dependent on the particular circumstances prevalent at the time. That is it focused on the more **bureaucratic** type of organisation that was emerging.

KEY TERMS

Bureaucracy, which literally means to work from the desk, is know more likely to be associated with red tape and an excessive use of rules and regulations. However Max Weber (whose work we will discuss later in this chapter) viewed this as a formal way of ensuring that decisions were not simply made on the whim of manager but rather that there would be clarity and standardisation which would ensure equity for all employees.

Fayol's principles of management relate to his view that a manager should:

- plan
- organise
- command
- coordinate
- control.

Management role	Road manager	Band manager
Plan	Plan the schedule of events for a particular tour.	Decide what type of events the band should be playing over the year.
Organise	Arranging transport, hotels, food, equipment, etc.	Select, from the various options identified above, events that can best fit into a schedule to meet the band, aims.
Command	Ensure that the road crew have confidence in road manager so that there are no conflicting instructions.	The band will have to have faith in the band manager in order to agree to go along with any schedule.
Coordinate	Get the band to the performance on time!	Match up the right road manager and band.
Control	Ensure that the road crew and band follow agreed procedures on tour.	Ensure that the road manager and band keep to contractual agreements.

Table 2.2 Fayol's principles applied to two different levels of management

Managers also perform different roles at different managerial levels within an organisation. We consider his definition in Table 2.2 where two different levels of management are involved. The road manager would view the job as more immediately meeting the band's requirements, an operational view. In contrast, the band manager would be considering longer-term goals for the band, a more strategic view.

1 Describe how managing a company of 250 people is different to managing a group of four people with regard to each of Fayol's five categories.
2 Which, if any, of Fayol's five categories is the most important and which is the least.

It is not just that different levels of management are required within the same type of organisation or industry, but managers need to be responsive to the particular environment and context they are working in. A manager on an oil rig in the North Sea, one of the most hostile working environments in the world, will be dealing with a different set of priorities than a manager of a children's nursery. However, both will have safety as a top priority and would need to respond immediately, with command, coordination and control, to anything that might threaten safety. Moreover, their colleagues will need to have confidence in the commands given in the event of an emergency, they will need to know that the manager has a plan for emergencies and is capable of organising everybody to effectively carry out the safety procedures.

Defining management

There have been various other definitions of management since Fayol, many of them criticised for being too prescriptive and not accurately matching what managers actually do on a day-to-day basis.

Knowing what a manager has to do does not make the job any easier and most managers feel that they are reacting to a number of different situations throughout the day without time to stop and reflect. But in all cases the manager should be making decisions which are in general agreement with the organisational aims. Thus one of many possible definitions of management is simply: 'Management is concerned with organising available resources to achieve organisational objectives'.

Of course managers need to manage through people to achieve any of their aims. So managers must also be able to **interpret** and delegate.

KEY TERMS

Managers must **interpret** the organisational objectives and ensure that they are effectively delegating tasks that meet those requirements.

Messages about organisational aims from within and without the organisation typically need to be interpreted and understood by managers who then need to communicate these organisational aims to staff. The manager also needs to pass on concerns from staff up to the next level of the managerial chain.

Nobody likes to pass on bad news and managers are often in a difficult situation when this occurs. Hence there is often a temptation to suppress bad news and stress good news. Managers do not enjoy passing on poor production figures to more senior managers as it may reflect on their managerial abilities.

Example

Some commentators blame the unforeseen difficulties in uniting East and West Germany with the over-optimistic production figures that arose in East Germany prior to reunification. These were likely to have occurred due to managers' fear, under the previous communist regime, of reporting bad news.

KEY TERMS

Delegating, or delegation, is the process used by managers to allocate responsibility for a particular task to an employee. Note that this is not simply allocating a task to an employee but trusting that they will deal with the task in the best way that *they* deem suitable.

The advantage of getting delegation right is that the best person for the job within the organisation is doing the job and the organisation is operating in an efficient way. The risk for the manager, of course, is that if delegation goes wrong it is the manager who is ultimately responsible.

One of the most difficult tasks that managers face, particularly new managers, is that of **delegating**. It is important to make the most effective use of the human resources within an organisation but this is no straight forward task.

Example

A football manager must effectively delegate the job of winning a football game to the team. The manager will not survive too long in the role if the team keep losing.

Figure 2.2 Sir Alex Ferguson

The manager must decide if the person has the appropriate skills for a particular job. If not who has, or do people need training, or should new staff employed?

This is an important point: all managers are judged on what they achieve through people. Being judged on getting the right person for the job, and delegating tasks effectively, is as important to a small restaurant owner as it is to a large multinational company.

Example

Gavin Neath was made Chairman of Unilever UK after 28 years with the company. It was clear that Unilever UK understood his capabilities. However, he was told on his appointment that he would be judged on the quality of the people he leaves behind.

REFLECTIVE QUESTIONS

1 Imagine that you have been performing your job well for a number of years and have just been promoted to supervisor (a common enough scenario). Do you now trust someone else to do one of your previous tasks, or do you delegate? Remember that you will be judged on what that person does.
2 Can you think of a time when somebody has given you an instruction, a boss or teacher at school, which has not been clear but you have been too afraid to ask for clarification. Is this your fault or the message-giver's fault?
3 You are likely at university, or school, to have worked within a team. If things went wrong what, if anything, did you do? What should you have done?

2.3 Some of the various approaches to management

Most of our current understanding of management has been formed from the turn of the nineteenth century and this development has progressed through a number of well-known approaches. We consider the three of the main ones below, in chronological order.

Classical approach

The principle on which much of the research was undertaken by writers on the classical approach was that common sets of rules and procedures could be determined. An example of this is in Table 2.1, where Fayol laid out 14 generic principles of management.

This approach focuses on the formal structural of the organisation and its purpose, and the planning of work.

- **Formal structure**

Knowing where 'things fit' inside a large organisation was a concern for Max Weber (1864–1920), a German sociologist. He considered the bureaucracy of the organisation. Although bureaucracy is now associated with 'red tape', due to its over reliance on rigid rules and paperwork, advocates of bureaucracy point out that the rules ensure that employees are not arbitrarily treated but are treated uniformly within the rules. Thus it would be more difficult for a manager to favour one employee ahead of another because of personal likes and dislikes.

- **Planning of work (Scientific management)**

Where the formal structures took an overview of the organisation, often theoretical in nature, other researchers were looking in detail at the process of individual jobs with a view to improving the efficiency of particular tasks. One major viewpoint was that of selecting the right person for the job and that there was a 'right' job for everyone. This attracted criticism from a number of quarters, from trade unions to the House of Representatives in the USA.

CASE STUDY

The famous study of Bethlehem Steel Corporation by Frederick Winslow Taylor (1856–1915), the 'father' of what became known as scientific management, dramatically increased both production and wages for men employed in handling pig iron.

Taylor, working as a management consultant, picked a particular worker, a Dutch labourer named Schmidt, and gave exact instructions on how and when he should work and rest. These instructions enabled Schmidt to increase his workload from 12.5 tons per day to 47.5 tons per day, a dramatic improvement that lasted for 3 years! He also increased his wages by 60 per cent over his fellow labourers.

Not all men employed at the steel corporation were capable of achieving Schmidt's output and Taylor went to great lengths in selecting the right man for the right job. However, all achieved increases in output when following Taylor's methods.

Taylor, along with others such as Henry Ford, Henry Gantt (a colleague of Taylor at Bethlehem and famous still for the Gantt chart) and the Gilbreths, used scientific methods based on facts to achieve their results. They contributed not only to improved organisational efficiency but improved a number of working conditions for employees.

However, there were many who opposed scientific management as it reduced the human role to that of a machine and gave the worker no say in their job role. Also, although Taylor did not view it this way, many employers used the carrot-and–stick approach as jobs could now be more rigidly controlled.

CASE STUDY

Frank Gilbreth (1868–1924) and Lilian Gilbreth (1878–1972)

This famous husband-and-wife team gave birth to 12 children and perhaps this is what drove them to make optimum use out of every activity, which became their way of life.

They were convinced of the value of accurate measurement to determine the one best way of doing a task, be it buttoning up a shirt or laying bricks. Indeed Frank had worked in the building trade and he reduced the bricklayer's motions of laying bricks from 18 per brick to just five.

Human relations approach

The classical approach was more about scientific approaches to management than human aspects and needs. This changed around the early 1920s with the advent of the human relations approach and the famous Hawthorne Experiments (1924–1932).

These famous experiments at the Western Electrical Company in the USA had four distinct phases:

- **The illumination experiments** (1924–1927) Workers were split into two groups, one group had the lighting altered while the other group's, the control group, lighting remained constant. This experiment returned the surprise result that both groups productivity grew, even when one group had the lights dimmed!
- **The relay assembly test room** (1927–1929) Here workers who were involved in repetitive boring tasks were put into a small group, still doing the same jobs but subject to a generally more friendly and informal manner. A number of changes were made in a controlled way (shorter breaks, longer breaks, etc.) but there was a general increase in productivity. It was starting to look as if extra interest in the workers by management might be becoming beneficial.
- **The interviewing programme** (1928–1930) Interviews were held with staff to determine their view of supervisors and general work conditions. This programme, with over 200,000 interviews, was starting to show that relationships between employees were important.
- **The bank wiring observation room** (1932) This experiment centred on a group of 14 men working together who were allowed to set their own work patterns within the set day. Natural leaders and a set level of output soon arose that was adhered to by the individual members of the group, even though money incentives were offered to increase them.

There are many theories that surround people's assumptions about how to best motivate and manage employees. Douglas McGregor (1906–1964), basing much of what he did on Maslow's hierarchy of needs (see Chapter 6), outlines two opposite types of manager, the **Theory X** manager and the **Theory Y** manager, and this has proved to be a useful guide to a range of managerial types.

At one end of the scale we have a **Theory X** manager. Here, the manager would be reluctant to leave a workforce without some way of checking that they would carry on working while being unobserved. This assumption would lead a manager to assume that most employees would need to be coerced in some way if organisational aims are to be met.

KEY TERMS

A **Theory X** manager would typically hold the view that the average worker is inherently lazy and that they will do their best to avoid work whenever possible.

At the other end of the scale we have the **Theory Y** manager. They would take the general view that the workers are more likely to be productive without someone leaning over their shoulder. That is they view their workforce as one that is willing to work to the best of its abilities given the chance.

KEY TERMS

A **Theory Y** manager works under the assumption that the average employee is prepared to accept responsibility if they are given the correct support mechanisms.

---

1 Do you know a Theory X or Theory Y manager?
2 What type of manager, according to McGregor, would you say Margaret Thatcher was?

Example

Considering different cultural considerations W.G. Ouchi (1981) recommends Theory Z. This was based on the successful Japanese model of managing people who were used to long-term employment, in many cases a lifetime with one company. Here the emphasis was on trust along with greater involvement and input from the workers in the organisation.

Figure 2.3 Theory X versus Theory Y manager

Contingency approach

As the search for one universal best way of managing was faltering, another view was developing that suggested that there was no generic 'one best way' suitable for all organisations. The importance of considering the different situational context of each organisation is known as the **contingency** approach.

KEY TERMS

We are used to dealing with different situations in our everyday life. If we go to catch a plane and it fails to arrive we would expect the company to have some **contingency** plan to fall back on, i.e. organise another plane, and accommodation and refreshments if there is going to be a long delay.

This approach suggests that management techniques are changed to suit the particular circumstances. This not only applies to different organisations but also to different departments within an organisation and even to different employees within a department.

REFLECTIVE QUESTIONS

Can you think of an example of a manager, or teacher, who may have treated two people differently? It may be that what you might have thought of as favouritism was in fact an attempt to get the best out of both by using different methods.

2.4 What managers do

Having given the wide use of the terms 'manager' and 'management' some thought it is time to consider what it is that managers actually do.

One survey of almost 300 managers and what they actually did, as opposed to what we think they do, was undertaken by Luthans (1988). The outcome of this survey was grouped into four categories, with a percentage average time spent on each category allocated as follows:

- Traditional management (32%) – planning, controlling and making decisions
- Communication (29%) – exchanging information, verbally and on paper
- Human Resource Management (20%) – motivation, disciplining, general staffing difficulties, training and staff development.
- Networking (19%) – socialising with people outside the immediate department.

 1 If you were in charge of a bar in a student union, what proportion of time do you think should be spent on each of the activities in Luthans' classification?

2.4.1 Changing environment

Managers must constantly monitor changes in their environment, both externally and internally. There are many examples of what, with hindsight, appeared to be management blunders. One of the most quoted is IBM's decision not to immediately enter the market for desktop computers as they could see no reason at the time for anybody having a home computer!

Example

Marconi's fortunes have changed dramatically in recent years. From being a company well known for technology and financial prudence and being the supplier of choice to British Telecom, it failed to make their preferred list of eight main suppliers in May 2005 and has since been taken over.

Managers are often very busy just keeping things going day to day, and none of us can see into the future. However, managers need to set aside time to engage with questions concerning the internal and external environment to ensure that they are at least aware of possible changes that will affect their organisation.

REFLECTIVE QUESTIONS

Imagine you are the manager of a small local opticians and a large national chain of opticians are about to open up next to you. How would you react to this new external threat?

2.5 Managing people and resources

Managers need to make the most effective use of both people and resources. This would be a lot easier if a manager had an endless supply of suitably qualified people and adequate resources. However, in practice most managers have to cope with fewer people and resources than they would like. It is important that they make best use of both.

Managing people

Mary Parker Follett (1868–1933), a woman ahead of her time in a predominately male-oriented management society, recognised the value of people to the manager and organisation. Her definition of management was simply *the art of getting things done through people* and she referred to it as an art, rather than a science.

Although managers can appear to hold sway over staff, it is more often the case that they are dependent on their staff, and are generally judged by the performance of the staff. How then do managers get staff to achieve organisational goals? There are a number of ways of getting people to achieve organisational aims. These are based on types of power. We generally, as a society, accept a manager's right to manage, and indeed this is enshrined in employment law.

The following are five of the most well-known types of power that can exist in organisations.

- **Positional power (or Legitimate power)**
  This is the power that resides with the manager from the position they hold within the organisation. Hence we would expect the person appointed as office manager to manage the office.
- **Expert power**
  People will often turn to specialists within organisations for expert advice. Accountants are a good example of this as they can often make decisions in the organisation that are difficult for non-specialists to challenge.
- **Reward power**
  Organisations can use incentives, bonuses for example, as an aid to achieve organisational aims. These can have dramatic effects if they are valued by employees.
- **Coercive power**
  This is in some sense the opposite of reward power, in that employees would know that some sanction would occur if they did not meet management objectives.

● **Referent power (Charisma power)**

Sometimes the managers own personality and reputation can be enough for employees to follow them. If Sir Alex Ferguson became the manager of another football team he would carry with him referent power and his new players would be more willing to heed his advice than advice from a new, unknown manager.

Example

An extreme use of coercive power was used on black workers in gold mines in South Africa, who would often be whipped if they were not perceived to be working hard enough. Organisational aims were certainly being met as these miners were the most productive in the world. However, organisations have an ethical responsibility to balance power with control. Society is not prepared to, nor should it, accept profit at any cost.

REFLECTIVE QUESTIONS

You have just left university and been placed as a junior manager with responsibility for four members of staff. You are on a six-month probation period and know that you will be judged on results. What type of power are you likely to have?

Managing resources

Balancing adequately the available resources (the organisation's facilities, employees, materials, physical assets, etc.) is at the heart of most managers' decisions.

We all balance decisions about resources. Time is a resource that we can't replace. Many nights we have to make a decision about how to best 'spend' time. Do you set the alarm clock and go to bed early enough to have a leisurely breakfast before going to work, or do you set it later in order to stay up longer the night before and then rush out in the morning? You can't do both, although many people try!

Managers have to match existing resources to current needs. Given a set budget, how should it be spent? More staff, better machinery, relocation to a new factory? These are examples of the longer-term decisions, which managers must consider. For some companies in the UK, faced with rising wage costs compared to some international competitors, relocating abroad has become a real option.

Figure 2.4 Call centre

Managers also face more immediate, everyday resource priorities. Some are more urgent than others, and often affect more than one resource.

Example

Can an intensive care ward manager in a hospital risk moving a patient when the bed is needed urgently for another patient? The decision may have a number of other factors involved in the background, the immediate availability of specialists, the chance of getting a suitable bed elsewhere, coordinating staff to do the move, etc. Managers often need to deal with a complexity of issues around what may appear a single decision, even one as important as life and death.

REFLECTIVE QUESTIONS

Marianne is in charge of a small fast-food home-delivery service. If an order is waiting to go out, should she make the delivery team wait until another order comes in, as it is expensive to deliver to just one customer in one area of town, or wait and risk losing the first customer's order in future?

It is possible to work very efficiently without being effective, and it is important for managers to understand the difference if they are to make the best use of available resources.

Example

It is pointless if a department produces 50,000 widgets per year, if only 20,000 are required for the jobs on order. The department would view themselves as very efficient ('nobody in the company can produce as much as us') but the manager who allowed this to happen is not making effective use of the company's resources.

The difficulty for managers is that they are usually too busy dealing with everyday management tasks referred to as 'fire fighting', (members of staff ill, late deliveries, machine breakdown, etc.), to stop and take a general overview.

CASE STUDY

'Fire prevention, not fire fighting, must be practised. Most corporations still reward highly those managers who act as fire fighters. In a survey, 75 per cent of US managers said good fire fighters get fast promotion. But there is no reward for fire preventers. Two years ago I was having a discussion with a General Motors executive who was extremely proud of his fire-fighting teams, and he was telling me how one team had solved a difficult problem. "What my team did was disassemble the complex product completely and put those pieces back together again. Problem solved, and money saved for the organisation." I asked him what the root cause of the problem had been, but he could not reply. I then asked how his team could guarantee that the problem would not come back. Again, no answer. This way of operating, curing rather than preventing, is common in many organisations, from North America to Asia, and from Europe to Australia.'

(Source: Subir Chowdhury, 2000:7)

 ## 2.6 Some emerging issues around management

Organisations and managers now have to focus more on social responsibility and **ethics**. It is no longer the case that 'business is business' as the old saying goes, which was taken to mean that in business anything goes! Managers now need to take into account the people who are affected by their decisions.

KEY TERMS

Ethics concerns behaviour that we view as a society to be right or wrong. Moreover, it is not just about what the manager thinks is morally acceptable, it is about what any stakeholders affected by a decision feel is right or wrong.

Ethics

Being seen as an organisation to be ethically correct is increasingly important. However, these decisions are not always clear-cut and it is important to consider the perspectives of all involved.

REFLECTIVE QUESTIONS

Imagine that you have been offered a 20 per cent pay rise, dependent on reducing your workforce from ten to eight people. However, you have worked closely with this team for a number of years and consider them as good friends who have helped you in your managerial career to date. What would you do?

Social responsibility

Social responsibility is relatively easy to define but, particularly when it concerns large corporations, **Corporate Social Responsibility** (CSR), it is much harder to relate into practice as not everybody agrees on what the responsible thing to do is.

KEY TERMS

Corporate Social Responsibility is the responsibility that an organisation has to take decisions that show concern for the environment and all stakeholders connected to, or affected by, the organisation.

CASE STUDY

Almost 50 years ago, Milton Friedman, building on a firmly held economic principal, argued that 'There is one and only one social responsibility of business, to use its resources and engage in activities designed to increase its profits as long as it stays within the rules of the game' (1962: 133). However some organisations, like Enron at the beginning of this century, will endeavour to bend the rules of the game to breaking point. In fact, the corrupt business practices at Enron, an US energy trading company, caused major panic on stock markets around the world.

Moral dilemmas for managers are not new but the increasing focus on ethical issues is moving higher up a manager's list of priorities. Ethics, or social responsibility, did not appear anywhere with respect to outside stakeholders in Fayol's list (See Table 2.1).

2.7 Summary

The chapter began with an introduction to management and how we have come to accept the term now almost without question. It then considered the historical background and influences, which led to some present-day theoretical managerial approaches.

Management was then defined and we considered what it is that real managers actually do. We saw that they need to constantly monitor the environment, both within and external to the organisation, and ensure that they are effectively organising their limited resources. Increasingly they are required to manage these resources in a way that society deems socially responsible.

KEY IDEAS

Some of the main points covered in this chapter are listed below. If you feel unsure about any of them, then revisit the appropriate section. If you would like some additional reading on the topic, try the books listed below in recommended reading.

What do we mean by management?
- A manager was described simply as someone who gets things done through other people.
- According to Fayol, management consists of Planning, Organising, Commanding, Coordinating and Controlling.
- Managers perform different roles depending on their managerial level within an organisation.
- Managers must interpret organisational objectives and ensure that they delegate tasks appropriately.

Some of the various approaches to management
- The classical approach to management considered the formal structure of an organisation, its bureaucracy, and the details of particular processes, scientific management.
- The human relations approach began to look more at workers' needs and motivations.
- The different situational aspects of management, the contingency approach, suggested that management techniques are changed to suit particular circumstances.

What managers do
- Luthans' survey points to managers spending their time on traditional management (32%), communication (29%), human resource management (20%) and networking (19%).
- Managers constantly monitor changes in the environment for change.

Managing people and resources
- It is possible to work very efficiently without being effective and it is important for managers to understand the difference if they are to make best use of resources.
- Types of power that a manager can use with people to achieve organisational aims are positional, expert, reward, coercive and referent power.

continued . . .

. . . continued

Some emerging issues around management

- Organisations and managers now need to think more about social responsibility and ethical issues.
- Corporate Social Responsibility is the responsibility that an organisation has to take decisions that show concern for the environment and all its stakeholders.
- Ethics is concerned with those activities that we view as a society to be right or wrong.

1 Give an example of how each of Fayol's principles is applied to an organisation of your choice.

2 Think of a situation you have been in, either at work or in university where you have been efficient but not effective.

3 Do modern managers need to be aware of the historical development of management?

4 Can an organisation be successful and be socially responsible?

RECOMMENDED READING

If you would like to learn more about some of the issues in the sections within this chapter you might like to consider the following books.

What do we mean by management?
A good general management standby is Laurie Mullins' book *Management and Organisational Behaviour*. It contains far more than is needed for our purposes, but it is a useful reference book if you are intending taking your studies further.

Some of the various approaches to management
Paul Thompson and David McHugh's book, *Work Organisations*, gives an excellent and critical overview of the important issues around the emergence of large organisations and management. A book worth persevering with if you want to deepen your understanding of management and organisations.

What managers do
Management the New Workplace, by Richard Daft and Dorothy Marcic gives an easily understandable overview, with lots of examples, of the various aspects of the management role.

Managing people and resources
Managing people is adequately covered in Mullins and in Daft and Marcic (see above). However, if you are more interested in the operational side of managing the resources the *Operations Management*, by Nigel Slack, Stuart Chambers and Robert Johnson covers everything in great detail.

Some emerging issues around management
There is so much great stuff emerging from new research about management that it is hard to pick one book! However, *Management 21C* by Subir Chowdhury has a collection of articles by key thinkers on some of the issues that managers and organisations will face in the future.

USEFUL WEBSITES

www.dti.gov.uk Lots of useful information and data here on the Department for Trade and Industry web site.

www.managers.com The Chartered Institute of Management website. One of the main professional managers training organisations in the UK.

www.ft.com Very good for up to date information (as is the daily newspaper!) but you will have to pay for a lot of it should you want more detail.

www.cbi.gov.uk The Confederation for British Industry, they have a vested interest in good management.

www.cipd.co.uk The web site of the Charted Institute of Personnel Management, a very useful resource for practising managers.

REFERENCES

Adams, S.H. (1950) *Sunrise to Sunset*. New York: Random House.

Chowdhury, S. (2007) *Management 21C*. London: Prentice Hall.

Czinkota, M.R., Ronkainen, I.A., Moffett, M.H. and Moynihan, E.O. (2001) *Global Business*. Orlando: Harcourt.

Daft, R. L., and Marcic, D. (2007) *Management and the New Workplace*. Canada: Thompson.

Friedman, M. (1962) *Capitalism and Freedom*. Chicago: Chicago University Press.

Luthans, F., Stajkovic, A., Luthans, B. C. and Luthans, K. W. (1988) 'Applying behavioural management in Eastern Europe', *European Management Journal,* vol. 16, no. 4, 466–74.

Mullins, L. J. (2002) *Management and Organisational Behaviour*. 6th edn. Harlow: Pearson Education Ltd.

Ouchi, W.G. (1981) *Theory Z*. Reading: Addison Wesley.

Slack, N., Chambers, S. and Johnston, R. (2001) *Operations Management*. 3rd edn. Harlow: Pearson Education Ltd.

Thompson, P. and McHugh, D. (2002) *Work Organisations*. 3rd edn. Hampshire: Palgrave.

3 Strategy, Mission and Stakeholders

'However beautiful the strategy, you should occasionally look at the results.'

(Sir Winston Churchill, 1874–1965, British statesman)

CHAPTER OUTLINE

3.1 Introduction
3.2 What is 'strategy'?
3.3 Strategy and the mission statement
3.4 Strategy and stakeholders
3.5 Different levels of strategy
3.6 Ways to deliver strategy
3.7 Problems with strategy
3.8 Summary

CHAPTER OBJECTIVES

After carefully reading and engaging with the tasks and activities outlined in this chapter, you should have a better understanding of:
- what we understand by the terms strategy, mission statements, and stakeholders
- the role of strategy
- the link between strategy and mission statements
- the link between strategy and stakeholders.

3.1 Introduction

Have you ever wondered why organisations do certain things? For example, why did Tata Motors take over the Jaguar and Land Rover brands? Why did B&Q start trading in China? Why did Wal-Mart take over Asda? The answer to these, and many other 'why?' questions that you might have about organisations lies in their strategy(ies).

As you will see as the chapter unfolds, organisations do not just have one strategy. There are different levels of strategy (corporate, business, and functional), and organisations need to take many things into account in their strategy formulation and implementation. This chapter takes into account two of these important factors (mission statements and stakeholders). However, organisations also need to consider issues such as their micro and macro external environments (which are covered in greater detail in later chapters of this book).

3.2 What is 'strategy'?

Many people will be familiar with the phrase 'if you don't know where you're going, how will you know when you've got there?' **Strategy** is simply about knowing *where* you want to go, and then planning *how* you are going to get there. In our opening example of Tata Motors, Tata may have wanted to open up new markets in higher end motors and may have seen the purchase of the two high-end brands as a vital step in achieving this, as well as an in-road into the UK. B&Q may have felt that they could not grow their market share much further in the UK, so in order to grow they needed to find new markets elsewhere in the world. Wal-Mart may have wanted to gain a foothold in the UK market, and what better way of doing that than to take over one of the 'big 4' (Tesco, Sainsbury's, Asda, and Morrisons).

KEY TERMS

Strategy is about deciding *what* business the organisation should be in, *where* the organisation wants to be, and *how* the organisation is going to get there.

Although people often use different terms to describe strategy, such as strategic management, and strategic planning, essentially strategy is all about working out what needs to be done and how. Traditionally, organisations set out a **vision** and/or **mission statement**, and then set **goals** and **objectives**, which should be in line with their stated vision and/or mission. Organisations then design their strategy(ies) for detailing how they will go about achieving this.

As the chapter unfolds you will see, however, that in reality strategy setting/ planning is rarely such a neat affair: strategies can change, alter or disappear entirely, and new strategies can emerge. This is not necessarily to be regarded as a negative thing. It is actually very important to the success of any business that it monitors both its micro and macro external environments, so that it can adapt appropriately to opportunities and threats that may emerge. For example, when the bank Northern Rock got into financial difficulty Virgin worked up a bid to take it over. Had Virgin been successful this would have been a good example of an emerging strategy; taking advantage of an opportunity presenting itself in the market.

For most organisations the main purpose of developing their strategies is to perform well in the market, i.e. compete in the market for long-term success. Organisations find it helpful to identify how they will compete, and what will give them higher levels of profit (or other appropriate measure of performance; not all organisations are driven by profit as a key performance indicator). Strategies need to identify the source(s) of competitive advantage for the company, and how these can be achieved, i.e. what the organisation's **competitive strategy** is.

KEY TERMS

A **vision statement** gives an *outline* of what an organisation wants to be. Its purpose is to provide inspiration.

A **mission statement** is a broad statement of the scope of an organisation's customers, products and services, which aims to distinguish it from other, similar organisations. Typically, a mission statement should detail the level of performance the company aims to achieve.

A **goal** is something that an organisation is trying to achieve. It is a desired future state, and enables the organisation to direct its efforts towards its achievement. Goals can be fairly ambiguous, whereas objectives are more precise.

An **objective**, or rather a set of objectives, details *exactly how* an organisation is going to achieve its goal(s). An objective should be specific, measurable, achievable, realistic, and time-bounded (SMART). They can be classified as primary objectives (those that must be achieved if the organisation is to survive, e.g. profit, sales, and market share), and secondary objectives (which are a measure of the efficiency of an organisation. They are critical for success, but may not affect survival for some time, e.g. customer care, and product development.)

Competitive strategy is the basis on which the organisation plans to achieve competitive advantage in the market place.

Creating strategies can be a time consuming job, so it stands to reason that there ought to be some important benefits from this investment of time.

Benefits of strategy formulation include:

1 **A reduction of uncertainty** – managers need to look ahead to the future, anticipate change (for example, through undertaking PEST and SWOT analyses), and to develop options (contingency plans) for responding in appropriate ways.
2 **Helping to link short term to long term** – strategies can help people in the organisation to see where everything fits together, and why they are doing what they are doing for the long term. This may help gain commitment through improved understanding of the long-term direction of the organisation.
3 **Enablement of control** – the setting of objectives provides standards against which performance can be measured.

Figure 3.1 provides a diagrammatic summary of the key strategic concepts presented so far in the chapter.

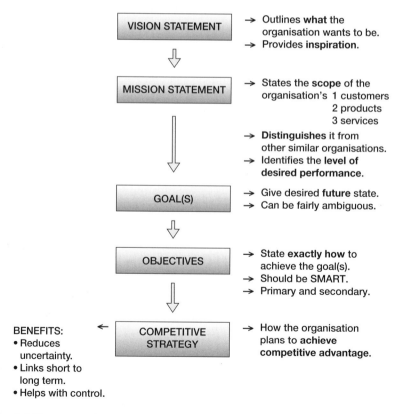

Figure 3.1 Key strategic concepts

1 What is strategy?
2 Why is strategy important?

3.3 Strategy and the mission statement

An organisation's mission should underpin everything it does. Strategies should be formulated that work towards achieving it. Many mission statements also detail the underlying beliefs and values of the organisation. For example, the RSPCA's mission states that it will prevent cruelty, promote kindness and alleviate the suffering of animals, but that they will work within the law. Prevention of cruelty, promotion of kindness, alleviation of suffering, and working within the law are the underlying beliefs and values of the organisation.

According to Dobson et al. (2004) there are four key aspects that mission statements should clarify:

1 The principle business or activities of the organisation.
2 The key aims or objectives of the organisation.
3 The key beliefs and values of the organisation.
4 The main stakeholders of the organisation.

You should be able to see the mission of an organisation 'played out' through its strategies and behaviour. One way of establishing if this is happening is to use the Ashridge Mission Model (Campbell and Young, 1991). The model looks at how closely aligned the following four elements are:

1 Mission
2 Values
3 Strategy
4 Standards of behaviours.

If the four elements are closely aligned then the mission is being realised in practice. If there are discrepancies, then the mission is not being realised in practice. This can sometimes happen where senior managers (who are normally 'in charge' of strategy formulation) might believe the vision is too idealistic, rather than being realistic and achievable. So, if strategy formulators in the organisation believe the mission is too idealistic to be turned into reality, for example because of current market conditions, strategies may be formulated to enable the organisation to survive, and ideally thrive, despite what the mission may say. There seems to be no practical sense in creating strategies that are in alignment with the mission, if it is thought this may damage the organisation; this would be folly. This highlights one of the main criticisms of mission statements, which is that they can sometimes be too idealistic.

Example

Some examples of mission statements are provided below to illustrate the variation in articulation across a range of different types of organisation.

Asda – To be the UK's best value retailer exceeding customers' needs always.

BBC – To enrich people's lives with programmes and services that inform, educate and entertain.

easyJet – To provide our customers with safe, good value, point-to-point air services. To effect and to offer a consistent and reliable product and fares appealing to leisure and business markets on a range of European routes. To achieve this we will develop our people and establish lasting relationships with our suppliers.

RSPCA – The RSPCA as a charity will, by all lawful means, prevent cruelty, promote kindness to and alleviate suffering of animals.

Starbucks – To inspire and nurture the human spirit – one person, one cup, and one neighbourhood at a time.

1 What is a mission statement?
2 Why should the mission statement be taken into consideration in strategy formulation?

3.4 Strategy and stakeholders

Organisations also need to consider the needs of their **stakeholders** when they are formulating *and* implementing their strategies. There are two aspects to this. First, the organisation has to meet the needs of certain stakeholders in relation to ensuring that it reaches its goals, whether that is to make a profit and be a market leader, or as may be the case in a not-for-profit (NFP) organisation, this may be to offer best value for money in the provision of their products/ services. Second, the organisation needs to ensure that it meets the needs of a whole different set of stakeholders by ensuring that the way it operates does not have any unavoidable adverse impact, which links to the concept of **Corporate Social Responsibility (CSR)**, i.e. organisations need to ensure when they are formulating and implementing their strategies that they do not unavoidably adversely impact on other stakeholders or the environment.

Stakeholders can be internal to the organisation, e.g. employees, shareholders, departments, internal customers, internal suppliers, and external to the organisation, e.g. customers, suppliers, local community, pressure groups, the media, government, the law, and the environment. They can also be classified

KEY TERMS

Stakeholders can be individuals or groups that may be interested in, and/or may be affected by the plans and activities of an organisation, or the behaviour of any member of that organisation.

Corporate Social Responsibility (CSR) is about having an awareness of how the organisation can impact on stakeholders and the environment, and is about accepting responsibility to manage decision making, including strategy formulation and implementation, for the wider good.

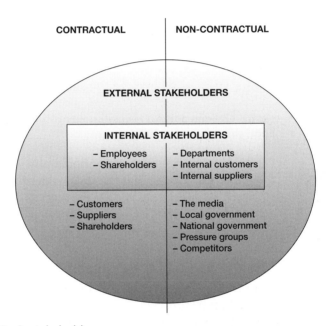

Figure 3.2 Basic stakeholder map

as contractual or non-contractual, i.e. some have a legally binding contract with the organisation, such as employees and suppliers, whereas others do not, e.g. the media.

NB: Figure 3.2 does not contain a definitive list of stakeholders, merely illustrative examples.

Nutt (2002) demonstrated the importance of understanding stakeholders in terms of organisational performance. Nutt showed that half of strategic decisions failed because decision makers did not adequately address stakeholder needs. This demonstrates that strategies can fail if stakeholders are not considered in strategy formulation and implementation.

Level of interest in the organisation

	Low	High
Low	**A** Minimal effort	**B** Keep informed
High	**C** Keep satisfied	**D** Key players

Power to influence the organisation

Figure 3.3 Eden and Ackerman's stakeholder power and interest matrix (Source: Eden and Ackerman, 1998)

Part of the consideration that should also be taken into account relates to the *power* and *interest* that the stakeholder has in relation to the organisation. However, as previously noted, the idea of responsible corporate behaviour should also be taken into consideration, even where a stakeholder may not have much power over the organisation.

Eden and Ackerman (1998) created the concept of the power-interest matrix (see Figure 3.3) to help see where stakeholders are *at a particular point in time* in terms of two dimensions: level of interest in the organisation, and power to influence the organisation. Stakeholders can of course change from one category to another as and when circumstances may change. Organisations can place their stakeholders on the matrix, and use this as a tool to help them to identify who the most influential stakeholders are, and this may help in formulating more effective strategies. Eden and Ackerman proposed a different way of managing each quadrant: minimal effort needed, keep the stakeholders informed, keep the stakeholders satisfied, and for key players ensure as far as possible that they get what they want/need.

ACTIVITY

- Choose an organisation that you are familiar with, and list its internal and external stakeholders. Then identify which are contractual and non-contractual.
- Draw up a power and interest matrix, and place the internal and external stakeholders you have just identified onto the matrix. Remember that some

stakeholders can move around the matrix at different times, so you need to place the stakeholders in the quadrant you think they are in at this point in time.

● Identify the objectives of your chosen organisation, and explore how your stakeholders both help and hinder the organisation in its achievement of those objectives. NB: to limit this exercise it would be useful to perhaps choose two internal stakeholders and two external stakeholders. Use examples to illustrate the points that you make.

1 What/who are stakeholders?
2 Why is it important to know who your stakeholders are when you are formulating your strategy[ies]?
3 How can you prioritise the needs of your stakeholders?
4 Stakeholders can change quadrants on the power/interest matrix.
   a) Under what circumstances might a stakeholder move from one quadrant to another? Give a couple of examples to illustrate your points.
   b) What implication(s) can this have for strategy?

(3.5) Different levels of strategy

There are different levels of strategy within an organisation:

1 Corporate – concerned with *what* business(es) the organisation should be involved in.
2 Business – concerned with *how* to succeed in the chosen business(es).
3 Functional – the means by which the business strategies are carried out. For example, research and development strategy, finance strategy, marketing strategy, human resources strategy, and so on.

Example

The Virgin Group, like all large businesses, will have a *corporate strategy* that sets out what its long-term objectives are in terms of what businesses it plans to be involved in. There will be a number of *business strategies* as the organisation is involved in a number of businesses, e.g. airline, mobile communication, digital TV, trains, holidays, and music. That is, each business unit/area (you might see these referred to as SBUs – strategic business units) will need its own business level strategy. As the business areas Virgin has are diverse, it is likely that each business area of Virgin, i.e. each SBU, will have a series of *functional strategies* specific to the needs of each SBU. Of course, as you would imagine, these strategies will be confidential as they will contain commercially sensitive information.

KEY TERMS

Corporate strategy sets out the long-term objectives and policies of an organisation, enabling people to see its purpose, direction, and scope.

Business strategy sets out how the organisation plans to succeed in a given business area.

Functional strategy refers to the strategies by which each function, e.g. marketing, product development, production, and human resources, will support the achievement of the business strategy.

SBU is a commonly used acronym for a **'strategic business unit'**. A SBU is where an organisation has a number of products and/or services that are closely related in some way, and so it is meaningful to treat them as a unit/area that needs its own specific set of strategies.

Corporate strategy

Questions that an organisation considers at this level revolve around *what* business(es) it should be involved in. Should it keep one of its business areas, or should it get rid of it? Should it diversify into new areas, or stay as it is? Should it stay local, or expand to regional, national, or international? These types of decisions are top-level *directional* decisions. At this corporate level, strategies can aim for growth, stability or renewal.

- A growth strategy – aims to *increase the amount* of business undertaken by expanding the range of products and/or services, and/or the markets it serves.
- A stability strategy – aims to continue offering the *same* products and/or services to the *same* type of customer. Public sector organisations often engage in this strategy as they typically do not have much opportunity, or even desire to grow. Small business owners also often engage in this strategy as a way of staying in sole control of their business.
- A renewal strategy – follows a period of trouble for the organisation. If there has been poor performance then management will need to make *major changes* to its strategies to return profits to acceptable levels before it can consider stability or renewal as alternative options. Our example of Dell is a good illustration of a company that used a renewal strategy approach.

Managers can use Ansoff's (1987) product/market matrix (see Figure 3.4) as a tool to help develop and achieve their chosen strategy. Growth can be achieved by focusing on one or more of the quadrants. Stability can be achieved by staying with the existing product(s) and service(s). Renewal can be achieved by withdrawing from some existing products/services and markets, followed (in some cases) by entering into some new product(s)/service(s) and/or market(s).

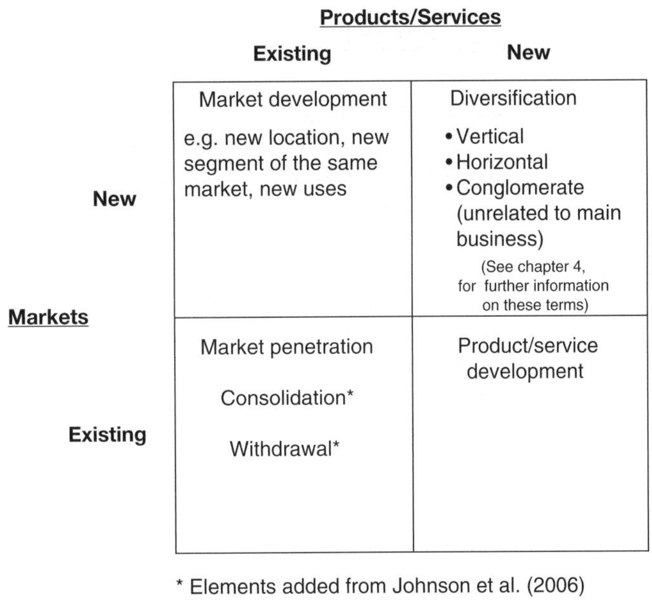

Products/Services

	Existing	New
	Existing	**New**
New	Market development e.g. new location, new segment of the same market, new uses	Diversification • Vertical • Horizontal • Conglomerate (unrelated to main business) (See chapter 4, for further information on these terms)
Existing	Market penetration Consolidation* Withdrawal*	Product/service development

Markets

* Elements added from Johnson et al. (2006)

Figure 3.4 Ansoff's product/market matrix

Example

Dell changes strategies in bid to renew sales

The business model successfully used by Dell for many years was to focus on corporate customers, and to provide customisation for each order, such as adding extra memory. Dell machines could only be purchased online, which helped to keep costs down, thereby helping make the price of the products competitive. However, the market started to change. Growth started to move away from corporate markets to the individual customer and away from richer countries to the emerging markets. The emerging markets posed a particular problem for Dell because in these countries consumers were not as comfortable with online shopping, preferring instead to buy in-store. In addition, PCs were becoming more powerful, and therefore people were less likely to need to buy a PC from a supplier that offered the option of increasing the size of the hard drive, i.e. this feature was no longer a particularly attractive unique selling point for Dell. Profits were falling, and strategies needed serious attention for Dell to regain market share.

Dell changed their strategy for location of sales. Although they continued to sell online, they started to sell in shops, particularly in the emerging economies. Through product development the company also worked on the visual image of their products away from dull black boxes to design products to build what owner Mr Dell called 'brand lust'. In other words, Dell acknowledged that what the product looked like was an important issue in sales.

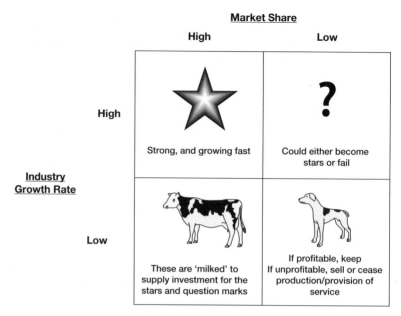

Figure 3.5 Boston consulting group (BCG) matrix

Dell also diversified into managing the IT systems of its customers; a strategy that was working well for competitors Hewlett-Packard. To help do this, Dell purchased several companies already in business providing these services; an example of growth by acquisition.

Managers can also use the Boston Consulting Group (BCG) matrix (see Figure 3.5) as a tool to help them to decide which businesses (SBUs) or products/services they should keep or get rid of. Managers need to place their SBUs (or products/services) on to the matrix according to the rate of industry growth and current market share. Once all SBUs (or products/services) have been entered on to the matrix, managers can use this summary of the organisation's portfolio to help them make strategic decisions as to which to keep, and perhaps which to get rid of.

Stars

Stars are characterised by a high rate of growth in the industry/market, and a high market share. These SBUs or products/services are important for the organisation because they are doing well, and also have the potential to expand (because industry growth rate is high). However, stars need investment. For example, in the case of a product, if sales are growing the organisation may well need to invest money in building more plants so they can make more of their product. If they are making more, then they need to invest more money into their distribution channels. Expansion requires human resource investment, and so on. As the industry or product reaches the maturity stage of the industry/product life cycle there is less growth, less or no investment is needed, and the star product can be moved to the cash cow quadrant (assuming market share remains high).

Cash cows

Cash cows are SBUs or products/services that have high market share, but where growth potential is low or has stopped, i.e. the market may be saturated. Investment for cash cows tends to be low, so these SBUs or products/services should be profitable for the organisation. They should provide cash surplus for the organisation, which can be used to invest in star SBUs or products/services and/or question marks. They are called cash cows because of the idea that they can be 'milked' to provide funds for other areas of the business.

Question marks

Question marks are SBUs or products/services that have high industry growth rates but low market share at the moment. Investment in the question mark could go either way; it could become a star, or it could fail.

Dogs

The dog has low potential for industry growth, and low market share. Unless something can be done fairly quickly to increase market share substantially these SBUs or products/services need to be *considered* for selling off, or in the case of an individual product/service, consideration may be given in terms of ending production/provision. However, if the dog is still profitable, or perhaps is integral to the mission of the organisation, it may be kept.

ACTIVITY

On a piece of A4 paper, create the four quadrants of the BCG matrix. Think of examples of products or services that fall into each of the categories, and place them on your matrix. Jot down why you think they belong in the quadrant you have placed them. After you have done this, take one of your question marks and one of your dogs and devise a strategy for each that you think may result in a growth of market share.

1 What are the three different levels of strategy, and how are they different from each other?

2 What are the three types of strategy considered at corporate level, and how are they different from each other?

3 What tools/models can managers use to help them make their strategic decisions? For each tool/model briefly explain *how* they are helpful in terms of making strategic decisions.

CASE STUDY

Pringles (owned by Proctor and Gamble) were launched in the USA in October 1968, and in terms of expanding their market, were introduced to Europe in 1990 in Sweden, followed by the UK in 1991, Germany and Austria in 1996, Portugal, Greece and Norway in 1998, France, Spain, Italy, Denmark and Finland in 1999, and Holland and Switzerland in 2000. Pringles are also available in Russia, Belgium, Canada, Latin America, China, South Korea, Australia and New Zealand.

Pringles now have an extensive range of products, in terms of flavours, pack sizes, and full-fat/low-fat options, which has grown steadily over the years. Proctor and Gamble's strategy for these changes over the years has been based on research into the changing tastes and wants of consumers. For example, as consumers have become more health conscious, the Pringles Light range was introduced. As consumers came to expect more exotic flavours, Pringles responded with a range of new flavours. In addition, to give consumers more flexibility in how/where their Pringles could be eaten, Pringles responded with different pack sizes.

1 The introduction of Pringles into new countries represents an example of what type of strategy?

2 The introduction of new flavours and pack sizes represents an example of what type of strategy?

3 At what strategic level are these Pringles examples?

Business strategy

Questions that an organisation considers at this level revolve around the choice the organisation has over *how* to compete in their chosen market(s). Michael Porter devised two types of competitive advantage; low cost, and differentiation. Low cost, as the name implies, involves the organisation using low price as their strategy for competitive advantage. Differentiation involves the organisation making the product or service concerned somehow special in the market, i.e. making it stand out from the competition in some way; making it special/distinctive/unique, rather than low price. An example of this in the food retailing market would be Aldi (cost/price) versus Marks and Spencer. An example from the motor industry would be the Ford KA (cost/price) and the Lexus sports coupe convertible (differentiation). If you look on YouTube, you will be able to see TV advertisements for supermarkets and cars that will enable you to see their differentiation strategies coming through.

From his basic premise of cost leadership and differentiation, Porter devised three generic strategies (see Figure 3.6) that an organisation could use to develop and maintain competitive advantage in the market:

1 Cost leadership
2 Differentiation
3 Focus (which can be cost focus, or differentiation focus).

Cost leadership

Cost leadership is a strategy where the organisation *competes on price*, rather than, for example, quality or advanced features. Economies of scale are needed with this strategy and organisations opting for this need to ensure they are efficient and keep their operating costs at a minimum. In itself, a low cost strategy does not guarantee a competitive advantage; customers *also* have to regard the product(s) and/or service(s) as representing value for money. Examples include Argos, and easyJet.

Differentiation

Differentiation is a strategy where the organisation offers a product or service that is somehow quite *distinct* from its competitor(s). Again, the customer has to value the distinct element(s) of difference.

There are different ways/forms of differentiating. For example, you can differentiate on quality, e.g. Marks and Spencer food, or a Rolex watch. You can differentiate on design and technology, e.g. Apple computers, and Dyson cleaners. You can differentiate on service, e.g. Hilton hotel versus a cheap bed and breakfast. You can differentiate on reliability and safety, e.g. Volvo cars. You can differentiate on brand, e.g. Coca-Cola and MacDonald's are widely recognised brands. There are more. . . durability, serviceability, sophistication and so on.

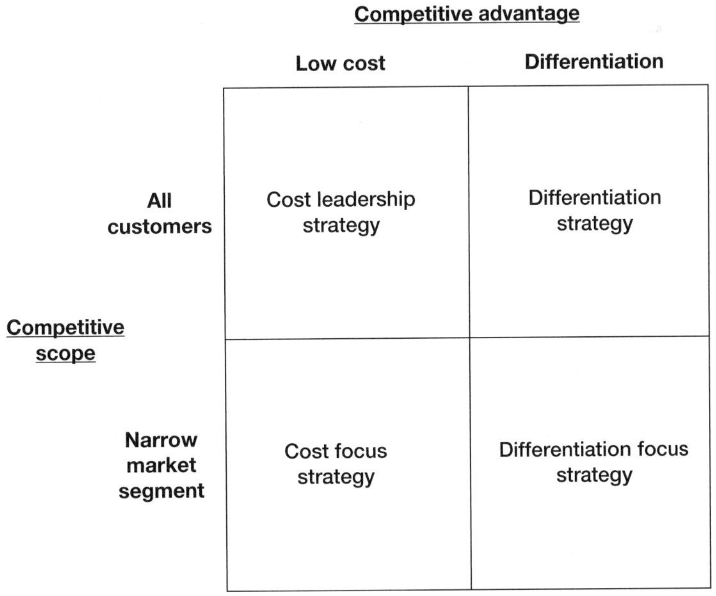

	Competitive advantage	
	Low cost	**Differentiation**
All customers	Cost leadership strategy	Differentiation strategy
Narrow market segment	Cost focus strategy	Differentiation focus strategy

Competitive scope

Figure 3.6 Porter's generic competitive strategies

Focus

Focus is a strategy where the organisation targets *narrow segments* of the market. This can be by consumer group or geography. Examples of consumer groups are teenagers, gamers, the retired, fitness fans, clubbers, professionals, extremely wealthy, business people, and so on. You can have a cost leadership focus or a differentiation focus. Examples include Sheila's Wheels, car insurance aimed at women drivers (this has the focus of women who drive), BUPA (private health care), Bentley motors (luxury transport for very well-off people), first-class and business-class air travel (for customers with bigger wallets), SMART cars and electric cars (still a narrow target market at present), SAGA holidays for the over 50s, and designer clothes.

Porter originally suggested that organisations would need to choose either a cost leadership strategy *or* a differentiation strategy. However, examples of successful organisations following *both strategies at the same* time led Porter to rethink this idea. As a result he suggested that although it is possible that some organisations can make progress on both strategies at the same time, they should aim to have a commitment more to one than the other.

Example

Supermarkets are a good example of organisations with *both* cost leadership and differentiation strategies. Asda and Tesco, for example, both have a cost leadership strategy. You can see this play out in their TV advertising campaigns, which try to portray their companies as the cheapest provider of your weekly shopping. However, when you walk around either store (or any of the major supermarket chains for that matter) there is also evidence of differentiation strategy in their own brand product range. For example, Asda has introduced a 'Free From' range for customers with food allergies and intolerances, 'Asda Organics', their own 'economy' brand (Smart Price) and more 'exclusive' brand (Extra Special). All the major supermarkets have this strategy for their own brand goods.

Next time you go shopping, keep a look out for the differentiation strategy in action. However, as Porter suggests, these organisations should have a stronger commitment to one strategy than the other; in our example this would be the cost focus strategy.

ACTIVITY

Search for Asda and Tesco TV advertisements on YouTube to see the strategies they employ in their campaigns.

ACTIVITY

- On a piece of A4 paper, create the four quadrants of Porter's Generic Competitive Strategies.
- List a few examples of products and services that you can think of that come under each of the strategies. Identify different examples than those provided in the chapter. For differentiation, cost focus and differentiation focus strategies, be sure to note down *how* the product/service is differentiated or focused. For example, Club 18-30 holidays would be cost focus; they are relatively low cost and focused on a narrow age range.

ACTIVITY

Identify two *very different* organisations that compete on a cost leadership strategy (you might use two from the previous activity) and *explain how* they do this, i.e. find out what they do that enables them to keep their prices low.

1 What is the purpose of business level strategy?
2 How is business level strategy different to corporate strategy?
3 Describe and explain the three strategies devised by Porter to help organisations develop and maintain competitive advantage in the market.

Functional level strategy

To ensure that business strategies are achieved, an organisation needs its functional areas to work toward their achievement. This means for example, that if an organisation has a differentiation strategy that relies on technology and innovation, its Human Resources strategy will need to be aligned to this business strategy to ensure the organisation employs the right mix of people to make this happen. The marketing and advertising strategy then needs to ensure that customers actually find out about the product and want to buy it. The finance strategy needs to ensure that adequate finance will be available when and where it will be needed to make it happen, and so on.

1 What is the purpose of functional level strategy?
2 What could happen if one or more functional area of an organisation fails to support the business strategy? Use examples to illustrate your points. One example to help get you started is provided in 'Toys Recalled in Lead Paint Scare below.

Example

Toys Recalled In Lead Paint Scare

In 2007, several Fisher-Price toys had to be recalled following fears that the paint used in their production contained unacceptably high levels of lead. In total, 83 types of Chinese-made toys were recalled. More than 94,000 units of the affected toys had already gone on sale in the UK and Irish Republic, and the recall involved almost one million toys in total.

This is a good example of how a functional area (in this case production) can seriously impact on the achievement of the goals and objectives of an organisation. New strategies were certainly needed to ensure, as far as possible, that such problems did not occur again.

3.6 Ways to deliver strategy

There are three basic ways in which an organisation can deliver its strategies:

- through internal development
- through mergers and acquisitions (also discussed briefly in Chapter 4)
- through joint developments and alliances.

Internal development

Strategies can be delivered through redeploying or expanding the resources the organisation has available. For example, if an organisation has a strategy for providing a completely different type of service than they are currently providing, rather than make all current staff redundant because they are not currently able to provide the new service, the organisation could look to retrain some staff, redeploy others, and take on some new staff with the required knowledge and skill set to support those who are being trained up. This is an example of a functional strategy; in this case a Human Resources strategy.

Mergers and acquisitions

These are quick ways of building market share and gaining entry into a new market, or segment. For example, Wal-Mart acquired Asda, thereby gaining entry to the UK market and growing its retail market share globally. Our Dell example also shows how acquisitions are used to deliver a service growth strategy. Mergers and acquisitions are also used, for example, to gain control of knowledge, technology, production, and distribution capacity. For example, if an organisation smaller than yours has developed a specific technique or piece of technology that you can use to maximise something your organisation produces or provides, acquiring or merging with that company will 'buy into' what you need. This reduces the power that company may have had over you, and removes or reduces the chance that competitors will be able to access the technique or technology for a while, helping you gain or maintain your position in the market.

Joint developments/ventures and alliances

In order to develop a product or service it is sometimes prudent to create a joint development/venture or an alliance with another organisation. You might do this if it is not possible or desirable to merge with or acquire the organisation concerned. These options are less risky than mergers and acquisitions, and any associated risk is spread among the partners. Some of these types of arrangements are contractual, while others are more of a 'gentleman's agreement'. What is important is that *both parties are benefiting* from the arrangement.

Example

Borders and Starbucks benefited from an alliance untill Borders folded at the end of 2009. Many Borders stores had a Starbucks cafe and people who perhaps otherwise may not have gone into Borders, may have done so for the coffee shop, and made a purchase from Borders at the same time (and vice versa). Some Tesco stores also have a Starbucks or Costa Coffee cafe.

ACTIVITY

Undertake some research to discover which companies have:
- merged with another company
- been taken over (acquired) by another company
- undertaken a joint venture or alliance with another company.

Discuss *why* you think these things happened, and what the pros and cons might be.

CASE STUDY

Three-way joint venture bags environmental awards

Envar Limited (a waste management company) teamed up with Shotton Paper Mill (owned by UPM Kymenne) and United Utilities to undertake a joint venture (JV) aimed at reducing their carbon footprint and use of landfill, winning them two environmental awards in the process.

A lot of waste residue is produced by the paper industry and from wastewater treatment. The challenge of what to do with the waste, in terms of reducing its impact on the environment, led to

continued . . . ▶

◀ | *. . . continued*

the formation of this three-way joint venture. The result of the JV was a reduction in fuel costs for the mill, reduced use of landfill, and a supply of fertiliser for farmers.

How did they do it? The mill built a combined heat and power plant to turn some of their waste into ash by combusting it with forestry cuttings. United Utilities, following on from trials, found that this ash could be used as a substitute for lime, which was traditionally used to stabilise sewage sludge. Substituting the lime for ash meant that the United Utilities waste product could be recycled by using it as an agricultural fertiliser. The ash from the paper mill no longer had to go to landfill, and the sewage could now be recycled as fertiliser.

Not only is this a good example of a joint venture, but also one of a socially responsible business practice, which would not have been possible by the organisations working in isolation.

1 What are the benefits of the joint venture strategy to the organisations involved in this example?

2 Are there any possible drawbacks to working on this kind of joint venture?

1 What are the three basic ways an organisation can deliver its strategies?

2 What might be some advantages and disadvantages of:
   a) internal development?
   b) mergers and acquisitions?
   c) joint ventures and alliances?

3.7 Problems with strategy

There are organisations that have done well without having formal strategic plans. Conversely, there are organisations that have done badly, despite having them. So, planning in a strategic way does not necessarily guarantee success. Strategic thinking and planning has its limitations, particularly with regard to its ability to forecast accurately, and to respond to changes in the micro and macro external environments.

The basic idea of strategic planning is to look to the future; to make some forecast, and create a strategy (plan) for how to get there. However, managers do not have crystal balls, so the best they can do is to use their knowledge and experience to give it their best (informed) guess. Because managers are unlikely to have all the information they need to make their 'predictions' and create their plans, they may opt for more cautious strategies. However, some managers may create a range of strategies for different circumstances. You might call these contingency plans. So, if the first strategy (plan) cannot be realised for some unforeseen reason, then strategy (plan) B can come into operation. However, it would be difficult for an organisation to have a strategy (plan) for every possible eventuality. However, contingency planning is a useful way for dealing with uncertain futures.

This idea of alternative, back-up plans, that are dependent upon how the future pans out has led some writers, such as Henry Mintzberg, to the idea that strategy should be *emergent:* it should emerge as circumstances change. That is not to say that traditional strategic planning, where analysis has been undertaken, and plans created based on that analysis, should be abandoned. Rather, that there should be flexibility in the system. For example, one should not persist with a plan just because it was well researched. If things change (as they are likely to do), so must the plan. Plans need to be adapted, and sometimes perhaps, in extreme cases scrapped. In environments that are fast changing, for example in high-technology markets, strategies may need to emerge quickly as a result of technological advances.

Figure 3.7 shows this idea of the emergent strategy. At the beginning there was an intended strategy, but due to some uncertainty, some of that intended strategy was not put into effect, which leads to what we can call the deliberate strategy. Then there may be some unexpected events that impact on the business, and the deliberate strategy needs to be amended; leading to the emergent strategy. The combination of the deliberate and emergent strategies leads to what eventually happens, which we can call the realised strategy. So, realised strategy (what actually happens in the end) emerges from a combination of planning, changing circumstance, and adaptation.

Example

If you wanted to get from Liverpool to Paris you may have an intended strategy of flying there direct using easyJet from Liverpool John Lennon Airport. That is how you initially intend to get there. However, your taxi is late picking you up from your house to get you to the airport and you miss your flight. You ask if there are any other flights that day, and are told that there are no available seats. However, the assistant suggests that you may still be able to get to Paris that day via Eurostar. You deliberately amend your strategy (because after all, you have a choice to stick to your original strategy if you wait until another day). So, some of your intended strategy is binned, i.e. the part about flying there direct. You still have a deliberate strategy to get to Paris that day, but the strategy that emerges is that you will do this using an alternative mode of transport. So, the two streams of decision making (the deliberate strategy to get to Paris that day, and the emerging strategy of the use of an alternative means of transport) come together to form what we might call the actual realised strategy. The realised strategy is not exactly how you had originally planned it, due to unforeseen circumstances, but you got there in the end, albeit slightly later, and having cost you more (since you did not get a refund on your plane ticket).

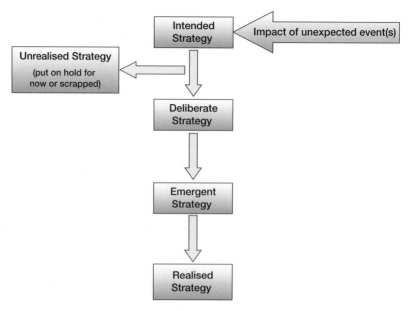

Figure 3.7 Mintzberg's intended, deliberate and realised strategies

ACTIVITY

Think of an example from your own life that illustrates Mintzberg's idea of intended, deliberate and realised strategies. Draw up your own diagram to illustrate this, and add a brief explanation in the form of bullet points to each part of the diagram.

1 What factors might prevent an original (intended) strategy from being the final 'realised' strategy? Give examples to illustrate your thoughts.

2 Some people might say that they will stick to their original plan, no matter what. What could happen if decision-makers insisted on sticking to their original (intended) strategy, despite changes in their micro and/or macro external environments?

3.8 Summary

This chapter has provided an introduction to strategy, and has briefly explored how and why mission statements and stakeholders fit into strategic thinking. There is clearly a lot to consider in terms of formulating and implementing strategies, and models such as those introduced in this chapter can help managers to structure their thinking and decision-making. However, decision-makers also need to have an understanding and appreciation of the impact of the wider external environment when they are formulating and implementing their strategies. What is important is that strategies are formulated to take into account a wide range of sources of information, and that they are reviewed and amended in light of changing circumstances.

KEY IDEAS

Some of the main points covered in this chapter are listed below. If you feel unsure about any of them, then revisit the appropriate section. If you would like some additional reading on the topic, try the books listed in recommended reading.

● **What is strategy?**
Strategy is simply about knowing *where* you want to go, and then planning *how* you are going to get there.

● **There are different levels of strategy**
Corporate strategy is concerned with *what* business(es) the organisation should be involved in. *Business* strategy is concerned with *how* to succeed in the chosen business(es). *Functional* strategy is the means by which the business strategies are carried out.

● **Strategy can be achieved in three basic ways:**
  1 Through internal development
  2 Through mergers and acquisitions
  3 Through joint developments and alliances.

● **Mission and stakeholders are important in strategy formulation and implementation**
The mission and stakeholders of an organisation need to be taken into consideration in the formulation and implementation of an organisation's strategies. There is an important link here to corporate social responsibility (CSR).

● **Understanding the external environment is important for strategy formulation and implementation**
Organisations need to be aware of what is happening, or could happen, in their micro and macro external environments. This knowledge and understanding is vital in ensuring appropriate strategies are devised, and that strategies are amended appropriately as circumstances change. These changing circumstances could be opportunities or threats.

REFLECTIVE QUESTIONS

1 Do mission statements always have to be the central guiding force in corporate strategy formulation? Explain your answer.
2 Supermarkets are a good example of organisations that have *both* cost leadership and differentiation strategies for their own brand goods. Why do you think supermarkets do this? What are the benefits of this strategy?
3 What do you think the advantages and disadvantages are of using models such as the BCG matrix and Ansoff's product/market matrix in helping determine strategic decision-making?
4 Why is CSR an important factor in strategic planning and implementation?

RECOMMENDED READING

Strategy

For a text that has a good chapter on strategy, with helpful illustrative examples, see Naylor, J. (2004) *Management.* 2nd edn. Harlow: Pearson.

For a more detailed text on strategy see Johnson, G., Scholes, K. and Whittington, R. (2008) *Exploring Corporate Strategy.* 8th edn. Harlow: Pearson.

Mission statements

For a brief, easily digestible read on mission statements and their value see Mullins, L.J. (2007) *Management and Organisational Behaviour.* 8th edn. Harlow: Pearson.

Stakeholders

The following sources are useful expansions to the introduction provided in this chapter:

Ansoff, I. (1987) *Corporate Strategy.* Revised edn. London: Penguin.

Boddy, D. (2008) *Management: An Introduction.* 4th edn. Harlow: Pearson.

Campbell, A. and Young, S. (1991) 'Creating a sense of mission', *Long Range Planning,* vol. 24, no. 4, 10–20.

Frooman, J. (1999) 'Stakeholder Influence Strategies', *Academy of Management Review*, vol. 24, no. 2, 191–205.

Pajunen, K. (2006) 'Stakeholder influences on organizational survival', *Journal of Management Studies,* vol. 43, no. 6 1261–1288.

USEFUL WEBSITES

Ansoff's matrix
www.mindtools.com/pages/article/newTMC_90.htm
Ashridge Mission Model
www.12manage.com/methods_campbell_ashridge_mission_model.html
BCG Matrix
www.mindtools.com/pages/article/newTED_97.htm
Contingency planning
planningskills.com/askdan/6.php
Industry life cycle
www.enotes.com/small-business-encyclopedia/industry-life-cycle
Porters' generic competitive strategies
www.12manage.com/methods_porter_competitive_advantage.html
Product life-cycle
www-rohan.sdsu.edu/~renglish/370/notes/chapt11/index.htm
www.netmba.com/marketing/product/lifecycle/
www.12manage.com/methods_product_life_cycle.html
www.referenceforbusiness.com/management/Or-Pr/Product-Life-Cycle-and-Industry-Life-Cycle.html
Stakeholder analysis
www.mindtools.com/pages/article/newPPM_07.htm
Stakeholders – interests and power
tutor2u.net/business/strategy/stakeholders-interests-and-power.html

Stakeholder mapping
www.12manage.com/methods_stakeholder_mapping.html
Strategic management
www.quickmba.com/strategy/

REFERENCES

Ansoff, I. (1987) *Corporate Strategy*. Revised edn. London: Penguin.

Campbell, A. and Young, S. (1991) 'Creating a sense of mission', *Long Range Planning*, vol. 24, no. 4, 10–20.

Dobson, P., Starkey, K. and Richards, J. (2004) *Strategic Management: Issues and Cases*. Oxford: Blackwell.

Eden, C. and Ackerman, F. (1998) *Making Strategy: The journey of strategic management*. London: Sage.

Johnson, G., Scholes, K. and Whittington, R. (2006) *Exploring Corporate Strategy*. 7th edn. Harlow: Prentice Hall.

Nutt, P.C. (2002) *Why decisions fail: avoiding the blunders and traps that lead to debacles*. San Francisco: Berrett-Koehler.

4 Structure, Size, and Growth

'Every company has two organizational structures: the formal one is written on the charts;
the other is the everyday relationship of the men and women in the organization.'

(Harold S. Geneen, American Businessman, 1910–1997)

CHAPTER OUTLINE

4.1 Introduction
4.2 What do we mean by organisational structure?
4.3 Types of organisational structure
4.4 Organisational size
4.5 Organisational growth
4.6 Summary

CHAPTER OBJECTIVES

After carefully reading and engaging with the tasks and activities outlined in
this chapter, you should have a better understanding of:
- what we mean by the term organisational structure
- why structure is important
- some key issues for consideration in organisational structure design
- different types of organisational structure
- organisational size and growth.

4.1 Introduction

Organisations vary in size and structure. Some organisations can be very small,
such as a local butcher's shop, and some very large, such as Microsoft. Some

organisations can be based in one particular geographic location, while others can have locations all around the world. Some start out small, and grow into larger organisations over a period of time, using various ways in which to do so. One thing that is clear is that structure, size, and growth are closely intertwined. Generally, in small organisations there is little need for formal structuring, but as organisations grow, they invariably require more formalised organisation. This chapter aims to introduce you to some of the key ideas involved in **organisational structure**, size and growth.

KEY TERMS

Organisational structure refers to the way in which jobs are formally arranged.

Example

Historically, organisations changed rapidly in the Industrial Revolution. As factories became established in towns, labour moved from the countryside in search of work. Largely, people had been used to managing their own motivation and labour, but working in the factories required structure and order to ensure effective functioning could occur. Although structure, hierarchy and order was not a new phenomenon (it had existed for a very long time in the military, for example) this type of rapid growth in the size of organisations was breaking new ground for commercial enterprise at the time. These changes in the organisation of work led to the development of scientific management theory.

4.2 What do we mean by organisational structure?

The way an organisation organises itself in terms of who does what, and who reports to whom, is basically what organisational structure is concerned with. The structure of an organisation needs to ensure that it is able to achieve its mission and objectives in an effective and efficient manner. In other words, an organisation needs to be structured in an appropriate way to get things done, while also enabling a degree of flexibility that will enable it to meet what can often be fast-paced changes in the external business environment.

Sometimes, management may decide that the structure of an organisation needs to change, and this is referred to as **organisational design**.

KEY TERMS

Organisational design is the development of, or changes to, the structure of an organisation.

1 Under what kind of circumstances might a company need to alter their structure?
2 What kind of impact could restructure have on the employees of a company?
3 How could a company manage a restructure to minimise the potential impact on employees?

ACTIVITY

Undertake some research to identify an organisation that has gone through some form of restructure over the last few years.

1 Explain how the structure has changed.
2 Suggest some reasons why the change may have been undertaken.

There are six key issues to consider in terms of organisational design.

Key issue	Summary of what this means
1 Specialisation	Work is divided into specific jobs.
2 Departmentalisation	Jobs are grouped together, often by function, e.g. human resources, marketing, and sales.
3 Chain of command	Explains who reports to whom.
4 Span of control	The number of staff a manager can effectively and efficiently manage at a given time.
5 Degree of centralisation	Concerned with the question of whether decisions are made higher up the **hierarchy**, or further down the hierarchy, i.e. is decision-making **centralised** or **decentralised**?
6 Formalisation	Concerned with the level of formality required in the behaviour of staff, e.g. the extent to which rules and procedures need to be followed.

Table 4.1   Key issues to consider in organisational design

KEY TERMS

Hierarchy refers to the levels of management/authority in an organisation.

Centralised is a term used to describe an organisation where decisions are taken by senior staff high up in the organisation, i.e. by chief executives and senior managers, and then cascaded down through the hierarchy.

Decentralised is a term used to describe an organisation where decision-making is allowed to occur much lower down the hierarchy of the organisation, e.g. through middle managers, or line managers, thus allowing for faster decision-making to take place.

Example

The army is an example of a formalised organisation, with a 'rigid' chain of command. The degree of centralisation of decision-making is high, although lower ranks are of course permitted to make decisions on the ground (although in line with the orders that have been passed down). Span of control varies depending on the work area concerned. Work is divided into specialist jobs, and like all organisations, there is departmentalisation.

Understanding the six key issues is important later on in the chapter when we consider a range of different organisational structures that organisations use (see Section 4.3). Let's look at each of them now in a little more detail.

Specialisation

The term specialisation is a more recent term for 'division of labour', and has its roots in scientific management. In the early twentieth century, Henry Ford used the idea of dividing up the tasks that went into producing a car so that employees could focus on one (or a small number) of tasks, and so become better and faster at them, and as a result standardise and increase production. These type of jobs are generally thought of as being repetitive, and these days there is concern that such jobs are boring and do not provide a great deal of job satisfaction, which *can* lead to, among other things, stress, high absenteeism, high staff turnover, and poor or inconsistent quality.

In a response to the problems inherent with such narrow job specialisation, employers have devised management techniques such as **job rotation** and **job enrichment**, in an attempt to alleviate some of the associated problems. However, not all specialised jobs are this routine in nature. In our example of the British Army for instance, staff specialise in particular aspects of army work, but their daily activities are not necessarily *routinely monotonous,* for example, like someone who may work on a production line. So it is routine monotony that is the key problem in terms of specialisation.

KEY TERMS

Job rotation is where an employee is moved from one task/job to another. The motivation for managers doing this includes the alleviation of negative psychological states such as boredom, and to help reduce negative physiological problems such as repetitive strain injury. Psychological alertness is also needed to reduce mistakes and accidents. Job rotation is also used to train staff in other areas, which offers a number of benefits for the organisation and employee.

Job enrichment is a term used to describe the addition of some element(s) of work that will make a person's job more rewarding in some way. This is often achieved through giving the jobholder more responsibility and/or additional tasks to perform.

Today, work specialisation is still a common feature in many organisations. You would commonly see task specialisation in production line environments. For example, in vegetable packing houses you would have staff that specialised in delivering the vegetables to be processed, those who grade the vegetables by size and quality, those who remove poor quality produce, those who wash, those who trim, and those who package.

As previously mentioned, specialisation is not just a feature of production line environments. All organisations have staff who are specialists in a functional area, e.g. management accountant, payroll officer, head chef, librarian. While

Figure 4.1 Staff working on a production line, performing specialist roles

these jobs are certainly not as narrow in focus as repetitively performing one or two functions on a production line, they nonetheless represent examples of job specialisation. In these types of jobs, some staff request job rotation (sometimes called secondments) to provide some variety to enrich their experience of work.

ACTIVITY

Undertake some research on your own to explore how *routine monotonous specialised* jobs impact on:

- the employee
- the quantity of work undertaken
- the quality of work undertaken

Alternatively, work in groups to discuss the above issues.

Departmentalisation

After jobs have been specialised, organisations often group people with particular specialisms into departments, e.g. finance, marketing, human resources, catering, and so on. Sometimes people with a particular specialism are not grouped together: instead they act in their specialist role within another department. For example, an IT technician may be placed in each faculty in a university. There will also be an IT services department however, where the majority of the IT technicians will be based. The idea of having the specialists together in a department is that this will help to coordinate the work of those staff in a more organised and integrated way, while having a technician within a faculty helps facilitate a quicker response to daily issues.

Departmentalisation can take different forms, and it is on this basis that organisation structure charts are drawn up (see Section 4.3).

ACTIVITY

On your own, or in a group, undertake some research to find at least one organisational example to illustrate each of the following forms of departmentalisation:

1 Functional departmentalisation
2 Product departmentalisation
3 Division departmentalisation
4 Geographic/regional departmentalisation.

Form of departmentalisation	Summary of what this entails
Functional	Here the organisation is structured around traditional functions such as marketing, sales, finance, production etc.
Product	Here the organisation is structured around the products (or services) it produces. For example, each major product (or service) will have its own functional departments to service them.
Division	This is an extension of product departmentalisation. A division may have several products (or services) within it and all of those products (or services) in that division will have their own functional departments to service their needs.
Customer	Customer structures are organised around categories of customer, for example, business customers (**B2B**), and private/retail customers.
Process	This type of structure groups jobs based on product or customer flow.
Geographic/regional	This is where jobs are grouped on the basis of their geographical position. For example, a company could have a Marketing Director for each of the following areas: Europe, Asia, America, and Australia.

Table 4.2   Different types of departmentalisation

KEY TERMS

B2B is an acronym that stands for 'business-to-business'. B2B means that one business is selling directly to another business, rather than to individual retail consumers.

Chain of command

Chain of command is a phrase used to describe the line of authority in an organisation that extends from the top to the bottom. The chain of command is important in establishing lines of authority, i.e. who reports to/is responsible to whom. Employees need to know who has legitimate power to make decisions.

Example

The MoD (Ministry of Defence) commands the Army through two headquarters and a number of smaller headquarters in different parts of the world.

The following diagram illustrates a broad view of this chain of command (as at mid-2009), although a much more detailed chain of command exists.

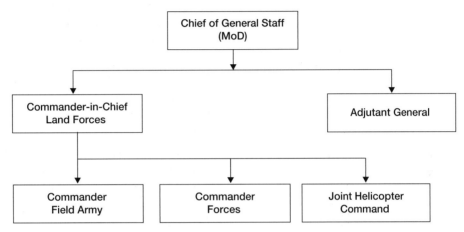

Figure 4.2 Illustration of the chain of command in the British Army
(Source: Adapted from www.armedforces.co.uk/army/listings/l0006.html)

Span of control

Span of control refers to the number of employees that a manager can effectively and efficiently manage at a given time. The idea is that the wider the span of control, the less layers of management an organisation is likely to have. As organisations have sought to become more cost effective, often through **downsizing** by stripping out layers of middle management (frequently called delayering), this has led to the enlargement of the span of control of many managers, i.e. in flatter, leaner organisations spans of control are likely to be much wider. This has implications in respect of where decision-making should lie (centralisation versus decentralisation). If a manager has more staff to oversee they may well need to cascade down some decision-making in order to continue to function effectively.

KEY TERMS

Downsizing is where an organisation deliberately reduces the number of staff it employs. The aim is to improve the performance of the organisation. Similar phrases that you may come across to describe such a phenomenon are de-massing, re-engineering, restructuring, and rightsizing.

Degree of centralisation

Degree of centralisation is concerned with where decision-making takes place in an organisation. If decisions are made by individuals who are senior in an organisation, and then passed down the 'ranks' to be put into action, this is said to be a highly centralised organisation (as in the Army example shown in Figure 4.2). At the opposite end of the continuum, you might get an organisation that delegates the decision-making to employees who are at the 'coal face'. This type of organisation would be said to be a highly decentralised organisation.

It is important to note that no one organisation would ever be fully centralised or decentralised. This is because it would simply not be possible or desirable for every decision ever made in an organisation to be made either by senior management, or by employees at the 'coal face'.

Formalisation

Some organisations are more formal than others in the way they are structured, and therefore the way people behave toward one another.

There are two issues to consider in terms of formalisation:

- how standardised the jobs are in the organisation
- how much employee behaviour is influenced by rules and procedures

The higher the degree of formalisation of a job role, the less discretion the employee has in terms of how they carry out their role(s). Where job roles are highly formalised you will see a situation where everyone is required to perform the same job role in the same way, therefore resulting in a standard, and consistent way of doing things.

Example

When looking for a new motor insurance quotation, many people telephone call centres of insurance companies in search of the best deal. It is highly likely you will be asked the same type of questions, and dealt with in the same manner no matter which insurance company you ring. Similarly, if you call the same company on several occasions you are likely to speak to a different customer services operative, but you are likely to receive a standardised service.

In organisations that are formalised you will find that job descriptions are clear and adhered to by the employee (versus an organisation where job descriptions may be quite fluid), and there will be many clearly stated rules and procedures to be adhered to in the formalised organisation.

Figure 4.3 Call centres are examples of a standardised working environment

So, there are some organisations that are more formalised than others. However, within an organisation there may be some sections or departments that are more formalised than others. For example, you might find within a university that the Registrars Office would be a more formalised environment than, say, the Careers department. The key issue with formalisation is however, how much discretion and autonomy the employee has in how they perform their job.

ACTIVITY

Work-related stress is an important and intensely researched aspect of organisational life. Find out what academic researchers and the Health and Safety Executive have to say about the role of discretion/autonomy in terms of work-related stress. ▶

Discuss whether increasing discretion/autonomy is possible and desirable in all types of work. Give examples to illustrate your points.

1 What kind of impact do you think de-layering has on managers in an organisation?

2 When a manager's span of control is increased, how might this impact on their subordinates?

3 What kind of impact could de-layering have on the quality of work undertaken?

4 Why is it undesirable to have all decisions made in an organisation by employees at the 'coal face'?

(4.3) Types of organisational structure

Organisations can be structured in different ways, and we have already looked at some of the key issues. Generally speaking, the larger the organisation, the more likely you are to find a greater degree of specialisation, departmentalisation, centralised decision-making, and formalisation.

In your reading on organisational structure and size you may well come across the following phrases used to describe organisational structure:

- mechanistic model
- organic model
- tall organisation
- flat organisation
- simple structure
- functional structure
- product structure
- divisional structure
- customer structure
- geographic or regional structure
- matrix structure
- team structure
- virtual organisation (sometimes called network or modular structure).

We will briefly consider each one. If you would like to know more about any of them, additional reading is suggested at the end of the chapter.

Mechanistic and organic models of organisational structure

The mechanistic and organic models of organisational structure represent two extreme models of organisational design: at one extreme, the mechanistic model, and the other, the organic model.

The following table details the main characteristics of each model.

Feature	Mechanistic model	Organic model
Tall or flat?	More likely to be tall	Flat
Specialisation	More than likely	Less likely
Departmentalisation	Extensive	Some
Chain of command	Long	Short
Span of control	Narrow	Wide
Degree of centralisation (where the decision-making occurs)	Centralised	Decentralised (highly participative decision making)
Knowledge location	Knowledge located at the top of the hierarchy	Knowledge widely spread throughout the organisation
Formalisation	High	Low
Information/ communication	Limited Mostly downwards (vertical) communication	Comprehensive Upward, downward, and lateral/horizontal communication
Staff focus	Loyalty and obedience is important	Being committed to goals is the most important thing
Associated terms	Bureaucratic	Cross-hierarchical Cross-functional teams

Table 4.3   Characteristics of the mechanistic and organic models of organisational structure

Tall organisations

The term 'tall organisation' refers to a type of organisational structure that is characterised by many layers of management. With a tall organisation structure you are likely to get narrower spans of control, as there are more layers of management, and more specialised work. Tall organisations tend to be slower at decision-making because there are more layers of management to go through, and they also tend to be slower in responding to changes in the external business environment (for the same reason).

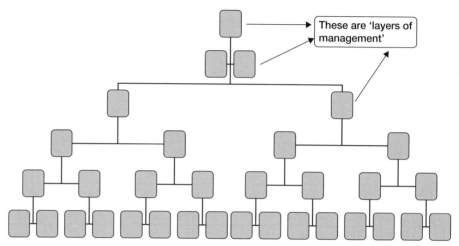

Figure 4.4 A tall organisation

Figure 4.4 illustrates an organisation with six layers of management. Organisations can, of course, have more layers than this.

Flat organisations

The opposite idea to the tall organisation is the flat one. The term 'flat organisation' refers to a type of organisational structure that is characterised by few layers of management. With a flat organisation you are likely to get wider spans of control; as there are less layers of management a manager will have more people to oversee. Flatter organisations tend to be more responsive to changes because decision-making has fewer layers to go through, and hence is generally quicker.

The flatter structure can sound more appealing if you consider that it can offer a faster, more responsive decision-making climate, which is thought to be more appropriate when the external environment is uncertain and fast changing. However, a major disadvantage of the flatter organisation is that managing in this kind of organisation can be more challenging, as the range of situations encountered by a manager is likely to be much wider than in a tall organisation.

The fewer levels of management, the more varied the tasks the manager is likely to have. The manager in a flatter organisation needs to have a wider range of knowledge, skills and abilities. So, in flatter organisations where layers of management are stripped away, the work does not simply disappear, it is taken on by fewer managers, and in this way their workload and variety increases, which is much more challenging.

Figure 4.5 A flat organisation

1 Why might organisations strip away layers of management?
2 What types of phrases are used to describe this 'stripping away' of levels of management?

Simple structure

If you had your own small business it is likely you would have a simple structure to your organisation, at least to begin with. This means that there would be you, as the owner, and a number of employees. There is unlikely to be any need for departmentalisation and formalisation. The decision-making would be centralised to you, the owner-manager, and your span of control would be as wide as the number of staff you employ.

As small organisations grow, it is unlikely they will remain as such simple structures. When an organisation employs more people, the tasks become more specialised, and the organisation more formalised. There are different structures an organisation could use when this happens; functional, product, divisional, customer, geographic/regional. We will now look at each of these in turn, starting with the functional structure.

Functional structure

The functional structure is organised in terms of functional areas, e.g. marketing, finance, human resources, and so on. Specialist knowledge is grouped into these areas. The different functions need to work together to achieve the goals of the organisation.

As with all structures, there are advantages and disadvantages, which are summarised in Table 4.4.

Product/service structure

As the name suggests, this structure is organised around the products (or services) the organisation produces. Each product will have its own functional departments to service it (so each product is like its own business in this respect). Each product or service would therefore be seen as its own **profit centre**.

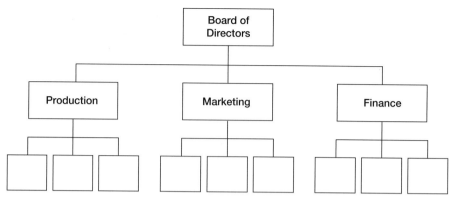

Figure 4.6 Functional structure chart

Advantages	Disadvantages
Suited to small- and medium-sized organisations.	Can have problems with coordination between the functional areas.
Suited to organisations with a small number of products.	Functional areas may have a narrow view of the goals of the organisation, which could impede the organisation.
Helps with the specialisation of functional knowledge.	Functional groups focus on their own specified areas, and therefore customers may experience a 'patchy' service.
Helps to reduce duplication of functional resources.	As the functional areas are focused on their own area, this could result in a slower response to changes in the market.
Helps with the coordination of functional areas.	

Table 4.4   Summary of advantages and disadvantages of the functional structure

KEY TERMS

Sections of a business are often divided into **profit centres**. Each area has its own profit centre, from which expenses are deducted from the profits that area makes. This makes it easier to see which areas of the business are making a profit, and how much.

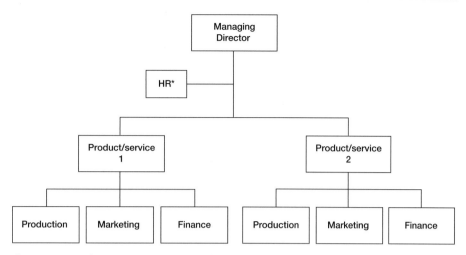

Figure 4.7 Product/service structure chart

* When an organisation is structured by product or service, or by geographical location, it may be the case that certain aspects of support services/functions, such as HR, might be delegated to individual units. However, it is likely that overall responsibility would lie with an overarching department. This may be the case for any of the major functions, not just HR, which is the example given in this illustration.

Advantages	Disadvantages
Enables the organisation to specialise in particular products (or services).	There can be duplication of functions (as you can see from the diagram).
Enables managers to become experts in their industry.	There is a danger that each division can lose sight of the overarching goals of the organisation because they are focused on their own specific product (or service).
Enables the organisation to get closer to their customers.	

Table 4.5   Summary of advantages and disadvantages of the product (or service) structure

Divisional structure

The divisional structure is an extension of the product structure. Here, a division is made up of several products that are normally related in some way. Each division will be serviced by its own dedicated functional areas.

As with the functional structure, there are also advantages and disadvantages (see Table 4.6).

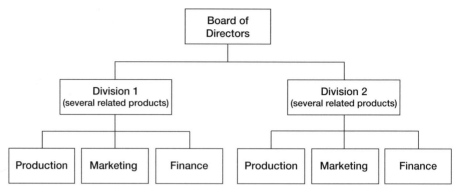

Figure 4.8 Divisional structure chart

Advantages	Disadvantages
As the products are 'lumped together' into divisions this cuts down on the number of functional departments you would have had if using the functional structure, which saves on staffing, and streamlines customer service for customers purchasing products from that division.	This structure is only appropriate for large organisations, who have a lot of products, across a diverse range.
Coordination and cooperation across products in a division can be facilitated.	Since there are still divisions, there are likely to be problems coordinating between those divisions.
	The objectives of the division might conflict with the overall objectives of the organisation, which could lead to conflict and/or reduced cooperation.

Table 4.6   Summary of advantages and disadvantages of the divisional structure

Customer structure

Not surprisingly, a customer structure is organised around the customer. This structure is useful where different types of customers might purchase different products, in different quantities, or have different needs. For example, business-to-business/industrial sales might be very different than sales to individual retail customers; the former likely purchasing in bulk, the latter, individual items.

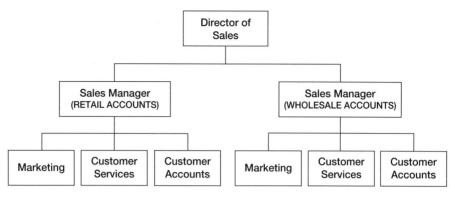

Figure 4.9 Customer structure chart

Advantages	Disadvantages
Helps the organisation to develop a better understanding of the different types of customer it has, which should enable the organisation to better meet the needs of their customers.	Can lead to duplication of functional resources, because each customer area would be serviced by its own functional areas.
Enables the organisation to respond faster to the changing needs and preferences of their customers.	There can be problems in coordination between customer units and the objectives of the organisation.

Table 4.7   Summary of advantages and disadvantages of the customer structure

Geographic/regional structure

Some organisations are structured in terms of geography. For example, a company operating in the UK might have geographic areas of South West, North West, and so on. An organisation trading beyond the UK might have geographic areas such as UK and Northern Ireland, France, Belgium or Spain (of course, depending upon where they trade). As with the product and divisional structures, it is often the case that individual geographic areas are treated as their own profit centres.

NB: Some companies may combine a geographic and division structure, and some geographic with product.

Matrix structure

The matrix structure is a fairly contemporary organisational design. It is a combination of two other organisational structures, e.g. a combination of functional and divisional.

So far, all the organisational structures discussed in this chapter results in an employee having one direct person to report to. As the matrix structure is a combination of two organisational structures, the result is that employees in this type of structure end up having two people to report to. Some authors refer this to this as a 'dual reporting relationship', and others as the 'dual chain of command'.

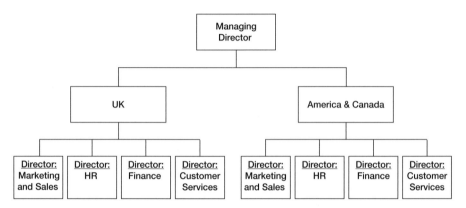

Figure 4.10 Geographic/regional structure chart

Advantages	Disadvantages
Can assist in the development of in-depth knowledge and understanding of a particular geographic market, governments, and competitors within the specific areas concerned.	Can lead to problems in coordination and communication between the regions.
Can help to develop a sense of accountability (and possibly competition) for the performance of managers of the different areas.	Can lead to over-competitiveness between regions, which could inhibit cooperation.
Each region should be able to respond faster to changes in their immediate external environment.	There will normally be duplication of functional services, as each region would be serviced by its own functional areas.
	Each region may have its own production facilities, which may not necessarily be the most efficient and effective way.

Table 4.8   Summary of advantages and disadvantages of the geographic/regional structure

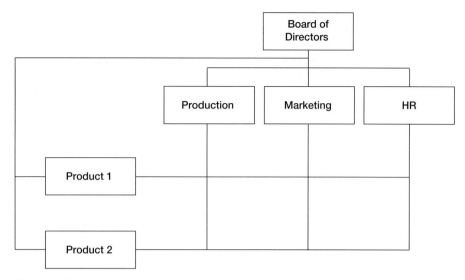

Figure 4.11 Matrix structure chart

How does it work? Let's consider an example of functional combined with product (see Figure 4.11). In this example, specialists from different functional departments may be assigned to work on particular projects, both with people from different functional areas than themselves, and with product areas. For example, a product manager could assign staff to his/her team from functional areas as necessary, to achieve what ever their objective is. If a member of staff is assigned to join the team from marketing, that person would have two 'bosses'; their normal boss in marketing, and the product manager in charge of the project.

Advantages	Disadvantages
Helps information flow in an organisation because people from different areas are working together more.	When you have two bosses this makes supervision and evaluation more complex.
Can improve the quality of decisions because different opinions from different perspectives are brought to the table.	Accountability for decisions can be spread because more people are involved in the process from different areas.
It can be particularly useful in changing and complicated business environments because the knowledge and skills needed can be quickly brought in from areas of the organisation as needed.	Where a team is made up of individuals from different departments/sections, who may have different views and objectives, this can lead to different perspectives and possibly dysfunctional conflict.

▶

Advantages	Disadvantages
Staffing is well utilised through this 'borrowing' approach as and when needed.	There can be communication difficulties as specialists may use language specific to their work specialism that others may not be familiar with.

Table 4.9   Summary of advantages and disadvantages of the matrix structure

Team structure

The team structure is very similar to the matrix structure in its basic idea, which is to draw personnel from different areas of the organisation to work on a specific project. Unlike the matrix structure, these teams are often 'self-managed'. Staff can be drawn from any area, and from any level of the organisation. The team may be from across functions or from within a single area – in which case it would look like a mini version of the department concerned.

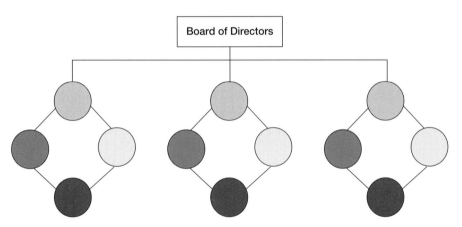

Figure 4.12 – Team structure chart (N.B. different shading indicates staff from different areas/departments)

Advantages	Disadvantages
They can offer greater flexibility, lower costs, and a faster response than other structural options in terms of delivering the project(s) in hand.	They may do none of the things opposite if the team is unable to meet regularly because they do not have sufficient time to give to the project.
Staff can be drafted in when the skills and expertise are needed (as long as such personnel exist in the organisation).	The team members may take time to reach an effective stage (Tuckman), which may delay functional outputs.

▶

Advantages	Disadvantages
Management delegate responsibility to the team rather than 1 individual, so the team is mutually accountable for delivering (this could also be a disadvantage however!).	Some teams may find the concept of self-management daunting, and may work more effectively with identifiable leadership.
Less hierarchical division among team members.	Although team structures are not based on a hierarchy, in practice, where members of the team are at different levels in the organisation, there will still exist a degree of 'separation' and possible deference to the views of more senior staff.

Table 4.10   Summary of advantages and disadvantages of the team structure

1 If a team is brought together for a 'project' of some sort, whereby the members are from different functional areas *and* from different levels (seniority) within the organisation:

a) What kind of issues might arise?

b) How might these issues impact on the effectiveness of the team?

The virtual organisation

The virtual organisation (sometimes called the network or modular structure) is where an organisation undertakes some of its core business functions, but **outsources** the rest to a network of other businesses. The organisation basically hires in specialists from outside of the organisation as and when they are needed.

KEY TERMS

Outsourcing is where an organisation has a contract with another organisation to supply a product or service that they need as part of their business undertakings. This is also referred to as 'contracting out'.

ACTIVITY

Visit the home page for Virgin (www.virgin.com/Companies)

How would you characterise the structure of this company?

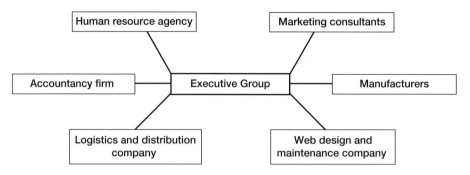

Figure 4.13 A virtual organisation

Advantages	Disadvantages
Can allow managers to focus more on the core activities of the organisation, which may help them to become better at this and thereby gain competitive advantage.	Non-core activities that have been contracted-out cannot be forgotten, and need attention (which takes staff time and skill) to ensure they are delivered appropriately so they do not negatively impact on the running of the organisation.
Can help reduce staffing costs. However, out-sourcing can also be expensive.	The contracted-out activities need good coordination.

Table 4.11 Summary of advantages and disadvantages of the virtual organisation

4.4 Organisational size

As we have already mentioned earlier in this chapter, the size of an organisation affects its structure. The larger the organisation is the more specialisation, departmentalisation and so on. Larger organisations tend to be much more mechanistic. The aim of this part of the chapter is simply to introduce you to the different ways in which organisation size is measured. We will then go on to explain some of the ways in which organisations can grow in Section 4.5.

The size of an organisation can be measured by a number of factors, such as:

- turnover – how much revenue the organisation is bringing in
- value of output – how much output/product/service the organisation is producing, in monetary terms
- capital employed – the amount of money that is invested in the organisation
- level of employment – the number of staff employed at the organisation.

Level of employment is broken down into the following categories:

- Micro firm   0 – 9 employees
- Small firm   0 – 49 employees (includes micro)
- Medium firm (**SME**)   50 – 249 employees
- Large firm   250+ employees

(Source: Department for Business, Innovation and Skills (BIS))

KEY TERMS

SME is an acronym that stands for 'small- to medium-sized enterprise'.

ACTIVITY

1 Identify one company for each of the following classifications by level of employment:
- micro
- small
- SME
- large.

2 For each organisation identify how it is structured.
3 Discuss how you think the size of the organisation has influenced its structure.

CASE STUDY

The Home Office is a large organisation, and in January 2007 the UK Government split it into two separate departments (Department of Justice and Department of Security).

1 Why do you think the Home Office was split into two departments? (Your answer should be related to problems associated with its size.)

2 What kind of impact (both positive and negative) might this restructure have had on:
   a) the organisation
   b) the people working for it
   c) the people who need to access the information and services provided by it.

Organisational growth

Many organisations start out small, and grow over time, through different ways. Some grow into very large corporations indeed (as shown in the case study on Cadbury-Schweppes below), while other organisations remain relatively small (often out of choice, i.e. the owner wishes to remain in control of their company). Greiner (1972, as cited in Capon, 2004) developed a model of organisational growth, which proposed that over time, as an organisation grew through change, it would experience various crises (in leadership, autonomy, control, and red tape), and how it dealt with those crises would determine the direction it took next.

Typical ways that organisations grow are through:

- vertical integration
- horizontal integration
- conglomerate diversification.

Let's briefly consider each of these in turn.

Vertical integration

This is where the organisation moves backwards and/or forwards into activities that are related to the organisation's products and services. Johns and Saks (2005:492) define this strategy for growth as 'the strategy of formally taking control of sources of organizational supply and distribution'. A company can take control of another company by acquiring it, or may join forces with it through a merger (see Chapter 3, Section 3.6 for more on mergers and acquisitions). An example includes breweries that run their own pubs (where they only sell their own drinks).

Horizontal integration

Horizontal integration is where an organisation develops activities that complement its existing business, i.e. products and/or services that are the same, or similar to what they already do. Like vertical integration, there will be some link between existing and new activities. Like vertical integration, horizontal integration usually occurs through mergers and/or acquisitions.

Conglomerate diversification

Unlike vertical and horizontal integration, conglomerate diversification is where an organisation grows by expanding into completely different products/ services. For example, supermarkets have branched out into clothing, banking and insurance, which are nothing to do with their core business of food retailing. Virgin is also an excellent example of a corporation that grew by building a diverse portfolio of products and services. The idea here is to grow, but to spread the risk by not 'having all their eggs in one basket'. This strategy for growth is also used when there is no/little scope for growth in the core market, so in order to expand the company has to move into different products and/or services.

ACTIVITY

Find an example of at least one company for each of the following ways in which an organisation can grow:

a) vertical integration
b) horizontal integration
c) conglomerate diversification.

Describe how each of the organisations grew in these ways, i.e. chart the 'event(s)' that occurred. This may include several 'events' over a long period of time.

CASE STUDY

Cadbury Schweppes is a good example of how an organisation has grown from small organisation to a globally recognised brand.

John Cadbury opened a small grocery shop in Birmingham in 1824, and functioned as a sole trader (and would have been classified as a micro company). By 1831 he had changed his business from a grocery store to the manufacture of drinking chocolate and cocoa. In the 1840s John went into partnership with his brother, Benjamin (and became known as 'Cadbury Brothers of Birmingham'). In 1861 John Cadbury retired, and his two sons, Richard and George, took over the family business. In 1878 Richard and George, and their 200 employees (now an SME) outgrew their premises, and in order for the company to keep growing, they needed to find new premises. So, in 1879 they built a new factory on the banks of the Bourn Brook (which was to become known as 'Bournville' [ville is the French word for town or city]).

Within ten years the number of employees grew from 200 to 1,200 (now a large company). After the death of Richard, the sons of Richard and George, joined George to run the business, and turned the company into a private limited company. New products swiftly followed, and the business expanded. By the turn of the century the new factory at Bournville employed around 2,500 workers. After the First World War the Bournville factory was redeveloped, enabling mass production. In 1919 Cadbury merged with J.S. Fry and Sons, and in 1969 merged again with Schweppes, making Cadbury Schweppes Plc (a world leader in confectionary and soft drinks in the UK and abroad, with factories all over the world, and a large range of household brands), who employ around 55,000 workers. In 1995 Cadbury expanded into China, and established a factory in Beijing. Also in 1995 Cadbury Schweppes acquired Dr Pepper/Seven-Up Companies Inc. (and shortened its name to Dr Pepper/Seven-Up Inc.). In 2003 Cadbury Schweppes acquired Adams (famous for chewing gum). In May 2008 Cadbury Schweppes demerged from its Americas drinks arm, Dr Pepper Snapple (new name Dr Pepper Snapple Group).

continued . . .

◀

. . . continued

In early 2010 Cadbury is in the process of being acquired by the giant American company Kraft.

Focus on structure:

1 Visit the website for Cadbury Schweppes (or access their most recent Annual Report and Accounts online), and using the knowledge you have gained from this chapter, classify the current over-arching structure of the company.
2 Using your knowledge of organisational structure and your research on Cadbury Schweppes, draw a basic structure chart that shows how you think the company is structured.
3 As the company grew, how do you think the increasing size might have impacted on the structure of the organisation?

Focus on size and growth:

1 Use the information provided in the case study to identify the key ways in which Cadbury's has grown over the years. (Hint: if you have not already done so, reading through Chapter 3 on strategy, mission and stakeholders will also help with this activity.)
2 Why do you think the company made the decisions to grow in these ways?
3 Why do you think the company decided to 'shrink' a little by de-merging with Dr Pepper Snapple Group?

 ## Summary

This chapter has introduced a wide range of issues pertinent to the study of organisational structure. Organisational structure can be very simple in small organisations, but can become much more complicated as organisations grow in size, and change, for example through mergers and acquisitions.

KEY IDEAS

Some of the main points covered in this chapter are listed below. If you feel unsure about any of them, then revisit the appropriate section. If you would like some additional reading on the topic, try the books listed in recommended reading.

What do we mean by organisational structure?
● Organisational structure is the way in which jobs in an organisation are formally arranged; who does what, and who reports to whom.
● There are many different types of organisational structure.

continued . . . ▶

◀ *. . . continued*

Why is organisational structure important?

● The structure of an organisation is important because it needs to ensure that the organisation is able to achieve the mission and objectives of the organisation, in an effective and efficient manner.

Key issues in organisational structure

● An organisation needs to be structured in an appropriate way to get things done, while also enabling a degree of flexibility that will enable the organisation to meet what can often be fast-paced changes in the external business environment.
● Specialisation needs to be considered.
● Departmentalisation needs to be considered.
● Chain of command needs to be considered.
● Span of control needs to be considered.
● Degree of centralisation of decision-making needs to be considered.
● Formalisation needs to be considered.

Issues to consider about organisational size and growth

● When organisations become too big, problems can occur that require workable, effective solutions.
● Organisations do not always carry on growing. Sometimes they decide to become smaller, for example, through selling off parts of the company, through de-mergers, and through redundancies.

REFLECTIVE QUESTIONS

1 Some organisations can become so big that they experience problems in terms of organisational efficiency and effectiveness. What advice could you offer an organisation in this situation?
2 Think of a situation you have been in, either at work or in university, where you have worked in a team structure.
   a) What problems did you encounter?
   b) Why do you think these problems occurred?
   c) What could you have done to improve the situation?
3 The matrix and team structures appear to be good ideas when projects need expertise from different functional areas. Reflect on the problems staff might experience working in these structures.
4 Do you think it is important for an organisation to regularly review its structure? Provide a rationale for your answer.

RECOMMENDED READING

Organisational structure and size

Boddy, D. (2008) *Management: An Introduction.* 4th edn. Pearson: Harlow.

Hitt, M.A., Black, J.S. and Porter, L.W. (2005) *Management.* International edn. Pearson: Upper Saddle River, NJ.

Makawatsakul, N. and Kleiner, B.H. (2003) 'The Effect of Downsizing on Morale and Attrition', *Management Research News*, vol. 26 nos. 2–4, 52–62.
Mullins, L. (2007) *Management and Organisational Behaviour*. 8th edn. Harlow: Pearson.
Robbins, S.P. and Coulter, M. (2007) *Management.* 9th edn. Upper Saddle River, NJ: Pearson.
Thornhill, A. and Saunders, M.N.K. (1998) 'The meanings, consequences and implications of the management of downsizing and redundancy: a review'. *Personnel Review,* vol. 27, no. 4, 271–295.

All of the textbooks provide useful expansion on the introductory points raised in this chapter. They provide useful illustrative examples. They are easy to read, and highly recommended as sources to further your knowledge and understanding in this subject area. The journal articles offer you a more in-depth look at the impact of changing size and structure.

Organisational growth
Capon, C. (2004) *Understanding Organisational Context: Inside and Outside Organisations*. 2nd edn. London: Prentice Hall FT.
Capon provides more detailed reading on Greiner's (1972) organisational growth model.

USEFUL WEBSITES

www.managementhelp.org/ Provides a wide range of business related information, including organisational growth.
www.managementhelp.org/org_thry/new_forms.htm Provides information on new organisational structures (includes network structure, virtual organisations, self-managed teams, learning organisations, and self-organising systems).
http://epress.anu.edu.au/info_systems/mobile_devices/ch11s04.html Greiner's five phases of organisational growth.
www.berr.gov.uk/ Organisation size – definitions of organisational size can be found at the website for the Department for Business, Innovation and Skills (previously known as the Department for Business Enterprise and Regulatory Reform – BERR – and prior to that known as the DTI).

REFERENCES

Capon, C. (2004) *Understanding Organisational Context: Inside and Outside Organisations*. 2nd edn. London: Prentice Hall FT.
Department for Business, Innovation and Skills (BIS) (online). Available at: www.berr.gov.uk/.
Johns, G. and Saks, A.M. (2005) *Organizational Behaviour: Understanding and Managing Life at Work.* 6th edn. Toronto: Pearson.

5 Communicating across the functions

'*The greatest problem in communication is the illusion that it has been accomplished.*'

(George Bernard Shaw)

CHAPTER OUTLINE

5.1 Introduction
5.2 What is communication?
5.3 Functions of communication
5.4 Flow of communication
5.5 Challenges to effective communication
5.6 The impact of technology on communication
5.7 Summary

CHAPTER OBJECTIVES

After carefully reading and engaging with the tasks and activities outlined in this chapter, you should have a better understanding of:
- what communication is
- the function of communication within organisations
- the variety of ways in which communication occurs in the organisational context
- some of the barriers to effective communication
- some of the impacts that technology has had on communication in organisations.

5.1 Introduction

In this chapter we will largely focus on **internal communication** within organisations, although we will briefly touch on communication between organisations when we consider technology and communication. Without effective internal communication, no one will know what is really going on, and serious problems can arise, particularly in terms of control, coordination, and the negative impact it can have on employees. Information can get lost somewhere in 'the system': it can be distorted, misunderstood, and so on. Being able to communicate effectively both within and across the functions of an organisation is therefore of vital importance.

> **KEY TERMS**
>
> **Internal communication** is communication that occurs within an organisation, as opposed to between an organisation and individuals and companies outside of the organisation.

5.2 What is communication?

Many people think the answer to this question is simple and straightforward. However, as can be the case with many words we use every day, it is a little more complicated than most people realise.

Some people make the assumption that **communication** is purely the *transmission* of information. However, this is just part of the picture.

Communication involves the following two fundamental principles:

1 The sender *transmits* information to the receiver.
2 The receiver *understands the meaning* of the message that was sent.

You may see definitions of communication that include that there should also be *feedback from the receiver* to the sender, although this does not necessarily have to happen in order to be able to say that communication has taken place.

What is most important in the process of communication is that the sender and receiver are in agreement (consensus) about the meaning of the message. If they are not, then the communication has not been **effective** and there will be some degree of misunderstanding (which could happen for a number of reasons, which we will explore later on in the chapter). So, another important aspect to consider is effectiveness.

You will also come across the terms **formal** and **informal communication**.

KEY TERMS

The term **communication** refers to the process of sending and receiving of information, where both parties understand the meaning of the message being conveyed.

The term **effective communication** refers to the degree to which the sender and receiver both attribute the same meaning and understanding to the message that has been conveyed.

Interpersonal communication is communication that occurs between two or more individuals.

Organisational communication refers to how communication takes place within an organisation.

Formal communication refers to communication that follows the chain of command (see Chapter 4) in the organisation. It is also used to describe communication that is necessary in order for an employee to undertake their job.

Informal communication refers to communication that occurs between colleagues, such as the 'grapevine', but is not specified by the structural hierarchy of the organisation.

1 What are the key elements of effective communication?

2 What do you think the advantages and disadvantages might be of informal communication in an organisation?

Example

Asda makes use of technology to improve formal communications for training and corporate briefings. A few years ago the supermarket chain Asda installed a satellite training and communications system to play purpose-shot videos for staff. This enabled some paper and mail-based communications to be replaced. The system enabled corporate briefings and training sessions to be easily rolled out to all staff.

5.3 Functions of communication

There are four main functions of communication in an organisation:

1 To control and coordinate (people and activities).

2 To provide information.

3 To help motivate staff.

4 To enable staff to express their emotions.

Controlling and coordinating (people and activities)

This is one of the most important functions of formal internal organisational communication. If people do not know what they should be doing, when, where, and with whom, for example, there will be chaos and inefficiency. Work may be duplicated, or alternatively, not undertaken at all.

Examples of formal control could include where staff are formally disciplined by the use of both verbal and written forms of communication, with the aim of controlling or improving their behaviour. Other examples of communication being used to control and coordinate include health and safety signs, and sounds, e.g. the fire bell. Body language can also be used effectively to control someone; sometimes all it takes is a stern look from a colleague and the message is transmitted quickly and quietly (that they want someone to be quiet or to change the subject, for example).

So, communication is not just about the spoken and written word. Sounds, images, and body language are also important facets in communication, particularly with regard to controlling and coordinating the activities of people.

Example

Health and safety signs are a good example to illustrate the power of images in controlling/ coordinating people. Such signs also cut across language barriers. Familiar examples include the green safety signage such as fire exit and first aid, and the yellow warning signs such as danger of electric shock.

Figure 5.1 Health and safety signs

Providing information

Within organisations, there are masses of communications occurring every hour of every day. People are very often communicating in order to provide information, both within a section/department, and across the various functions. Most of this type of communication arrives in written format, whether it is in formal reports, via articles on an intranet, or in emails. However, sometimes information is provided verbally, for example through meetings, presentations, and speeches. The challenge is to choose the *right* form of communication for the purpose and audience. Later in the chapter we will look at some of the problems associated with communication, many of which relate to the methods used.

Communication to help motivate staff

While this is not necessarily an obvious function of communication to some people, it is important that leaders and managers understand the vital role that communication can play in terms of motivating, and conversely, demotivating staff. For example, setting goals, and then providing positive constructive feedback to an employee on how well they are doing can help to motivate an employee (see Chapter 6). Having positive, **two-way communication** in an appraisal can also help to motivate staff. Lack of information or ambiguous information can work to demotivate staff. There are many other examples, but these function to illustrate the point. The main lesson here is that not paying sufficient attention to the impact your communication can have on the receiver(s) may mean that opportunities to motivate staff are lost, or conversely, you inadvertently demotivate staff as a result of the communication that has taken place.

KEY TERMS

Two-way communication is where the receiver provides feedback to the sender.

Enabling the expression of emotion

People spend a good deal of time with their co-workers. For many people, work colleagues are an ongoing source of social interaction. Part of this interaction involves the communication of both positive and negative feelings. To be able to express feelings of frustration to colleagues, for example, is an important safety valve, both for organisational and individual health.

1 How do people express their emotions through communication?
2 How does communication control/coordinate people?

ACTIVITY

Think of some examples where communication has helped to motivate you, and some where you have felt demotivated. What was it about these communications that lead you to be motivated/demotivated? What can you learn from these experiences that can help you to be a more effective communicator?

5.4 Flow of communication

In this section we will consider two aspects in relation to the flow of communication:

- the flow/process of interpersonal communication
- communication networks in organisations.

We will also consider:

- the direction in which communication can travel
- the channels/methods used in communication.

The flow/process of interpersonal communication

In its simplest form, communication flows from a sender to a receiver, through a selected **channel**. The sender **encodes** the message to be sent, sends it via the selected channel, and the receiver **decodes** the message.

KEY TERMS

When people refer to the communication **channel**, they are referring to the chosen method of communication, e.g. email, report. You may come across the term used to refer to whether the communication is in the formal or informal sphere. Sometimes the term 'media' is used instead of channel.

The term **encode** means that the sender turns the message they want to send into symbols. The most common symbol used in organisational communication is a person's normal everyday language (such as English), whichever your language happens to be. However, communication can be encoded in many different ways. For example, sign language, body language, sound, coding, and context specific jargon and acronyms.

The term **decode** is used to describe the process the receiver goes through in understanding the message that they have received.

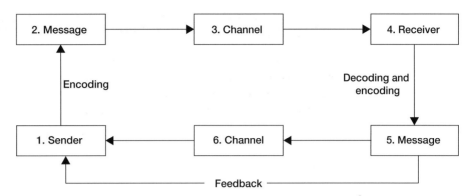

Figure 5.2 The process of interpersonal communication

The receiver may then respond to the message. In academic textbooks you will see this referred to as 'feedback'. The receiver encodes their message, selects their channel of delivery, and sends the message. This is received and decoded. This is of course a simple explanation of communication between two people. The process is illustrated in Figure 5.2, and is numbered to show the order we have just described.

There are many issues that can impact negatively on the *effectiveness* of communication, which will be considered later in the chapter.

Communication networks in organisations

In order to be able to understand how interpersonal communication takes place in the organisational setting, both *within* groups/teams/sections/departments, and *between* them, it is helpful to consider the range of **communication networks** that exist.

KEY TERMS

The term **communication network** refers to a number of patterns of horizontal and vertical flow of communication that can take place in the organisational setting.

Each network, whether formal or informal in its nature, tends to involve the same set of senders and receivers, i.e. on the whole, people tend to communicate with the same people, in the same way.

There are five common communication networks (patterns) that can be identified in organisations:

1 **The chain** – where communication passes through people in the formal chain of command, in the order in which people sit in that chain. Communication can be two-way.
2 **The wheel** – where the information passes through the leader.
3 **The circle** – occurs in groups/teams, where individuals communicate with people who are similar to them in some way.
4 **The all-channel** – where every group/team member communicates with every other group/team member.
5 **The clique** – where members of the group/team have different patterns of communication with different members, which results in unbalanced communication, i.e. some people will know more than others, and different information depending on who they choose to communicate with more.

Some authors also include the **grapevine**. This is an informal but important source of information in all types of organisation. Often, information that is communicated on the grapevine is not available through the formal channels. Some writers on the subject go as far as to say that the grapevine is the most important communication network. Noon and Delbridge (1993, as cited in Rollinson, 2005) provide a number of reasons why grapevines flourish. One of these points is that the grapevine can spread new information much faster than the formal channels. There is of course an inherent danger in the speed of the grapevine in that if the message is wrong, or partially wrong, then this can create problems. For example, if news spread rapidly via the grapevine that 20 per cent of employees are going to be made redundant, and this is wrong, the impact would create stress, panic and so on. Technically, this particular example would be classed as a **rumour.**

KEY TERMS

The **grapevine** is the informal channel of communication in an organisation.
A **rumour** is information from an unknown source that cannot be confirmed.

No one network is better than the other. Each has its advantages and disadvantages, and the choice of communication pattern should depend on the task to be completed, the people involved, and the culture of the organisation.

Example

UK managers worst in Europe for staff communication – leaving staff to find out important news via the grapevine and rumour

According to an article in *Personnel Today*, published in 2005, UK managers were said to be the worst in Europe for communicating with staff. According to the article, staff were often left to find out about important news through the grapevine and/or rumours. As a result, staff felt that they were left out of decision-making, and their motivation suffered.

To view the article, visit: www.personneltoday.com/articles/2005/04/04/29087/uk-managers-worst-in-europe-for-staff-communication.html

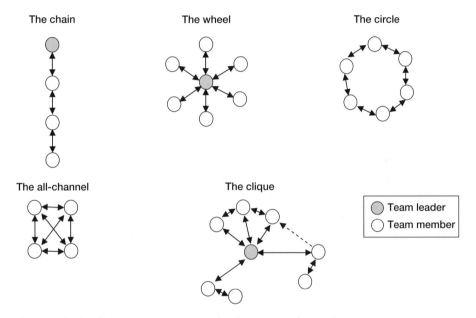

Figure 5.3 The five common communication networks

 ACTIVITY

Identify the main communication network that exists for you where you work. If you think you have one for formal communications, but another for informal communications, select the two and identify them clearly as formal and informal. Then, identify the pros and cons in terms of achieving effective communication. In light of the cons you identify, suggest ideas for improvements.

1 What is the difference between the grapevine and rumours?
2 What are the advantages and disadvantages to the informal grapevine?
3 What are the advantages and disadvantages of the clique pattern of communication?
4 What are the advantages and disadvantages of the all-channel pattern of communication?

Directions of communication

Communication can travel in different directions:

- downwards
- upwards
- horizontally
- diagonally.

Information that flows down from a manager, team leader or superior is referred to as downward communication. Information flows down the chain of command. When the rules of communication allow, information can be communicated back up the chain of command, i.e. upward communication. When there is downward and upward communication we call this two-way communication. If there is only downward communication we would call this one-way communication.

Information that is communicated between people who are at the *same level* in the hierarchy of the team/department/organisation is referred to as horizontal communication, in that these people are deemed, or perceive themselves to be on the same level. This kind of communication is more likely to be two-way, as communicators tend not to have any degree of authority over each other. Diagonal communication cuts across hierarchical levels and functional work areas.

Channels/methods of communication

As we have seen, people tend to communicate with the same people in fairly predictable patterns. We shall now go on to consider *how* people undertake their communication, i.e. what channels/methods they use.

There are so many ways that you can communicate with someone. A basic approach is to view communication as being either verbal (which includes oral and written communication) or non-verbal. Of course, oral and non-verbal communication such as body language occurs at the same time (except where you cannot see the person with whom you are talking, for example, over the telephone). New technology has also enabled new forms of communication to be possible, e.g. video conferencing, teleconferencing, and email.

Every channel/method of communication will have its pros and cons, and each one varies in its information **richness**.

Table 5.1, On pages 104–105, provides an overview of a range of typical communication channels/methods encountered in the organisational context, and some of their associated pros and cons.

KEY TERMS

Communication channels differ in their capacity to convey information, and this is referred to as their level of **richness**. Some methods of communication are regarded as richer than others, in that they have the ability to:

- handle multiple cues, e.g. aural and visual, simultaneously
- facilitate rapid feedback and
- be very personal.

Methods of communication are typically placed along a continuum of low-channel richness to high-channel richness. Richer forms are more likely to help ensure that a *shared meaning* occurs as a result of the communication.

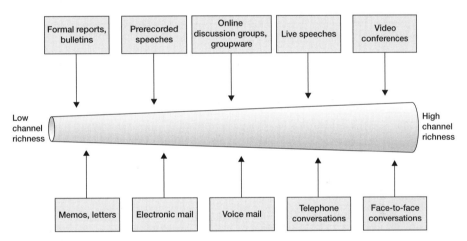

Figure 5.4 Information richness of some forms of business communication (Robbins, S.P. (2005) *Organizational Behaviour*. 11th edn. Harlow: Pearson)

ACTIVITY

Imagine that you work as a middle manager for an organisation. Your line manager has tasked you with exploring why the organisation has problems recruiting and retaining new staff. She has left it up to you how you can report back on your findings and recommendations. Identify *how* you would report back, and *why* you would use the particular method(s) you have selected. Identify the key aspects you would need to ensure you paid particular attention to in order to maximise the effectiveness of your communication(s).

Channel/ method	Pros	Cons
Oral communication		
Conversation	Enables two-way communication to occur, enabling you to clarify and explore issues. Can be vivid and stimulating (depending on the people concerned!). Enables you to adapt to the response of your audience.	Transient, i.e. unless it is recorded, the message is lost. You rely on your memory to recall what was said. Can be easy to misinterpret what someone says (particularly if you are listening to speech that is not in your first language).
Oral presentation/ speech	Can be vivid and stimulating. Non-verbal response of the audience can motivate better performance and/or prompt you to adapt.	Generally one-way (until questions are allowed), which can lead to some misinterpretation.
Telephone	Enables two-way communication to occur. Verbal response (including speed and intonation) enables you to adapt as appropriate.	Transient. Non-verbal communication aspect is missing (which can increase misinterpretations, and decrease the impact of the message).
Voicemail/ answer machine	Enables you to replay the message over and over until you are satisfied you have understood the message.	One-way communication (no way to check understanding/ask for clarification). Non-verbal aspect is missing.
Video conference	Enables two-way communication to occur. Non-verbal communication can inform the communication.	Need specialist equipment, therefore is more expensive than the telephone.
Internet conference via webcam	Enables two-way communication to occur. Non-verbal communication can inform the communication. Cheaper version of video conference.	Each person needs the appropriate equipment and training.
Written communication		
Memo Letter Email Report Fax	You can be more precise, and think about what you are saying, and amend where necessary before sending/submitting. Good use of written language should help to decrease the chance of misunderstanding. There for reference at a later date.	Easy to ignore. If you need to check your understanding of something, this is slower than verbal communication. You can misinterpret written communication (unless you follow up questions with the sender).

▶

Channel/ method	Pros	Cons
	For items sent via email and fax, it can be delivered quickly, and for email, to multiple people at one go.	
Non-verbal elements		
Gestures Facial expressions	If these are congruent/in line with the oral communication, it can significantly increase the impact of the oral communication. Help you to emphasise meaning.	Conversely, if gestures and facial expressions do not 'fit' with the verbal communication, they can cancel out much of the verbal message. Gestures and facial expressions are not universally understood, i.e. people from different parts of the world may interpret the same gesture in a different way for example. Over use/over the top use can distract people from the message to be conveyed.
Posture	A confident posture that is appropriate to the situation will have a positive impact on the communication.	Conversely, an inappropriate posture will have a negative impact on the communication.
Use of space	When you are in the same space as those you are communicating with, appropriate use of space can assert a level of dominance over others, and help you to get your message across.	Moving about too much can be off-putting, and detract from the message to be communicated.
Dress/clothing	Wearing attire deemed as appropriate for the occasion can help with face to face communication.	Conversely, attire deemed inappropriate by the audience concerned, can detract from the message you are trying to send.

Table 5.1   Communication channels/methods, and some of their pros and cons

5.5 Challenges to effective communication

In addition to some of the problems highlighted in Table 5.1, there are many challenges that stand in the way of achieving effective communication. Writers often refer to these as **barriers to effective communication**. These barriers are basically anything that can distort the message that is to be communicated. Authors often refer to the word **noise** to describe these distortions.

KEY TERMS

A **barrier to effective communication** can be anything that interferes with shared meaning occurring from the communication concerned.

The term **noise** refers to anything that interferes with the effectiveness of the communication.

These barriers to effective communication can occur at three levels:

- interpersonal
- organisational
- cultural.

Interpersonal barriers to effective communication

Interpersonal barriers to effective communication can affect communication between individuals, and between groups. Individuals who are trying to communicate may have different perceptions about the issue in question, and this may impact negatively on the effectiveness of the communication. That is not to imply that difference of opinion always results in negative/ineffective communication. However, sometimes it is easier and faster to reach a satisfactory conclusion when people have similar backgrounds in knowledge and experience. Individuals are also likely to have different past experiences, which results in what we refer to as a different 'frame of reference'. In discussing a subject, we draw upon our knowledge and past experience of the issue, i.e. we refer to what we know. When these experiences differ with those we are communicating with, we will have a different view of the issue in hand.

In addition, people have different personality traits. These differences will of course impact on how we communicate with one another. Our emotions can also impact on our communication. If we are particularly stressed, for example, we may well communicate differently than when we are in a 'normal' state of mind. What language we talk will also obviously impact on our ability to effectively communicate with others, as will our non-verbal communication. For example, non-verbal communication is not universally understood across different cultures, and therefore, when communicating with people from different cultural backgrounds, it is important to understand the differences.

Another important interpersonal barrier to effective communication is poor listening. Poor listening is responsible for many communication problems, because often, many people prefer to do the talking rather than the listening.

Also, people do not listen as attentively when they are tired, bored, and disinterested for example. Some people have to contend with a great deal of information and communication every day of their working lives, and many suffer from **information overload**, and these sort of people may be less inclined to listen carefully as they may be more likely to be cognitively (mentally) distracted during the process of your communication with them. So, listening, and grasping everything that is being communicated, is quite hard work. Therefore, when listening to verbal communication, many people miss a good deal of the information being transmitted, and this can result in mistakes.

KEY TERMS

Information overload is a phrase used to describe a situation where we are receiving more information than we can mentally/cognitively process at that moment in time.

CASE STUDY

Information overload!

In the modern workplace we have a wide range of ways to communicate with one another: face-to-face, telephone (landline and mobile), email, fax, Skype, text messages, and instant messaging, for example.

People will flag their emails to you as urgent or important, even if they aren't necessarily urgent or important to you – but you open them as a result, often interrupting your train of thought and putting you off your current task.

There's no doubt that we are interrupted at work from many sources, and this is impacting on our effectiveness and creating more stress as we struggle to focus and complete tasks among the wide range of incoming interruptions.

Organisations often respond by providing time management training, but it is not necessarily a problem that can be 'fixed' by this type of training.

1 What can you do as an individual to reduce the impact of the bombardment of incoming messages?
2 What can an organisation do to help reduce communication overload?

Lack of, or inappropriate feedback, is also another interpersonal barrier to effective communication. For example, you may be discussing a problem with another person, and you are suggesting a possible solution. If you receive no verbal or non-verbal response, how are you going to judge what that person actually thinks about your suggestion?

Other important barriers to effective communication include *filtering* and *information distortion*. Filtering involves the sender holding back part of the message. They may do this because they think the receiver does not need to know all the details, or perhaps because they think the receiver will not be interested in hearing everything – so the information is filtered, possibly impacting on the effectiveness of the communication. Distortion is slightly different to filtering, in that the change that occurs in the message occurs naturally as it is passed on through a series of senders and receivers, as in the case of the game 'Chinese Whispers'. There is no intentional filtering of the information, it just gets changed as it passes through a series of people. Where you have messages passing through several people in the chain of command this is a classic example of where communication can break down. The end message may not be anything like it was meant to be, as originated by the first sender. This is likely to be compounded by filtering as it is passed along.

In order to have *effective* interpersonal communication, it could therefore be argued that it is important to have an appreciation that the other person/people involved may well have a different perception than we do. Therefore we need to:

- be open-minded, and ready to discuss different opinions and perceptions
- listen carefully
- feed back what you understand to have been communicated, and what you think about it
- bear in mind the 'arousal' (interest) level of the other person/people involved
- consider that the message you get may have been filtered and distorted along the way, and so asking for clarification/feedback from the originator may also be important for certain communications.

Organisational barriers to effective communication

Principally, there are two barriers that impact on effective communication at the organisational level:

- functional barriers
- hierarchical barriers.

Functional barriers occur where people are communicating across the different functions of an organisation. For example, if someone from the finance department is communicating with someone from the marketing department, the two people concerned are from different functional backgrounds, and therefore may not fully understand each other. This can go deeper than simply not understanding the jargon that could be used in the communication. Failing to understand the reason behind why something needs to be done in a certain way can also impact on the effectiveness of the communication.

Then there are barriers that exist due to the hierarchical position of the individuals involved in the communication. For example, if a senior manager is talking to a shop-floor worker, there are likely to be barriers here. One of the barriers may be the type of language used. Another barrier may be that the worker lower down in the hierarchy may not wish to communicate their real views or feelings on a subject if they feel that it is not what the senior person wants to hear. This latter example is referred to as 'filtering'.

In addition to these functional and hierarchical barriers, we can also include grapevine and rumours here. Although we saw earlier in the chapter that the grapevine can be very helpful, it can also be a barrier to effective communication. It really does depend on the individual circumstance. Rumours and the grapevine can be barriers when the information they pass on is inaccurate.

Cultural barriers to effective communication

Perhaps the most obvious potential barrier in terms of communicating with people from a different culture is that of language – both the language itself and cross-cultural linguistic style. Of course, not everyone from a different culture has a different language, e.g. many people in the USA use English as their first language. However, there are several differences in how English is used in the UK, e.g. in spelling. Even within the same country we see differences, e.g. in terms of how colloquial words and phrases are used.

People from different cultures have been found to differ in their communication, and this is referred to in the academic literature as 'high- and low-context cultures' (see Table 5.2). Cultural similarity usually helps ensure more successful communication than cultural difference, i.e. the larger the cultural difference between the sender and receiver, the more difficult it will be to communicate effectively. For example, Germans are said to be a very low-context culture, and Asians very high-context culture; there is a large cultural difference in communication style. In this extreme example, one would expect communication between two such individuals to be hard work, and require a greater degree of understanding and commitment to the communication in order to achieve a successful outcome.

Low-context culture	High-context culture
Information must be provided in a very explicit/obvious way, mostly in writing.	Little needs to be in the written form, as most information is drawn from the social and/or business surroundings.
Preference for having clear, explicit guidelines and detailed background information.	Can work very well without a detailed specification and information.
Segmentation and compartmentalisation of information is common.	Information is very often drawn from the environment in which people find themselves.
Awareness of non-verbal cues is weaker.	Non-verbal awareness is much stronger, and more important.
Networking and individual interpersonal relationships are less important – functional ability is what matters.	Networking and individual interpersonal relationships are extremely important – relationships are what matters.
Knowledge is a commodity.	Information flows freely.
The message is most important, with the person and method being secondary considerations.	The channel/method used in the communication may be just as important as the message itself.

Table 5.2   Some characteristics of low- and high-context cultures

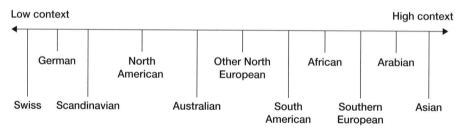

Figure 5.5 Examples of low- to high-context cultures

Organisational cultures also differ, and this too can impact on the effectiveness of communication. We won't dwell on this here as the focus of this chapter is communicating across the functions, rather than communicating between organisations. It is enough to mention that communication between two organisations can be easier where there is some common ground. For example, communication between two companies that are in the same sector will be easier than communication between two from very different sectors.

Workforce diversity is another issue that can impact on effective communication. As already mentioned, the more similar individuals are to one another, generally the easier they will find it to communicate together. This idea is referred to in sociological literature as 'homophily', i.e. we are attracted to people who are similar to us in some way that we view as significant. This idea is related to shared frames of reference. For example, in a new university class of students from different parts of the world, people are likely to begin by sitting in groups with other people from the same part of the world and communicate with each other in their native language.

There are other important differences that can impact on communication. Ethnicity, age, gender, social class, religion, sexual orientation, disability, and personality are good examples of other aspects of the workforce that impact on the achievement of effective communication.

ACTIVITY

Identify two very different examples of when you have experienced problems communicating effectively with other people. What do you think the barriers were to achieving effective communication in each case? Note down some possible solutions that might help improve effectiveness in similar situations in the future.

1 Why are some communication channels/methods 'richer' than others?
2 Identify at least five different channels/methods of communication, and list their pros and cons.
3 When we refer to 'noise', what do we mean?
4 Why is it easier to communicate more effectively with people who work in the same sector/industry than with people who work in a different sector/industry?

ACTIVITY

Think of one or two examples of where you have felt you have experienced 'information overload'. For each example, jot down how/why you think this happened. What were the effects this had on you and any work you were trying to complete? How did it impact on your ability to communicate effectively with others?

5.6 The impact of technology on communication

Information technology has radically changed the way people in organisations can communicate with each other. More information is readily available via

intranets for example. Previously, this information may have only been available in written format, and may not have been easy to locate. Thus, *more information is readily available to a wider audience, and it is generally quicker and easier to find.* Other methods of communication, such as email, fax, and instant messaging, have speeded up the delivery of information. It is not uncommon these days to hear employees refer to 'snail mail', and by that they are referring to the internal mail and/or the traditional postal system. Email, fax and instant messaging are delivered in an instant, but ordinary post is not, of course. And so, today, as technology gives us the immediate delivery of information, this is what we have come to expect as the norm.

KEY TERMS

An **intranet** is only accessible by the employees of the organisation. It uses internet technology.
There is also the **extranet.** Similar to the intranet, this communication system enables certain authorised personnel in an organisation to communicate through their network with certain outsiders, typically customers and suppliers.

Example

In 1999, the supermarket chain Sainsbury's launched a new corporate intranet and redeveloped its extranet. This was quite an innovative move at the time. The new system enabled employees and suppliers to access a new advanced knowledge retrieval facility to access workflow and information sharing systems, as well as information on product availability and promotion planning. As a result, stock control was improved.

Other technology that will be familiar to most of us in name, if not by experience, is teleconferencing and videoconferencing. Teleconferencing allows a group of people to talk with each other at the same time, using the telephone or email software. Videoconferencing allows groups of people to talk with each other at the same time and to be able to see each other. The benefits of both of these technologies are that people can communicate at the same time regardless of where they are geographically. This saves both time and money. Previously, if people wished to meet for the discussion they would have had to travel to the same location, which is often costly and time-consuming. The new technology also enables organisations to reduce the carbon footprint of their interaction, since they no longer need to travel to meet up.

Videoconferencing, having the benefit of being able to see other people, has an advantage over teleconferencing in that researchers consistently find that, in any given message, only half of the meaning is conveyed through the spoken word, with the other half coming across through body language (Clayton, 2003).

Perhaps less well-known to the non-business person is EDI (electronic data interchange). This technology enables organisations to exchange standard documents via their computer networks, e.g. orders and invoices. This can speed up the process, and reduce the amount of paperwork (as in the example of Sainsbury's).

Wireless technology has also had a huge impact on the way people communicate and work. Wireless technology has enabled people to be less reliant on their office, and thus be more mobile. Employees can use their laptops and mobile telephones to access their office from any location.

Example

Wireless internet helps Starbucks managers

Regional managers need to visit the stores in their regions on a regular basis. Prior to wireless they would need to drive back to their office every day to file reports, order supplies, etc. Wireless now enables them to use their laptops on site in any of their stores to do their job. Starbucks say that wireless internet has increased its managers' presence in stores as much as 25 per cent as managers now spend less time travelling to their offices.

(Source: TIME online at www.time.com/time/2003/wireless/article/starbucks_unwired_the_c01a.html)

1 In what ways has technology improved communication for organisations?

2 What advantage does videoconferencing have over teleconferencing? Why is this important in facilitating effective communication?

3 How has wireless technology influenced the way in which people can work?

4 According to Paul Waddington (1998) communication technologies such as voice mail, email, the internet, and video conferencing, can create the 'M25 effect', whereby more lanes just means more traffic. Paul argues that people create and distribute information through these channels because they can, not because it's useful.

  a) To what extent would you agree with this statement? Give examples to illustrate your point of view.

  b) If this is largely true, is there anything organisations can do to try to reduce the amount of information people send and receive through systems such as email, instant messaging, and text messages?

ACTIVITY

Jot down the different ways that you communicate with other people using information technology. Why do you use these methods? Do you use a different form of language when you use some, or all, of these methods? If so, why? What are the pros and cons of each of the methods you make use of?

CASE STUDY

Text message used to fire staff

2,400 staff from The Accident Group were made redundant by text message in May 2003. Text messages read 'Any staff who have not received an official briefing over the future of the company should ring 0161 605 5966.' On calling the number they received the following message 'If you have not been spoken to, you are therefore being made redundant with immediate effect. We would have preferred to have done this on a face-to-face basis. On the timescale available, this has not proved possible.'

The manner in which the company informed staff of their redundancies was largely condemned as wholly inappropriate, unprofessional, and extremely upsetting for those concerned. This is a good example of where communication technology was used in an inappropriate way.

1 Why do you think the organisation used text messages?
2 Why is text message, or similar methods such as email and instant messaging, deemed by most people as inappropriate in these circumstances?
3 What impact do you think the text messages had on the employees who received them?
4 What would have been a more appropriate way of dealing with this issue?

5.7 Summary

This chapter has provided an introduction to a range of concepts that are important in helping us to understand communication. It is clear that to achieve effective communication takes effort, and requires us to be aware of who we are communicating with, why, how, and the impact of our method(s) on the receiver. Organisations, and their members, need to understand all these issues as they work towards improving not just the efficiency, but also the effectiveness of their communications, not just within and across the different functions (the focus of this chapter), but also between organisations.

KEY IDEAS

Some of the main points covered in this chapter are listed below. If you feel unsure about any of them, then revisit the appropriate section. If you would like some additional reading on the topic, try the books listed in recommended reading.

What is communication?

- Communication refers to the process of the sending and receiving of information, where both parties understand the meaning of the message being conveyed.

What is effective communication?

- Effective communication refers to the degree to which the sender and receiver both attribute the same meaning and understanding to that message.

There are four basic functions of communication in an organisation:

1 To control/ coordinate (people and activities).
2 To provide information.
3 To help motivate staff.
4 To enable staff to express their emotions.

There are many channels/methods to communicate

- Each channel/method that you can use to communicate will have its pros and cons. What is important is choosing the right method(s) for the task in hand, and the audience.
- Each channel/method differs in its information 'richness' (it's ability to handle multiple cues simultaneously).

'Noise' can detract from the achievement of effective communication

- 'Noise' is anything that detracts from the message being received and understood in the way that was intended by the sender.
- This chapter has introduced to you a range of typical 'noise' factors that might impact on effective communication in the organisational setting.

REFLECTIVE QUESTIONS

1 Does good communication mean that the receiver must agree with the sender?
2 If formal communication enables an employee to perform their job role, why is there so much informal communication within an organisation?
3 Is it possible, and desirable, for a manager to restrict the opportunity for employees to informally communicate with one another?
4 Consider the informal grapevine that exists in an organisation. What kind of advantages and disadvantages does it provide?
5 Diagonal communication cuts across both hierarchical levels and functional work areas. What might be the problems encountered in this situation in terms of achieving effective communication?
6 To what extent would you agree with the argument that increased use and reliance on email and text messages have somehow eroded our abilities to communicate face to face, and that this is undermining working relationships?

RECOMMENDED READING

The following three texts have particularly good sections on communication:

Hitt, M.A., Black, J.S. and Porter, L.W. (2005) *Management.* International edn. Upper Saddle River, NJ: Pearson.

Robbins, S.P., Coulter, M. and Langton, N. (2006) *Management.* 8th Canadian edn. Pearson: Toronto.

Rollinson, D. (2005) *Organisational Behaviour and Analysis: An Integrated Approach.* 3rd edn. Harlow: Pearson.

Good texts that focus entirely on communication in organisations include:

Blundell, R. (2004) *Effective Organisational Communication: Perspectives, Principles and Practices.* 2nd edn. Harlow: Pearson.

Bovee, C. and Thill, J.V. (2007) *Business Communication Today.* 9th edn. London: Pearson.

A good text for exploring intercultural communication is:

Jandt, F.E. (2007) *An Introduction to Intercultural Communication: Identities in a Global Community.* 5th edn. London: Sage.

Of interest:

Lettice, R. (2008) 'NHS Direct launches text message service'. *The Register* (online). Available at: www.theregister.co.uk/2008/02/13/nhs_direct_sms_service/.

Waddington, P. (1998) 'Dying for information? A report on the effects of information overload in the UK and worldwide' (online). Available at: www.ukoln.ac.uk/services/papers/bl/blri078/content/repor~13.htm.

USEFUL WEBSITES

www.kwintessential.co.uk/intercultural-business-communication/tool.php Culture and its impact on communication – this site has useful information relating to culture and communication.

www.youtube.com/watch?v=S7QP8P_tPp0&feature=related Effective communication (including reference to channel richness) – video.

www.youtube.com/watch?v=8tIUilYX56E High and low context cultures – this gives a short media explanation.

www.personneltoday.com/articles/2008/01/28/44091/communicate-effectively-with-staff-how-to.html How to communicate effectively with staff.

REFERENCES

Berry, M. (2005) 'UK managers worst in Europe for staff communication', *Personnel Today* (online) 4 April. Available at: www.personneltoday.com/articles/2005/04/04/29087/uk-managers-worst-in-europe-for-staff-communication.html.

Clayton, P. (2003) *Body Language at Work.* London: Hamlyn.

Robbins, S.P. (2005) *Organizational Behaviour.* 11th edn. Harlow: Pearson.

Robbins, S.P., Coulter, M. and Langton, N. (2006) *Management.* 8th Canadian edn. Toronto: Pearson.

Rollinson, D. (2005) *Organisational Behaviour and Analysis: An Integrated Approach.* 3rd edn. Harlow: Pearson.

Waddington, P. (1998) 'Dying for information? A report on the effects of information overload in the UK and worldwide' (online). Available at: www.ukoln.ac.uk/services/papers/bl/blri078/content/repor~13.htm.

6 Leadership and Motivation

'Unless a variety of opinions are laid before us, we have no opportunity of selection, but are bound of necessity to adopt the particular view which may have been brought forward.'

(Herodotus, Greek historian, 5th century BCE)

CHAPTER OUTLINE

6.1 Introduction
6.2 What do we mean by leadership?
6.3 The difference between leadership and management
6.4 The search for leadership theories
6.5 Motivation
6.6 Early theories of motivation
6.7 Contemporary theories of motivation
6.8 Summary

CHAPTER OBJECTIVES

After carefully reading and engaging with the tasks and activities outlined in this chapter you should have a better understanding of:
● what we generally mean and understand by the term 'leadership'
● the differences between leadership and management
● some of the more established leadership theories
● some of the basics of human motivation
● some of the more established motivation theories.

6.1 Introduction

Why is it that some sports teams can change their manager and suddenly start to prosper? What do we mean when we say an organisation lacks leadership? Why did a nation decide to follow one particular man, Nelson Mandela, on his 'Long Walk to Freedom' (Mandela, 1994)?

The answers to these questions, and many like them, both intrigue and puzzle organisations. If they knew the answer to the question 'What makes a good leader or manager?' their recruitment policies would be that much easier. As it is, we are not too sure what it means to be either a 'good' manager or leader.

We have already made some implicit assumptions. First, that we can define what a leader is, and second, that it is the leader who is responsible for the organisation's success. As we shall see, both of these assumptions are not as straight forward as they first appear.

Academics have great difficulty in defining what a leader is, or pinpointing the reasons behind an organisations success, however leadership is widely recognised. Otherwise why would nations have decided to follow Mahatma Gandhi and Nelson Mandela? Both of them started out on their respective journeys without any formal authority. Some leaders can inspire such loyalty that people are prepared to sacrifice their lives for them. Other leaders (Julius Caesar for example) can make what were once loyal followers conspire to murder them.

This chapter begins to describe what we do know about leadership and how we make use of that information. This chapter also considers how and why people are motivated. Leaders and managers need to understand what motivates human beings to perform, and how they are motivated, so that they can develop strategies to maximise motivation to achieve high performance from their employees.

6.2 What do we mean by 'leadership'?

There are many different ways of classifying the term **leadership**. One of the difficulties with the classification is that there are some words that individuals may understand in different ways. An example of this is the word 'mother': everyone knows what we are talking about. But every mother is unique, so the view I have of my mother will be different to the view you have of your mother.

The word 'leader' is similar in that we have our own unique picture of what a leader is, which will depend on our own particular circumstances and experiences. Additionally, there are a number of different types of leader, displaying different characteristics.

Five of the more readily recognisable types of leader are:

- The **Traditional** leader. This is someone who assumes the leadership position by right. An example here is the present Queen. We all accept that a King or Queen is the natural leader by birthright, regardless of the person's ability to be a leader.
- The **Charismatic** leader. This is somebody who is viewed as a leader, and has gained influence, by the strength of their character, for better or worse. Examples are Florence Nightingale, Hitler and Napoleon.
- The **Situational** leader. Somebody who has influence because they are in the right place at the right time. We could have mentioned Churchill above as an example of a charismatic leader but he was also somebody who was in the right place at the right time when war broke out. It is interesting that Churchill lost his job once the war was over.
- The **Appointed** leader. This is by far the biggest category, as most leaders (and managers) are appointed to their position. Note that the appointed person could be an effective or ineffective leader and any appointed leader is dependant on many other factors for their success.
- The **Functional** leader. This person is ready to adapt their style to the particular circumstances that prevail. It is their performance that secures their leadership credentials, rather than who they are.

So, we tend to recognise the leaders in our society but the essence of leadership remains elusive and this leads to difficulties in defining what leadership is.

The historical connotations associated with the word 'leadership', derived in the Anglo-Saxon world from 'lead' (c. 800), to 'leader' (c. 1300), to 'leadership' (c. 1850) are deeply embedded in our culture (Rost, 1991). However, we need some kind of definition of leadership for our purposes. A leader can not be a leader without somebody to lead and they normally need to have some influence over them. Also, we need some activity or goal to be accomplished to identify the process of leadership.

KEY TERMS

So, we will define **leadership** here in line with the definition favoured by Northouse (2007), as: 'A process whereby an individual influences a group of individuals to achieve a common goal.' This view of leadership as a process also encompasses followers (the group of individuals led by the leader) rather than just the leader.

Let's consider two of the important parts that make up this definition.

- *Process* implies that there is an exchange going on between the leader and followers. That is, it is not simply focused on the leader and ignoring the followers, something that happened early on when researchers considered leadership as a trait (See Section 6.4).
- *Influence* can be assigned formally and informally but it must exist. A factory manager would have formal influence assigned to him or her, as would a general in the army, or a police sergeant. Some leaders emerge informally and followers identify strongly with them and their aims. For example, Martin Luther King influenced many Americans without having any formal authority over them.

CASE STUDY

Figure 6.1 Alexander the Great

Alexander of Macedon, 356–323 BCE, better known as Alexander the Great, was certainly a traditional leader who had great influence over his followers. In fact, in over 13 years as a ruler his followers only once refused to do as he asked.

He was the son of Philip II, King of Macedon, and was educated by the great philosopher Aristotle. On Philip's assassination in 336 BCE, Alexander, who was only 21, assumed the leadership position by right of birth. However, he had a number of enemies at home who he dealt with before restoring Macedonian power within Greece. Alexander then led his army victoriously through Asia Minor, Syria and Egypt and created an empire that ranged over three continents and by doing so, changed the nature of the ancient world.

6.3 The difference between leadership and management

Is there something different about leadership that means that a separate word to management is required? Why is it not just one of the many roles of management?

There are not many people who would describe their immediate manager as a leader, but people do recognise leaders. Bryman (1996) defines leadership by referring to 'creation of a vision' and management as a preoccupation with the 'here and now'. So the perception of the differences are that leaders are more visionary and have the ability to get the most out of their followers, while managers are more concerned with the day-to-day running of things.

Society views leaders as something more than managers. They are rare: as you will find if you try to name ten different ones you know. In contrast, managers are everywhere, at all levels within organisations. This does not mean though that managers are any less valuable than leaders. There are many excellent managers and plenty of poor leaders.

Of some help in making the distinction clearer (although not without its critics) is the following table based on work by Hollingsworth (1999). This former Squadron Leader recognised that there are many similarities between management and leadership, but also that there are six fundamental differences.

A Manager:	A Leader:
Administrates	Innovates
Maintains	Develops
Structure and systems oriented	People oriented
Control	Trust
Bottom-line focus	Focus on the horizon
Does things right	Does the right thing

Table 6.1 Fundamental differences between managers and leaders

Note in the table that the manager's role is very task oriented, and that the leader's role is more people oriented. This is also in line with Henri Fayol's view of management that we met in Chapter 2.

Both managers and leaders must make decisions. This is one of their key responsibilities and what most spend their day doing (Barnard, 1968; Donaldson, 1983). We are going to make a distinction between the types of decisions here as most decisions are routine and minor. Some though (e.g. redundancies, whistle blowing, promotions) are more significant. Society would generally consider the person making the more significant decisions as the leader, the manager making the more routine ones.

One quote from the Chinese philosopher Sun Tzu, who lived around 500 BCE, indicates that there is something distinctive about a leader's action and there is still much wisdom in these words for today's aspiring leader:

Go to the people
Live amongst them
Start with what they have
Build on what they know
And when the deed is done,
The mission accomplished
Of the best leaders
The people will say,
'We have done it ourselves.'

There is likely to be no agreement on clear distinctions between 'manager' and 'leader'. They are both complex interrelated areas. This does not mean that a lot of good research has not been valid but, for leadership in particular, the difficulties in defining leadership have led to some 'dogmatically stated nonsense' (Bernard, 1948).

The world and our understanding of management and leadership is also changing quickly. Some of the leadership theories that are more established are described in the next section.

6.4 The search for leadership theories

The importance of having the right leader to an organisation has led to a continual hunt for the one best way. What theory tells us is that there is not one best way: if there was we could simply apply that in every situation.

Being aware of the different theories and integrating them with practice will help to develop the aspiring leader. The following is a brief summary of some of the better-known ones, along with references if you would like to explore a little deeper.

Trait theory

This is concerned with seeking out the traits (the qualities and characteristics of a person) that leaders were thought to be born with. The research concentrated on determining what these traits were (Jago, 1982; Bass, 1990).

Note that this theory does not take into account the followers: it concentrates only on the leaders' characteristics. It also takes no account of any context that the leaders may find themselves in. However, the theory does allow a manager, or leader, to consider their own traits and work on any perceived weaknesses.

Positive points	Negative points
Sits well with most people's perception that a leader is born, not made.	Many studies and much research have failed to identify a comprehensive list of traits that all leaders possess.
Has identified the 'good' and 'bad' points that leaders can possess, so points to what a leader needs to work on to progress.	No agreement or evidence for what is a 'good' or 'bad' trait. What may be good in one context may not be appropriate in another.

Table 6.2   Positive and negative points about trait theory

Contingency theory

These theories take into account both the context and the situation and try to match up a particular leader to them, so unlike trait theory, it is not only reliant on the attributes of the leader. The theory proposes that an effective leader will be dependent on the setting (Fiedler, 1967; Hersey and Blanchard, 1992).

So, for example, depending on the type of relationship that exists between supervisors and workers, a particular type of leader could be chosen. If the relationship is a relaxed one, the organisation may decide they do not require a tough leader. However, if relationships were strained, the organisation could decide to appoint a leader with a firm style.

Path-Goal theory

This theory is all about employee motivation and how leaders motivate followers to achieve organisational goals. Here, the leader will work to remove any obstacles that are hindering the employees as they move towards their goal (Evens, 1970; House and Dessler, 1974). This theory extends contingency

Positive points	Negative points
Good background of research evidence for the theory.	No evidence from the research of why some leaders are more effective in certain situations.
Can help to predict what type of leadership skills will be most effective in particular circumstances.	Much of the research is based on the LPC (Least Preferred Co-worker) scale, which has been criticised by a number of researchers.

Table 6.3   Positive and negative points about contingency theory

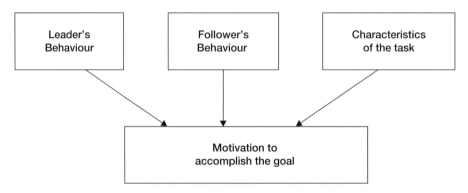

Figure 6.2 The main aspects of path-goal theory of leadership

theory by taking account of the leader in addition to the particular context of a task.

Although path-goal theory is seen as a pragmatic method of leadership it can become relatively complex very rapidly. The theory suggests that it is dependent on particular leadership styles being used at the right time to enable followers to achieve their goals.

Positive points	Negative points
Considers both the situation and the context and how different leadership styles should be used. It is a practical model.	Although it is a very practical model it can be difficult to apply owing to its complexity.
Concentrates on motivational aspects thus ensuring that a leader will continually seek out what followers expect in return for their best efforts.	The research has not really backed up the theory. The research has also failed to find a link between followers' motivation and a leadership style.

Table 6.4   Positive and negative points about path-goal theory

Transformational leadership

Here the focus is on how leaders achieve their goals by transcending the more normal *transactional* style. That is it considers how some leaders achieve more by focusing on their followers altruistic motives rather than the transaction of exchanging reward for performance. (Burns, 1978; Conger, 1999; Yukl, 1999).

The idea here is that followers' behaviour is *transformed* by the charisma of the leader who would achieve more than if a more usual *transaction* was used.

Positive points	Negative points
This appeals intuitively to followers who like the idea that they are with a charismatic leader with a vision.	Because it covers a broad spectrum of ideas it lacks clarity.
Some good research has been done to back up the ideas; in particular that it is an effective form of leadership.	Much of the research has been based around large organisations at senior level. Hence its relevance for other leadership levels is questionable.

Table 6.5   Positive and negative points about transformational leadership

KEY TERMS

Transformational leadership is about the ability to move followers to achieving more by focusing on objectives that transcend the normal leader follower exchange where tasks are completed without emotional involvement. Thus transformational leaders would typically have a strong sense of motivating others to go beyond the normal requirements of a task because of a particular belief (Gandhi being a good example).

Team leadership

Teams have become more essential to the differing organisational contexts that now exist and many employers rely heavily on an effectively led team. A lot of research has been done in recent years on effective teams and it has been consistently shown that one of the key factors in the team's success is effective team leadership (Larson and LaFasto, 1989; Zaccaro, 2001).

All the above theories require motivation. It should be clear by now that motivation and leadership are strongly linked and that leaders need to motivate their employees, followers or team members, etc. to achieve their goals. Think of a recent lecture you have been to. Would you be motivated to attend the next one? What exactly does motivate you – is it the lecturer, the subject matter, the

Positive points	Negative points
Team leadership models can help, in real life settings, to direct team members towards better and more effective teamwork.	While there is a lot of research on teams there is not much evidence of team leadership models being effective.
The role of the leader is fully integrated with the followers.	The models are difficult to apply in practice.

Table 6.6   Positive and negative points about team leadership

need to pass the course, or simply the company of the people you mix with in the lecture? As you can see, motivation is a more complex issue than it appears. The remainder of this chapter will explore different aspects of motivation.

 ## 6.5   Motivation

What motivates people to work hard and achieve success is a critical issue in organisations. If leaders and managers can understand what motivates their employees then it is possible for them to be more successful. For example, leaders and managers may be better placed to predict behaviour and manipulate/manage it. So, this part of the chapter aims to explain what **motivation** is, and how it works – invaluable knowledge for leaders and managers.

KEY TERMS

Motivation is concerned with the intensity, direction, and persistence of an individual's efforts in respect of achieving a particular goal.

There are many different opinions about what motivation is, and how it works. We refer to these as different theories of motivation. This chapter will present *some* of the early theories, as well as some more contemporary views on the subject.

There are three key issues to consider with motivation:

1 Effort/intensity, i.e. how hard a person is trying.
2 Direction, i.e. what the person is trying to achieve.
3 Persistence, i.e. how long a person will keep trying to achieve the goal(s).

It is important to understand that motivation varies *between* people, i.e. what motivates one person may not motivate another, and it also varies *within* a person, i.e. how motivated you are can depend on a number of factors.

ACTIVITY

This activity is aimed at helping you to see how levels of motivation can vary *within* a person.

Think of a recent example in your own life where, on the same day, you experienced different levels of motivation depending on the tasks/activities you were undertaking.

1 What task(s) were you undertaking that day where you were well motivated? Why were you motivated towards each of those tasks?
2 What task(s) were you undertaking that day where you were less motivated? Why were you less motivated towards each of those tasks?

Why do some people seem to be more motivated for certain activities than others? Think back to your time at school. Do you remember those students who became heavily involved in sport? What motivated some people to put a lot of effort into sport on top of their other studies? Why did some people give up their Saturday mornings to represent their school at sports?

The answers to these questions are complex, and would vary from person to person. Some people put in more effort than others. Some people persist over a longer period of time. And some people direct their effort to try to become professional sports people. Some people were motivated by **intrinsic** reward, e.g. sense of personal achievement, some by **extrinsic** reward, e.g. medals and trophies, and some by a combination of the two.

KEY TERMS

Intrinsic motivation is the motivation (driving force) that comes from *within* a person, and is related to psychological rewards such as belonging to a group or team, personal satisfaction in a job well done, and sense of achievement.
Extrinsic motivation is the motivation (driving force) that comes from *outside* of the person. For example, pay, company car, and perks of the job.

As previously mentioned, what motivates one person does not necessarily motivate another, and this is part of the reason why leadership and management are difficult, because, for example, a strategy you employ for motivating staff to achieve improved performance might work for some, but only serve to demotivate others.

For the purposes of this chapter we will look at a range of theories under two headings: early theories, and contemporary theories. The early theories are what are known as **'content' theories**, and all but one of the contemporary theories covered are known as **'process' theories**. There is general agreement that the process theories of motivation are more helpful in understanding human motivation in the workplace.

KEY TERMS

Content theories attempt to explain *what* motivates a person.
Process theories attempt to explain *how* people are motivated.

ACTIVITY

Think of some examples of strategies that people have used to try to motivate people, either in a working context or at home. Do you think each strategy would work on a range of different people? If so, explain why. If not, explain why not.

6.6 Early theories of motivation

Early theories of motivation were concerned with trying to establish *what* motivated a person; these are the 'content' theories.

Examples of well-known early theories of motivation include:

- the hierarchy of needs (Maslow, 1943)
- the two-factor theory (Herzberg, 1966)
- Theory X, theory Y (McGregor, 1960).

Maslow's hierarchy of needs

Maslow proposed that human motivation was influenced by our needs, and argued that these needs had a hierarchy of importance. He proposed that the lower-level needs had to be achieved (at least to a *satisfactory level*) before a person would be motivated by the subsequent level. In terms of motivating people at work, this theory implies that you need to understand what level the person is at in order to be able to select the most appropriate strategy to positively impact on their motivation. For example, attempts to improve motivation through self-esteem mechanisms will not be successful unless the lower-level needs of the individual have been achieved to a satisfactory standard for the person concerned.

If a manager attempts to motivate an employee through greater autonomy via a promotion (which does not include any pay increase), this would be highly unlikely to motivate the employee if s/he was having major financial problems. In fact, the extra responsibility would probably have a demotivating effect in this scenario. Therefore, it is important that managers know their employees well enough so that they do not make such errors. However, if this person had been offered a promotion with a significant pay increase and/or bonuses then the outcome would be likely to be different as the employee needs the money to satisfy their physiological and safety needs.

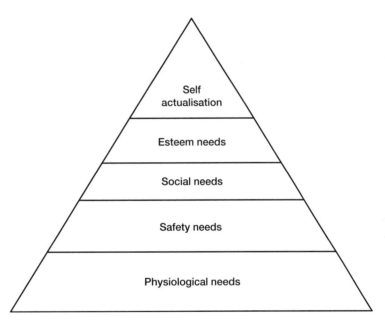

Figure 6.3 Maslow's hierarchy of needs

Need	Brief explanation
Physiological needs	This includes a person's need for, for example, food, drink, shelter, and sexual satisfaction.
Safety needs	This is a person's need for protection and security from emotional and physical harm.
Social needs	This is a person's need for belongingness, affection, friendship, and acceptance.

►

Need	Brief explanation
Esteem needs	This need is about a person's internal esteem needs, e.g. autonomy, self-respect, and achievement, and external esteem needs, e.g. attention, job and social status, and recognition for achievements.
Self-actualisation	This need is about a person's need to grow and become as much as s/he is capable of becoming, i.e. striving to be the best that you can be.

Table 6.7   Summary of the five needs

Two-factor theory

Herzberg's research concerning what employees felt made them feel exceptionally good or exceptionally bad about their job consistently showed there were two sets of factors that affected motivation at work. These two factors were referred to as hygiene (or maintenance) factors, and motivators (or growth) factors.

Hygiene/maintenance factors	Motivators/growth factors
Salary	Sense of achievement
Job security	Recognition
Working conditions	The nature of the work itself
Level and quality of supervision	Responsibility
Company policy and administration	Personal growth and advancement
Interpersonal relations	

Table 6.8   Hygiene factors and motivators

Herzberg found that no matter how good the motivators/growth factors were, they *would not* serve to motivate employees if the hygiene/maintenance factors were lacking. In other words, the first place to start in terms of building a motivated workforce is to make sure the hygiene/maintenance factors are attended to. Only then will the presence of motivators/growth factors impact in any positive way on employee motivation.

In 2003, research undertaken by Cubiks Consulting showed that 'pay was the chief cause of de-motivation. Only 6% of respondents considered a good pay rise to be highly motivating but an unsatisfactory pay rise emerged as the single biggest cause of employee unhappiness.' (Source: www.cubiks.com/aspx/document.aspx?documentid=330)

1 Which aspect of Herzberg's two-factor theory does this finding relate to?
2 Suggest some reasons why only 6 per cent of respondents considered a good pay rise to be highly motivating?

Theory X, Theory Y

McGregor was interested in finding out whether people were intrinsically or extrinsically motivated. Put another way, do we need to be motivated by others or are we self-motivating?

Theory X	Theory Y
Generally negative view of people	Generally positive view of people
Extrinsically rewarded	Intrinsically rewarded
Employees have little or no ambition	Employees exercise self direction
Employees do not like work	Employees accept responsibility
Employees try to avoid responsibility	Employees seek out responsibility
Employees need to be monitored closely	Employees enjoy the work

Table 6.9   Theory X, Theory Y summary

McGregor was of the opinion that theory Y most closely fitted the nature of employees, and that leaders and managers should lead and manage on this premise. However, real life is likely to be more complicated than such a simple dichotomy, and managers will no doubt find themselves in situations where they are managing some people who are more extrinsically motivated, and some who are more intrinsically motivated, and therefore a varied strategy for maintaining and improving motivation will be required.

(6.7) Contemporary theories of motivation

We do not use the term contemporary theories to describe theories that were recently developed. The theories are generally considered to represent *current thinking* in terms of explaining the motivation of employees.

Examples of well-known contemporary theories of motivation include:

- Equity theory, e.g. Adams (1965)
- Expectancy theory, e.g. Vroom (1964)
- Goal theory, e.g. Locke (1968)
- Cognitive evaluation theory, e.g. de Charms (1968)
- Reinforcement theory, e.g. Skinner (1971).

All of these are 'process' theories of motivation (theories seeking to find out *how* people are motivated), with the exception of reinforcement theory (which is a behavioural theory).

Equity theory

Adams (1965) proposed that people think about what they receive from doing their job, i.e. the job outcomes (such as pay, promotion, and perks) in relation to what they put in, i.e. the job inputs (such as effort, education, and experience), and they then compare themselves to similar others. If an employee feels that they are putting the same amount into a job, and receiving the same from it compared to a similar other, then they will be satisfied that they are being treated fairly (equitably): this is referred to as being in a state of equity. If, however, they feel that a similar other is receiving more, e.g. a higher wage or more perks, but they are only putting in the same amount of effort than they are, then they will see this as unfair (inequitable) and will be inclined to be demotivated by the situation. Alternatively, if a person compares them self to a similar other and thinks that they are receiving more than that person they *may* feel guilty about it.

So, we call this a process theory because the persons' brain is *processing the situation*, i.e. weighing it all up. It is important to note that experiencing a state of equity (fairness) does not necessarily motivate a person, but a state of inequity can result in demotivation (or guilt if they think they are getting more out of the situation). In this way, the theory is based on the concept of **distributive justice**.

KEY TERMS

Distributive justice is about how fair an individual feels the amount and allocation of rewards is among the individuals concerned.

What is also important in equity theory is the person's perception of the situation. This may not, however, be accurate. For example, if you thought you were being underpaid in comparison to a colleague who does the same job as you it is likely this would demotivate you. However, you could be wrong, i.e. you may have assumed this was the case, without actually knowing all the facts. It is therefore important that reward and promotion systems are transparent, as this can help to prevent, or at the very least reduce the chances of this kind of situation arising.

Although people talk a lot about equity in relation to rewards, typically pay, it is important to remember that pay is not the only reward that employees may use in their comparisons with similar others. For example, some people may use job titles, working environments, and number of support staff available to them as their basis for comparison (see for example Greenberg and Ornstein, 1983).

Adams argued that when there was a feeling of inequity the person concerned would be motivated to do something about it. Based on this premise, Walster et al. (1978) and Greenberg (1989) argued that an employee in this situation would make one of six choices:

1 They would alter their inputs, e.g. put less effort into their work.
2 They would change their outcomes, e.g. if you are working on a piece rate basis you could increase (or decrease) the number of items you made, even though for increasing output this may well lower the quality of your work.
3 They would distort their own perception of themselves, e.g. you might have thought you were a very good worker, but if you find out you do not get paid as much as a similar other then you might start to think you are not as good as you thought (this links to the ideas in self-efficacy theory).
4 They would distort their perception of others, e.g. you might try to explain away the reason a similar other gets paid more than you by highlighting what you think are particularly undesirable parts to their job.
5 They might choose an alternative 'similar other' to compare themselves against, e.g. you find someone you are doing better than, and start comparing yourself to them instead.
6 They might leave their job (and possibly the industry they work in).

Example

Imagine that you graduated six months ago and you have just landed your first job. You are very excited. The employer offers you £20,000 a year: this is the most money you have ever earned, so you are really motivated. Another graduate was taken on at the same time as you – same age, equivalent educational and experiential background. As you get to know this person, they reveal that they are on £25,000 a year, plus discounts, plus 5 days extra holiday than you. You are stunned. It appears your new colleague negotiated a higher starting salary and perks package, and you hadn't thought to do this. This is likely to demotivate you, as you see the situation as unfair (inequitable), and it could impact on your working relationship.

However, some people can be highly motivated by this type of situation, which is linked to self-efficacy (self-confidence). This scenario illustrates how complicated motivation can be, as everyone is different.

The practical implications of equity theory

Like all the theories of motivation covered in this chapter, equity theory has practical application to the 'real world'. Here are some key ones for equity theory.

1 For employees on hourly pay or salaries:
   a) Employees who feel over-rewarded *may* produce more than employees who feel they are equitably rewarded. This may happen if the over-rewarded employee feels guilty about the situation, and they may respond by increasing the quantity and/or quality of their inputs, until such time they feel there is a state of equity and they no longer feel guilty.
   b) Employees who feel under-rewarded *may* respond by decreasing the quantity and/or quality of their inputs, until such time that they feel there is a state of equity.
2 For employees who are paid by piece-rate systems:
   a) Employees who feel over-rewarded *may* produce fewer items, but in doing so may well produce better quality items than employees who feel equitably rewarded. An alternative response might be to produce more items. Either response aims to reduce the guilt felt by the over-rewarded employee, as they attempt to find a state of equity. However, where an employee opts to reduce the guilt by producing more items, this would only lead to greater inequity as they will receive more reward because it is piece-rate.
   b) Employees who feel under-rewarded *may* respond by decreasing their output, which lowers productivity. This type of response is a vicious circle as this will result in lower pay and an ever-increasing feeling of being under-rewarded. Theoretically, output should level off when the employee feels there is a state of equity.

Important concepts related to equity theory

As well as the concept of distributive justice, there are three other important concepts related to equity theory that impact on employee motivation, and therefore leaders and managers need to understand them.

1 Organisational justice

This is about *the overall perception* an employee has in terms of how fair they feel their workplace is. Employees are likely to view their organisation as a fair and just place to work if they feel the outcomes they receive *and* the way in which they receive them are fair.

There are two important concepts to consider in relation to further understanding the way in which people evaluate how they receive their rewards: procedural justice and interactional justice.

2 Procedural justice

This is about the perception an employee has in terms of how fair they think the *processes* are that lead to the distribution of rewards. It is concerned with *how* we get paid, and is regarded as being just as important as distributive justice. Two of the key issues here are with process control and explanations. For employees to regard the rewards procedure as fair, they have to feel that they have a certain amount of control over the reward outcome, and also feel that they had the opportunity to receive an adequate explanation. If distributive justice is lacking, procedural justice becomes even more important to employees. Procedural justice is linked to organisational policies and procedures, e.g. reward strategy (such as PRP, bonuses), and the appraisal system.

3 Interactional justice

This is about the perception the employee has in terms of the degree to which they feel they are treated with dignity, concern, and respect. Research shows that if people feel they are treated unjustly in such interactions, they will respond in some retaliatory fashion, e.g. they may talk in a derogatory way about the person concerned (Skarlicki and Folger, 1997), and this can impact on the morale and motivation of employees. Interactional justice is linked to the behaviour of supervisors and managers towards their subordinates.

This is all very interesting you might think, but why are any of these concepts important for a leader or a manager to understand?

The answer to this question is that leaders and managers need to realise that employees are sensitive to unfair procedures (whether this is real or imagined/perceived), and this is important if the leader or manager has to give any kind of negative information regarding rewards, for example, a less than expected pay offer. Managers need to ensure that they openly explain how the decisions were made, and that they consistently and without bias follow procedures, and interact in ways that promote dignity, concern and respect for workers. Additionally, this has to be done in such a way that the employees believe it, i.e. it is their perception that matters.

Equity theory assumes that over-rewarded employees will feel guilty about being over-rewarded, and will therefore respond to reduce this guilt.

1 Do you think employees always aware they are being over-rewarded? Explain your answer.

2 Why might over-rewarded employees feel guilty about it? What impact(s) could this have on working relationships with others?

Expectancy theory

This is one of the most widely accepted explanations of human motivation. It argues that a person tends to behave in a particular way based on the *expectation* that what they are doing will *result in a particular outcome*, and that the *outcome is deemed attractive* to the person. So, expectancy theory of motivation proposes that the amount of motivation a person has for a given task is the result of a mental process/calculation where the person considers the following three points:

1 Expectancy (or likelihood) – that they believe they will be able to achieve the task/outcome in question by exerting a particular amount of effort. In other words, how confident are we that we can do it?
2 Instrumentality – the degree to which the person believes that performing at a particular level will actually result in them receiving the final outcome they are striving for. In other words, if we do what we set out to, how much do we believe that we will receive the reward for doing it that we think we should get, or that we have been promised?
3 Valence (or attractiveness of reward) that the person places on achieving the task/outcome in question. Valence also takes into consideration the goals and needs of the person concerned.

This is also referred to as the EIV theory of motivation (expectancy, instrumentality, valence: Vroom, 1964).

Example

Imagine that you cannot drive a manual car yet, although you have an automatic licence and an old automatic car that gets you from A to B. However, your partner wants you to get a manual driving licence. You weigh this up. You think the likelihood you could pass a manual test is high, given enough practice, but you don't have the money to pay for lessons to practice in a manual car. Your partner pre-empts this rationale and promises to buy you a much newer car (manual or automatic; your choice) if you pass your manual driving test. A good offer. However, you weigh this up and consider that this offer is unlikely to materialise in reality (this is the instrumentality part of the process). In addition, you consider that actually, you already have a licence and you like your car, so you decide that, although you believe you could pass a manual driving test, you don't currently have the money to hire the car to practice in, and your partner is unlikely to follow through with the incentive of a newer car, and anyway, you already have a car . . . result . . . lack of motivation to do it.

Some people find the terminology used in expectancy theory can be off-putting. Put simply, this theory could be summed up by a series of questions that can determine the amount of motivation someone may have for a task.

1 How hard will I need to work to achieve the level of performance I am looking for?
2 Do I think I can actually achieve that level of performance?
3 What reward will I get if I reach that level?
4 How attractive/important is that reward to me?
5 Does that reward help me achieve any of my goals?

So, the goal(s) that a person has at any given time are vital in helping to explain a person's degree of motivation towards particular tasks.

If any element of the equation is missing, e.g. the person does not value the outcome, then there will be no or very little motivation.

If correct, expectancy (EIV) theory is important for managers, who would need to ensure:

1 Employees feel they possess the necessary skills, knowledge and abilities to do their jobs, at least to an adequate level (= expectancy).
2 Employees feel that if they performed their jobs well, or at least adequately, they would be rewarded (= instrumentality).
3 Employees feel the rewards offered for successful job performance are attractive to them (= valence).

This theory helps to explain why many employees fail to exert much effort in their jobs. This is because evidence shows that many employees do not believe that if they put in more effort this will have any impact on the reward they receive. Also, employees may not have the skill set to do any better, so irrespective of the amount of effort they put in, their performance will not improve, there will therefore be no impact on reward, and the result will be lack of motivation for the given task(s). The first point links to the organisation's reward system, and the second to training and development. So, the value of understanding how employees are motivated lies in helping managers to identify where improvements can be made in the organisation, e.g. the appraisal/reward systems and training, which could have a positive impact on employee motivation and performance.

ACTIVITY

Think of an example of something that you either needed or wanted to do, but failed. Use expectancy theory of motivation to analyse the possible reason(s) for your failure to achieve the desired outcome.

Goal theory

The basic idea behind this theory of motivation is that a person's motivation to behave in a certain way is strongly influenced by their goals/intentions. Locke (1968) argued that goals direct the behaviour and performance of a person.

Key aspects to this theory, which can assist managers, are that:

1 It is important for specific goals to be set (rather than vague statements such as 'do your best'). In this respect, the goals could be articulated more in the form of objectives.
2 The employee needs to accept the goal, which is best achieved through setting it together with the employee.
3 Commitment to the goal is essential. If the goal is not agreed in a participative fashion, but rather is assigned by the manager, the chance of gaining commitment from the employee may be improved if the manager clearly explains the purpose and importance of the goal.
4 Difficult goals, as long as they are accepted by the employee, lead to higher performance. However, the employee has to feel that they can achieve the goal, i.e. it has to be realistic otherwise motivation will suffer (note the link here to expectancy theory).
5 Feedback must be given (which needs to be complete, accurate, and timely) in terms of how the employee is progressing towards their goal. This results in higher performance, as long as that feedback is given in a constructive manner. Part of this process may involve revision of the goal, and/or identification of additional support required.

Robbins and Judge (2009) note, however, that there is evidence to show that goal theory works best when:

1 The person concerned *has* control over the task, as opposed to being reliant on other people to achieve it.
2 The task is simple, as opposed to complex.
3 The task is well learned, as opposed to something new and different.
4 When it is used in certain cultures, where individuals are reasonably independent, such as Canada, UK, and USA, and where people look for challenging goals, and where being a high performer is considered important in society.

According to Judge and Robbins (2009, p.220) they do however argue that setting specific, challenging goals for employees is the best thing managers can do to improve performance.

Example

Performance related pay (PRP) in schools

In 2000 the Department for Education and Employment drafted guidelines for the introduction of PRP to be used in schools to help improve standards.

The draft guidelines stated that an assessment would be undertaken of the progress made by pupils, and this assessment should be in terms of marks or grades from relevant tests or exams; which was claimed to be a common sense view.

Figure 6.4

Details of the criteria, which could allow some teachers to earn up to £2,000 extra, were published by the Schools Standards Minister. Opposition to the idea of assessing teachers based on the performance of their pupils was strongly articulated.

Expectancy and goal theory can help us understand why this PRP strategy probably would not work very well in practice in this industry.

For teachers of pupils with lower levels of ability this strategy is unlikely to help motivate staff, as they are unlikely to *expect* that they will be able to reach the set threshold level for payout, especially if they perceive that threshold (goal) to be unrealistic.

In addition, the proposers of this plan may not have considered the aspect of *reward valence*, i.e. how much the teachers would value the extra reward (a maximum of £2,000). Although this may sound like a lot of money to some people, when this is weighed up against the amount of effort required to get it, and that for many teachers the goals set may be perceived as unrealistic, this amount may not be valued enough to act as a significant motivating force. Therefore in terms of expectancy theory, this PRP strategy is likely to be lacking both expectancy and valence for many teachers.

Furthermore, if the system results in some teachers being able to achieve the set threshold simply due to either the school they work at, or the form they currently teach, this could well have a negative impact on team morale and cohesion, as reward is not necessarily as a result of performance (which links to the concept of distributive justice). On top of this, schools may find it difficult to recruit and retain teachers for lower-ability classes.

Cognitive evaluation theory

This theory might be particularly helpful in explaining changes in motivation where someone moves from being a volunteer to getting paid (or receiving some other tangible extrinsic reward) for doing the same work. For example, imagine you were volunteering for the RSPCA and found this intrinsically rewarding, and as a result of your experience you got a paid position with the RSPCA, doing pretty much the same thing as when you were a volunteer. The chances are you would experience an overall decrease in your level of motivation. Seems strange doesn't it? However, research by de Charms (1968) supports this explanation, and there have been a large number of studies that also support the theory.

The important point to take from the research on this theory is that when an organisation starts to give someone an extrinsic (tangible) reward, such as pay, for performing what they feel is an interesting task, the result is that the person's intrinsic interest in the task starts to decline. Part of the explanation for this seems to be to do with loss of control, i.e. where previously the person had control because they were voluntarily helping out with the task; this is gone when the person is tangibly extrinsically rewarded for doing it.

This theory has serious implications for reward practices such as performance related pay (PRP) and the provision of bonuses; as such practices represent forms of tangible extrinsic reward within contemporary working environments. According to this theory, the presence of such rewards is likely to be eroding the internal sense of satisfaction and motivation the employee might well have previously had toward the task. The tangible extrinsic reward is 'killing off' the intrinsic motivation.

In the previous paragraph we talked about 'tangible' extrinsic rewards; the opposite of which are intangible extrinsic rewards, such as verbal praise. The reason for making this distinction is that research shows that it is only the tangible extrinsic rewards that erode internal motivation toward a task. Verbal extrinsic rewards actually increase intrinsic motivation toward the task. The important managerial point of this is that, if you give someone a tangible extrinsic reward for doing something they begin to *rely* on this to motivate them to do the task, whereas if you give someone an intangible extrinsic reward (such as praise), this helps people to focus on the task and encourages them to do better. This is therefore an argument against the use of reward strategies such as PRP.

Self-efficacy theory (also known as social cognitive theory or social learning theory)

'Self-efficacy' is about your self-belief/self-confidence in your capabilities. The important idea with this theory is the person's *belief* in terms of being able to perform the task. The higher your self-efficacy, i.e. the higher your self-belief, the higher your confidence will be in terms of doing well at the task. In other words, if you believe you can do it, you are more likely to succeed (Stajkovic and Luthans, 1998). However, you also need the knowledge, skills and abilities to do the task in hand.

This theory helps us to understand why some people seem to work harder when they are given poor feedback, while in others the result of such negative feedback would be a reduction in motivation. Research shows that the former response is likely from someone with high self-efficacy, whereas the latter response is more likely from someone with low self-efficacy (Bandura and Cervone, 1986).

This is all very interesting, but how can it help a manager to improve an employee's motivation? The answer to this question is to use the idea of goal-setting to help increase the self-efficacy of the employee. If a manager works with an employee to set a challenging, but achievable goal, this sends the message to the employee that the manager believes s/he is capable of doing it. This in turn should increase the self-efficacy of the employee, which should improve their motivation toward more challenging tasks. At the same time, this should also lead to the employee setting themselves a higher threshold for their own performance.

Reinforcement theory

Unlike all the other contemporary theories of motivation presented in this chapter (which are cognitive theories), reinforcement theory is behaviouristic. Basically, this theory argues that *reinforcing* someone's behaviour will lead to behaviour repetition.

Reinforcement theory does not concern itself with internal mental processes, and focuses entirely on what happens when someone does, or as the case may be, does not do something. The response (or perhaps lack of response) to the behaviour encourages the person to do the same thing again and again. Writers on the subject generally agree that the theory does not fully explain human motivation. However, reinforcement is a key aspect in understanding motivation. There is no doubt that how you behave at work is influenced by the response you get. For example, if you take long breaks, but your supervisor never reprimands you about this, you are likely to continue to behave in this manner.

CASE STUDY

Teachers strike for more pay

Figure 6.5 Teachers' strike

In April 2008 the UKs largest teaching union, the National Union of Teachers (NUT) voted for a one-day strike over pay. The strike was in response to the 2.45 per cent pay rise that had been offered for 2008. The argument was that this was nowhere near the headline inflation rate of 4.1 per cent.

continued . . . ▶

◄ *. . . continued*

With a pay offer significantly under the inflation rate, this starts to erode the value of the pay packet in terms of what it can buy, and some also argue that it could be seen as indicative of teachers being undervalued as a profession in our society.

To attract top graduates and to retain good teachers, salaries need to be competitive with alternative sources of employment in the private sector. Paying below what you could expect to earn in the private sector will make recruitment and retention more difficult. In 2008 it was found that newly qualified teachers pay was roughly one-fifth lower than the average new graduate starting salary.

1 How do the early theories of motivation help us to understand why the teachers went on strike over their pay?

2 How does equity theory of motivation help us to understand why the teachers went on strike over their pay?

3 Which of the motivation theories is most helpful in understanding the strike action over pay, and why?

4 In an ideal world, according to motivation theory:
   a) How could teachers' motivation be improved?
   b) How could the 'brightest graduates' be encouraged into the profession?

CASE STUDY

Hotel attempts to combat high staff turnover through reward scheme

It is common knowledge that the leisure sector suffers from high levels of staff turnover. One group of four hotels in the UK decided they would try to do something about this for themselves by designing and implementing a reward and recognition package they hoped would help reduce their staff turnover.

Their scheme included cash awards of up to £150 to the person voted by their peers as employee of the month. Also included was a team reward system whereby every 12 weeks £1000 was awarded to the Hotel of the Season, and every year a £2,000 award for Hotel of the Year. Staff could spend the money on themselves as they saw fit. Also included in the scheme were discounted stays to family and friends.

1 Is this strategy of motivating staff content or process driven? Explain your answer.

2 What do you think the pros and cons of this approach might be?

3 In terms of the cons you identified, make suggestions for how the reward system could be improved in order to overcome the cons.

4 To what extent do you think this type of reward strategy is likely to result in improved motivation, both in the short and long term?

5 Does this approach make any underlying assumptions about the motivation of the employees?

6.8 Summary

This chapter has provided an introduction to leadership and motivation. As we have seen in our overview of leadership theories, motivation and leadership are inextricably linked. Leaders need to motivate their followers (employees, team members, etc.) to achieve their goals. However, as we have seen, motivation is not an easy concept to identify in a person. It varies both within a person and between different people. Having a good understanding of motivation will benefit both the leader and an organisation.

KEY IDEAS

Some of the main points covered in this chapter are listed below. If you feel unsure about any of them, then revisit the appropriate section. If you would like some additional reading on the topic, try the books listed in recommended reading.

What do we mean by leadership?
- There are many different ways of defining leadership and society does not share a common understanding of the term.
- Some of the more recognisable types of leader are: Traditional, Charismatic, Situational, Appointed and Functional.
- Leadership involves a process between followers and the leader, where some form of influence is used.

The difference between leadership and management
- Managers and leaders are different but not mutually exclusive. It is possible for a leader to manage and a manager to lead.
- Leaders tend to focus more on the future, while managers have more of an eye for the here and now.
- Both managers and leaders must make decisions. However, society would generally consider the person making the more significant decisions as the leader rather than the manager.

The search for leadership theories
- The importance of having the right leader in an organisation has led to a continual hunt for the one best way for a leader to act. However, the search continues.
- Theories on leadership include: Trait Theory, Contingency Theory, Path-Goal Theory, Transformational Leadership and Team Leadership.

Motivation
- Motivation in humans is complex, and many theories have been proposed to attempt to explain it.
- The main theories fall into two broad schools of thought: content theories, and process theories.
- The way a person thinks about motivation will influence the way s/he manages their employees.
- It is unlikely that any one theory of motivation can explain human motivation. Rather, an understanding of the range of theories can help a leader or manager to develop strategies that can help to maintain and improve employee motivation.

REFLECTIVE QUESTIONS

1 Think of a person you believe is a good leader. Would you say they were a Traditional, Charismatic, Situational, Appointed or Functional leader? Explain your answer.
2 The Prime Minister is the leader of the country. Is it better for the country if the Prime Minister is a transformational, rather than a transactional leader? Again, explain your answer.
3 What are the main lessons that a manager can learn from content theories of motivation in terms of maintaining and improving employee motivation?
4 What are the main lessons that a manager can learn from process theories of motivation in terms of maintaining and improving employee motivation?
5 Many organisations use forms of extrinsic reward to improve motivation and output. Examples include bonuses and prizes. Do you think this kind of strategy works on everyone? Discuss.
6 When people work for organisations such as charities, which perhaps do not pay as much as commercial organisations, how can we explain the level of motivation of these employees?

RECOMMENDED READING

What do we mean by leadership?
Leadership: Limits and Possibilities by Keith Grint, particularly Chapter 1, explores some of the issues that arise from trying to define leadership too tightly. The book manages to raise some of the many facets of leadership in a relatively accessible way.

The difference between leadership and management
For a slightly easier read than the more academic books mentioned, *Leadership Jazz* by Max DePree contains a number of excellent, and clear, leadership examples that have come about from his experience as a manager and leader.

The search for leadership theories
A good overview of leadership and the development and background to the better known theories can be found in *Leadership: Theory and Practice* by Peter G. Northouse, published by Sage. This book also manages to mix theory and practice in a readily accessible manner.

Motivation
Two excellent texts for more on motivation theories, and their application to the workplace are:
- *Management and Organisational Behaviour,* Chapter 7, by Laurie Mullins
- *Organizational Behavior,* chapter 6, by Stephen Robbins and Timothy Judge.
   Full references are provided in the reference section at the end of this chapter.
   Another interesting book is *The Enthusiastic Employee: What Employees Want and Why Employers Should Give It To Them,* by David Sirota, Louis Mischkind and Michael Meltzer (2005).

USEFUL WEBSITES

Leadership:
- The Leadership Trust
  www.leadership.org.uk
- The Northern Leadership Academy
  www.northernleadershipacademy.co.uk/portal/nlacommunity/homepage

NB: a word of warning here – there are many websites that claim to offer answers to leadership, so we suggest that you do not venture much further than the two sites given above for up-to-date, relevant material.

Cognitive evaluation theory:
http://changingminds.org/explanations/theories/cognitive_evaluation.htm
Employee Motivation, the Organisational Environment and Productivity:
www.accel-team.com/motivation/intro.html
Equity theory of motivation:
www.bola.biz/motivation/equity.html
Expectancy theory of motivation:
www.arrod.co.uk/archive/concept_vroom.php
Goal-setting theory of motivation:
www.mindtools.com/pages/article/newHTE_87.htm
Herzberg's two-factor theory of motivation:
www.accel-team.com/human_relations/hrels_05_herzberg.html
http://tutor2u.net/business/people/motivation_theory_herzberg.asp
Maslow's hierarchy of needs:
www.abraham-maslow.com/m_motivation/Hierarchy_of_Needs.asp
McGregor's Theory x, Theory y:
www.tutor2u.net/business/people/motivation_theory_mcgregor.asp
Performance related pay:
www.tutor2u.net/business/people/motivation_financial_performancepay.asp
Procedural justice in performance evaluation:
www.referenceforbusiness.com/management/Pr-Sa/Reinforcement-Theory.html
Reinforcement theory of motivation:
www.referenceforbusiness.com/management/Pr-Sa/Reinforcement-Theory.html
Self-efficacy theory of motivation:
http://en.wikipedia.org/wiki/Self-efficacy

REFERENCES

Adams, J.S. (1965) 'Inequity in Social Exchange, *Advances in Experimental Social Psychology*, vol. 62, 335–343.

Bandura, A. and Cervone, D. (1986) 'Differential Engagement in Self-Reactive Influences in Cognitively-Based Motivation' *Organizational Behavior and Human Decision Processes*, vol. 48, no. 1, 92–113.

Barnard, C.I. (1948) 'The Nature of Leadership' In: C.I. Barnard, *Organisation and Management: Selected Papers*. Boston: HBR Press.

Barnard, C.I. (1968) *The Functions of the Executive*. Cambridge, MA: Harvard University Press.

Bass, B.M. (1990) *Bass and Stogdill's Handbook of Leadership: A Survey of Theory and Research*. New York: Free Press.

Bryman, A. (1996) 'Leadership in Organisations' In: S.R. Clegg, C. Hardy and W.R. Burns (1978) *Leadership*. New York: Harper and Row.

Conger, J.A. (1999) 'Charismatic and Transformational Leadership in Organisations: An Insider's Perspective On These Developing Streams of Research', *Leadership Quarterly*, vol. 10, no. 2, 145–179.

de Charms, R. (1968) *Personal Causation: The Internal Affective Determinants of Behaviour.* New York: Academic Press.

DePree, M. (1992). *Leadership Jazz.* New York: Dell Publishing.

Donaldson, G. (1983). *Decision Making at the Top: The Shaping of Strategic Direction*. New York: Basic Books.

Evens, M.G. (1970) 'The Effects of Supervisory Behaviour on the Path-Goal Relationship', *Organisational Behaviour and Human Performance*, vol. 5, 277–298.

Fiedler, F.E. (1967) *A Theory of Leadership Effectiveness.* New York: McGraw-Hill.

Greenberg, J. (1989) 'Cognitive Reevaluation of Outcomes in Response to Underpayment Inequity', *Academy of Management,* vol. 32, no. 1, 174–184.

Greenberg, J. and Ornstein, S. (1983) 'High Status Job Title as Compensation for Underpayment: A Test of Equity Theory', *Journal of Applied Psychology*, vol. 68, no. 2, 606–613.

Grint, K. (2005) *Leadership: Limits and Possibilities.* New York: Palgrave Macmillan.

Hersey, P. and Blanchard, K.H. (1992) *Management of Organisational Behaviour*. 6th edn. Englewood Cliffs, NJ: Prentice Hall.

Herzberg, F. (1966) *Work and the Nature of Man.* Cleveland, OH: World Publishing.

Hollingsworth, M.J. (1999) 'Purpose and Values', *The British Journal of Administrative Management*, January/February, 22–23.

House, R.J. and Dessler, G. (1974) 'The Path-Goal Theory of Leadership: Some *post hoc* and *a priori* Tests' In: J. Hunt and L. Larson (Eds.), *Contingency Approaches in Leadership* Carbondale: Southern Illinois University Press, 29–55.

Jago, A.G. (1982) 'Leadership: Perspectives in Theory and Research', *Management Science*, vol. 28, no. 3, 315–336.

Larson, C.E. and LaFasto, F.M.J. (1989) *Teamwork: What Must Go Right/What Can Go Wrong.* Newbury Park, CA: Sage.

Locke, E.A. (1968) 'Towards a Theory of Task Motivation and Incentives', *Organizational Behavior and Human Performance*, vol. 3, 157–189.

Mandela, N.R. (1994) *Long Walk to Freedom.* London: Abacus.

Maslow, A.H. (1943) 'A Theory of Human Motivation', *Psychological Review*, vol. 50, no. 4, 370–96.

McGregor, D. (1960) *The Human Side of Enterprise.* New York: McGraw Hill.

Mullins, L.J (2007) *Management and Organisational Behaviour.* 8th edn. Harlow: Pearson.

Nord, W.R., Clegg, S.R and Hardy, C. (Eds.), *Handbook of Organisational Studies.* London: Sage.

Northouse, P.J. (2007) *Leadership: Theory and Practice,* London: Sage.

Robbins, S.P. and Judge, T.A. (2009) *Organizational Behavior.* Upper Saddle River, NJ: Pearson.

Rost, J.C. (1991) *Leadership for the Twenty-First Century.* New York: Praeger.

Skarlicki, D.P. and Folger, R. (1997) 'Retaliation in the Workplace: The Roles of Distributive, Procedural, and Interactive Justice', *Journal of Applied Psychology*, vol. 88, no. 3, 444–458.

Skinner, B.F. (1971) *Contingencies of Reinforcement.* East Norwalk, CT: Appleton-Century-Crofts.

Stajkovic, A.D. and Luthans, F. (1998) 'Self-Efficacy and Work-Related Performance: A Meta-Analysis', *Psychological Bulletin,* vol. 124, no. 2, 240–261.

Vroom, V.H. (1964) *Work and Motivation.* New York: Wiley.

Walster, E., Walster, G.W. and Scott, W.G. (1978) *Equity: Theory and Research.* Boston: Allyn and Bacon.

Yukl, G.A. (1999) 'An Evaluation of Conceptual Weaknesses in Transformational and Charismatic Leadership Theories', *Leadership Quarterly*, vol. 10, no. 2, 285–305.

Zaccaro, S. J., Rittman, A. L. and Marks, M. A. (2001) 'Team Leadership', *Leadership Quarterly*, vol. 12, 451–485.

7 Organisational Culture and Change

'There is something in all countries called management, but its meaning differs to a larger or smaller extent from one country to another, and it takes considerable historical and cultural insight into local conditions to understand its processes, philosophies and problems.'

(Hofstede, 1993, p. 88)

CHAPTER OUTLINE

7.1 Introduction
7.2 What is culture?
7.3 What do we understand by organisational culture?
7.4 Cultural change
7.5 Why we need change
7.6 Managing change
7.7 Summary

CHAPTER OBJECTIVES

After carefully reading and engaging with the tasks and activities outlined in this chapter, you should have a better understanding of:

- what society understands by culture
- some of the various classifications that help with our understanding of different aspects of culture
- cultural differences that make organisations unique
- differences between the managerial perspective and the social science viewpoint of cultural change
- reasons why organisations experience change and the difficulties associated with implementing change
- how to apply Lewin's and Kotter's techniques to assist in the change process.

7.1 Introduction

You have probably studied with a number of different tutors who have set different standards of expectation, both in class and for assignments. In so doing you have probably experienced a different **culture** in one tutor's class compared to another: one tutor may have fostered a relaxed casual atmosphere, another may have been more formal. To be successful as a student, you have generally to adapt to the atmosphere of the class.

KEY TERMS

Culture is the set of key values, beliefs and understandings shared by a group of people.

The same situation arises in organisations with employees who join the organisation adapting to the organisational culture. Culture, however, is difficult to classify and can be studied at a number of levels. It can also be very different in the various parts of an organisation. For example, most organisations would have a different culture in their marketing department compared to the culture of the finance department.

Example

A businesswoman arriving in Greece from the USA for the first time would have certain expectations from a business meeting in Athens. She would expect the meeting to be formal and business like from the start. The expectations from the local Greek participants however would be for a more social, less formal, approach, probably with some of the meeting taking place over a leisurely meal. Neither approach is wrong; it is just the way that people, dependent on their particular cultural background and experiences, are used to dealing with business meetings.

There are a number of influences on our own particular cultural environment: family and community expectations, educational experiences, religion, nationality, etc. Because people bring these cultural influences with them into an organisation, organisations are affected by, and in turn influence employees.

How and if culture can be managed, and who influences whom, are the subject of much academic debate and we will return to this important question later in the chapter. We begin by taking a closer look at what we mean by the word culture and then move on to consider its impact on organisations and the difficulties experienced when organisations attempt to change culture.

Figure 7.1 A business meeting

 ## 7.2 What is culture?

Culture (like leadership, Chapter 6), is easier to talk about than to define. It is very easy to talk about the culture of a particular country being different but not so easy to say why, and what the differences are.

CASE STUDY

Culture is not only restricted to nationalities. Within a 30-mile radius of Merseyside there are several different cultural identities. For example, St Helens and Wigan not only speak with pronounced different accents to people in Liverpool, but are also towns where rugby league is followed and played with a passion that is reserved for football in Liverpool.

Most people do not think too hard about their cultural identity, it is something that is just there. As Robbins (1992, p. 14) points out 'Culture is like fish to water. It is there all the time but the fish are oblivious to it.' Relating this to Merseyside, a schoolboy in St Helens would naturally play rugby. The same boy raised in Liverpool would most likely prefer to play football. He would have been influenced by the local cultural environment from the moment he was born without ever thinking consciously about it.

ACTIVITY

Think of a person of the opposite sex who is approximately your age and from the same local area. Do you think that there are cultural differences between you? You might find it helpful to consider differences in sport, music, food, recreation, reading, etc. to determine apparent differences.

Some aspects of culture are easier to spot than others. We talk about the visible and invisible **artefacts** of culture.

KEY TERMS

Artefacts are defined as man-made objects, thus they are interpreted within particular contexts and can change over time.

The visible artefacts of culture, such as language, symbols, dress and behaviour are easier to spot than the invisible artefacts. Invisible artefacts include people's values, beliefs and shared understanding. It is much harder to understand these deeper shared understandings held by a community, the invisible artefacts of their culture.

REFLECTIVE QUESTIONS

As well as cultural differences between countries and communities, think about some of the visible artefacts of you and your parents. For example, your dress and language is probably different to your parent's generation, although perhaps some of your invisible artefacts may be the same. One invisible artefact may be that every Saturday night you all sit down together for a special meal that you all enjoy. So perhaps there are different levels of cultural differences and similarities between the same communities.

The work of Geert Hofstede

Towards the end of the 1970s, Dutch professor Geert Hofstede undertook a major survey of national culture and its influence on the American company IBM, which at the time was operating in over 40 different countries. Hofstede's view was that culture is a type of mental programming that comes from sharing experiences within the same social environment and which affects overall behaviour.

His study identified four different dimensions of culture: power distance, uncertainty avoidance, individualism, and masculinity (Hofstede, 1980).

- *Power distance* considers the level of hierarchical distance between employees and managers. For example, is it a culture where employees are willing to engage in debate with managers, or would this be socially unacceptable behaviour? Some countries, e.g. Denmark and Sweden, find it difficult to accept inequalities between people and are classified by Hofstede as having a low level of power distance. Other countries are more comfortable with a higher level of power distance, e.g. France.
- *Uncertainty avoidance* relates to how comfortable a society is with uncertainty. In some cultures a handshake and a verbal agreement would be seen as binding and something both parties would be at ease with, while other countries would require the additional reassurance of a written contract. Germany is an example of a country classified as high uncertainty avoidance: here people feel uncomfortable about ambiguous situations. Singapore is an example of a country with a lower uncertainty avoidance culture.
- *Individualism* is concerned with how people feel about acting independently. Some countries are more likely to involve all members of the family in decisions, while in other countries people are more inclined to act independently. An example of a country with high individualism is the USA, while India is an example of a country with low individualism. In India, the group takes precedence over the individual, whereas in the USA, children would learn from an early age that individuals need to compete with each other to reach the top.
- *Masculinity and femininity* looks at the role played by gender in a society. Countries which are less masculine and more feminine are viewed as being more caring and supportive. In a country classified by Hofstede as having high masculinity, people would be viewed as more assertive and generally more work focused. Japan and Italy are viewed as high-masculinity societies, while Sweden and Norway were classed as low-masculinity societies with more emphasis on quality of life.

ACTIVITY

Think of your immediate family and the family of a close friend. Can you identify if they are different in terms of the dimensions of culture identified by Hofstede, e.g. power distance, uncertainty avoidance, individualism and masculinity?

Hofstede's work has been criticised by a number of authors, not least because it focused only on employees of one company and took no account of regional, as opposed to national, characteristics. There is also a criticism of what might be seen as provocative terms like 'masculinity' (Hofstede also refers to low masculinity as feminine). However, the survey is one of the largest to date (around 60,000 of IBM's workforce) and does make an important contribution to our understanding of national cultural differences.

CASE STUDY

It is not the case that Hofstede's study claims that one type of culture is better than another – it is simply a guide to classification. For example, Sweden, viewed as low with respect to power distance, uncertainty avoidance and masculinity is an example of a well-run and businesslike society.

Sweden covers an area greater than that of the UK and has a population of only around 10 million, yet they have a number of examples of organisational excellence that are respected throughout the world, e.g. Volvo, Ikea, Ericsson and Alfa Laval. Swedish people like to agree a way forward together, believe in equity for all and have a strong work ethic. This is perhaps why they have performed so well as a country over the last 100 years, particularly given their starting base as predominately a farming economy and its close proximity to Russia, something which many other countries struggled to cope with during the same period.

The country will probably continue to prosper in the next 100 years as it is continually looking for innovation and recognised as a 'future thinking' country. It has one of Europe's highest levels of broadband penetration and Kista, a region of Stockholm, is recognised as one of the world's high technology clusters, smaller but similar to Silicon Valley in the USA.

GLOBE

Following on from Hofstede's work, since the early 1990s the Global Leadership and Organisational Behaviour Effectiveness (GLOBE) research programme has extended our understanding of cultural differences between countries (Javidan and House, 2001). This has looked at nine different dimensions of national culture and is a major **longitudinal** study of over 800 different organisations in 62 countries. This has again been criticised for being too simplistic and not taking into account different subcultures within a nation.

KEY TERMS

A **longitudinal** study is a piece of research that has been undertaken over a longer than normal time span. So, for example, studying a child's growth over 10 years would be classed as a longitudinal study.

Hofstede's dimension	Low-scoring countries	Average-scoring countries	High-scoring countries
Power distance	South Africa Netherlands	England Brazil	Spain Russia
Uncertainty avoidance	Hungary Bolivia	USA Israel	Denmark Austria

Table 7.1   Snapshot of the GLOBE study

A snapshot of the GLOBE study considering only two dimensions of Hofstede's original four is shown above in Table 7.1.

1 Select a country you are familiar with from those listed in Table 7.1 above. Do you think from your experience that it fits in with the GLOBE study findings listed?

Both Hofstede's work and the continuing GLOBE project have attracted criticism. However, it has provided some empirical evidence that has added to our overall understanding of national cultures. It is also the case that countries are affected by their own particular laws and regulation, religious cultures, educational standards and language. So we should expect some similarities, even if they are very broad generalities.

7.3   What do we understand by organisational culture?

Walk into an Asda supermarket and look around carefully, then take a look at a Sainsbury's supermarket. They both sell groceries very successfully, but do it in different ways: Asda does this over a range of goods and makes a point of being seen as a cheap place to shop: 'that's Asda price'. Sainsbury's, on the other hand, is proud to offer a range of higher quality (and priced) goods. What do you notice about them? Their respective organisational cultures are clearly different and the culture of each organisation runs throughout the supermarkets. It is more difficult to state exactly what each organisational culture is, however.

One way of thinking about culture in organisations is simply as 'that's the way we do things around here'. Trying to pin down exactly what it is however is much more difficult. This is because the artefacts of any **organisation's culture** reside at various levels. As with communities, these artefacts include symbols, language, stories and beliefs that form part of a particular organisation's makeup.

KEY TERMS

Organisational culture is a relatively recent research topic. Most of the literature defining and analysing it originates from the 1980s. It refers to the artefacts, visible and invisible, that relate to one organisation and make it unique.

The definition given by Siehl and Martin (1984, p. 227) sums it up as: 'The glue that holds an organisation together through a sharing of patterns of meaning'.

CASE STUDY

IKEA, the successful Swedish home furnishing company, has characteristics that are unique to their organisation. The company thinks of a customer as coming for a day out, not simply to pop in to buy a piece of furniture and leave. It also aims to keep prices at 20 per cent less than its competitors and manages to do this thanks to the complex but integrated network of suppliers that it uses so effectively.

IKEA is the brainchild of Ingvar Kamprad, who realised that there was a need for cheap but stylish furniture. Although copied by other retailers, it was a different concept at the time it began and IKEA has managed to maintain an edge over its competitors.

Kamprad emphasises an informal, non-hierarchical business environment that fits in well with his fellow Swedish workers. But this belies an attention to detail that some may call obsessive. He will often not delegate questions to others but will go directly to front-line staff to determine what is going on in a particular area. Notice the contrast in this approach to a typical company CEO of the same size as IKEA in the UK. It is often difficult to get past their PA to speak to them and even rarer to see them on the shop floor. Kamprad is also different in that he will not travel anywhere first class, often resorting to public transport rather than a car.

One influential organisational culture theory is that given by Edgar Schein (1985). He identifies three levels of organisational culture; easily visible ones (artefacts) at the surface level of the organisation, at the next level there are behavioural norms and values of the organisation, and finally there are the basic **assumptions** that everyone in the organisation understands.

KEY TERMS

The basic **assumptions** of an organisation are the accepted beliefs that everyone takes as facts, not questioned or discussed but self evident truths within the organisation.

Schein's theory points to culture being maintained from inside the organisation, while at the same time being influenced by values introduced from outside the organisation. For example, a new manager might introduce some changes but only after they have been fully accepted by the organisation will they move from artefacts to deeper held assumptions. Hence, as can be seen below, cultures can change with interactions between different levels. However, it takes time for the underlying assumptions to be altered and fully accepted.

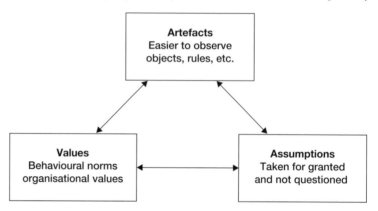

Figure 7.2 Artefacts, values and assumptions

As well as the cultural levels inside an organisation, different organisations have differing types of culture. The pre-eminent thinker Charles Handy (1993) classified four different types of organisational cultures. These are:

- **Power culture** has control resting in one, or a few key influential individuals. This can typically occur in smaller organisations where the owner has a lot of personal power.
- **Role culture** is typical of a bureaucratic organisation (see Chapter 2). Roles are clearly defined and it is the role, not the person that is the mainstay of the organisation. McDonald's is an example of an organisation with a role culture.
- **Task culture** refers to organisations where there is a clear focus on completing the task at hand. Influence in this type of organisation rests more with the task experts than with formal authority positions. A clinical hospital team would typically have a task culture, with appropriate experts all having a say in the task at hand.
- **Person culture** is typical of a university culture. Here, the people are the central focus, with particular professors creating certain research and teaching excellence. The structure of the organisation is there to support them and allow for change as professors' research interests alter over time.

Notice that the categories given by Charles Handy are not mutually exclusive as far as particular work environments are concerned. For example, working in a wine bar might be classed as a power culture if the manager had a lot of personal power and was the owner. However, another wine bar could just as easily have a role culture when the bar is part of a larger chain and the manager is an employee of the organisation. It is important to consider the culture of the particular environment you are studying and not to assume that all similar organisations fall into the same category, or even that the same culture exists throughout an organisation.

Organisational culture then, represents the often unspoken part of an organisation. It is difficult even for insiders to fully appreciate what it is, and it is particularly difficult for outsiders to pin down the essence of it. Indeed, it would require qualitative research using **ethnographic** methods to fully understand an organisation's culture.

KEY TERMS

Ethnography means cultural description and there are many ways of conducting this type of research. **Ethnographic** research into organisations can typically be thought of as observations and interviews.

Trying to determine and describe an organisational culture (doing ethnographical research) is difficult as it is not possible to know exactly what another person's values and feelings are. This is why researchers typically focus on the visible artefacts first in an attempt to begin to understand how employees understand their organisation's culture. These artefacts could be how an office is designed, how people dress in a certain part of a factory, particular slogans that a department may use, and so on.

The visible artefacts are not the culture, they are only a guide to help us to interpret the invisible artefacts. These invisible artefacts contain the underlying assumptions and beliefs that people within the organisation hold and understand. For example, an assumption could be that the company always looks after its employees. This would then subconsciously guide aspects of the organisation's behaviour in the way employees were treated.

ACTIVITY

Think about your own bedroom at home. What are the visible artefacts on display in your room that would help someone to identify you and your personality?

Figure 7.3 Does your bedroom look like this?

7.4 Cultural change

The culture of an organisation helps employees to make sense of the organisation and provides stability. People know where they stand in relation to the underlying assumptions of the company and this helps them to make sense of organisational activities. So when a change in the culture of an organisation is suggested, people will naturally feel uneasy, the usual environment that they have become accustomed to is about to change. Their underlying assumptions about the organisation are about to alter.

This unease about change means that changing culture is difficult and sometimes not possible. Schein (1985) talks about it taking place gradually over several years. It is worth pointing out here that cultural change is not the same as making a technological change, e.g. bringing in new machinery, which may require differing employee activities but not changes in the underlying organisational culture.

One important question to be raised here is the question of whether in fact the culture of an organisation can be managed. A number of popular writers in the 1980s (e.g. Peters and Waterman, 1982) began to argue that it can, and indeed should be controlled and managed if organisations are to become successful.

Other researchers (Smircich, 1983) are not convinced that culture can be managed or controlled and think that it is just something that is continually evolving and deeply rooted in the history of the organisation.

These two different perspectives about cultural change can be viewed as a **managerial perspective** and a **social science perspective**, with the managerial perspective aligning with Peters and Waterman's viewpoint, and the social science perspective aligning with Smircich.

KEY TERMS

A **managerial perspective** of culture is one where culture is viewed as something that can be attained as part of an overall management strategy. In other words, culture can be managed. The managerial perspective sees culture as something that an organisation has throughout (a unitary perspective of culture within the organisation) and this culture is passed on to employees who join the company through the process of socialisation.

The **social science perspective** takes the view that culture 'just is' and is something that cannot be easily described. It is continually evolving through social interactions between people and these interactions are the organisational culture. This organisational culture can have many different subcultures within departments and managerial hierarchical groupings.

CASE STUDY

The Chinese culture is one of the oldest in the world and has managed to retain a number of features consistently, not least the fact that it has been a highly centralised state for over 2,000 years. The social culture is characterised mainly by Confucianism, Collectivism, Renquing and Guanxi.

Confucianism advocates a common set of assumptions encouraging hard work, responsibility and teamwork ahead of personal advancement. Everyone knows their place and also who they must obey and respect.

There is a high value on collectivism in China, with a group orientation towards family and extended family members. The group is a source of identity, protection and loyalty.

In its ideal form, Renquing is an informal and unselfish give-and-take between people. In reality a close account of favours given and owed is kept and deep feeling of guilt and shame arise in those who fail to meet their obligations.

Guanxi can be considered as friendship based on mutual favours. This is often summed up succinctly as being about 'who you know, not what you know'.

The newer buildings in Beijing, Shanghai and Guangzhou seem to display a society with a western outlook. However, Western values are still only superficially embraced, and given the richness and history of Chinese culture it is hard to imagine that it will ever change.

REFLECTIVE QUESTIONS

Imagine that you are in a class of 30 students in a European university and five Chinese students join you for a year's study. Do you think that the students will alter the cultural dynamics of the class (social science perspective), or do you think that they will change to accept the established culture of the existing class (the managerial perspective)?

7.5 Why we need change

The last section considered some of the issues surrounding organisational change and the difficulties inherent in it. But why do we need change? Couldn't we just operate on the principle of: 'if it's not broken, don't fix it'? The answer is that companies must adapt to the environment if they are to survive. A good example of this is a company 30 years ago that manufactured typewriters. It would not have foreseen then that home computers would effectively put it out of business.

The typewriting company is an example of the changing market conditions. There is also increasing competition internationally, with ready access to goods from abroad, so companies need to change to adapt to this. Some organisations have changed by completely moving the company overseas.

Within 15 years from now, half of the world's wealth is predicted to come from India and China. It is hard to imagine that this will not impact on the organisational culture of many western companies.

There are also the everyday changes in government regulations that invoke change in organisations. In 2006, over 3,000 government regulations were introduced in the UK alone (e.g. the change in automatic retirement at the age of 65).

Change is also instigated in relation to company growth. For example, a company could outgrow its existing factory and need new premises, or it could increase its production in response to demand, which would require a new organisational structure.

So it appears that organisations will always need change, whether planned (a company introducing a new production technique) or unplanned (the typewriting company mentioned at the start of this section). There has been much debate of late about the pace of change being much more rapid than in previous years owing to the speed of technological innovation. However, the following quotation from 1922 indicates that this is not a new phenomenon.

Never before in the history of mankind have so many and so frequent changes occurred. These changes that we see taking place all about us are in that great cultural accumulation which is man's social heritage. It has already been shown that these cultural changes were in earlier times rather infrequent, but that in modern times they have been occurring faster and faster until today mankind is almost bewildered in his effort to keep adjusted to these ever increasing social changes.

(Ogburn, 1922)

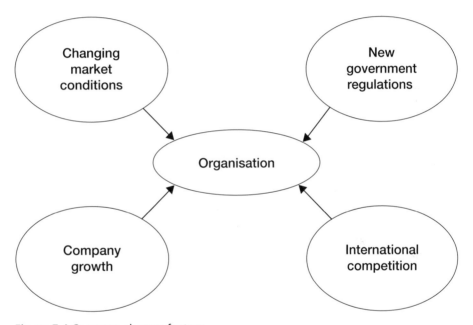

Figure 7.4 Common change factors

CASE STUDY

For many companies in the former East Germany, the fall of the Berlin wall in 1989 suddenly changed their working environment. They now faced the prospect of working in an unprotected capitalist market and competing with global organisations, something their new compatriots in the former West Germany had been doing successfully for the previous 30 years. They also had to adapt to new working conditions, which generally meant moving from large production operations towards team working conditions.

The effects of this changed environment 20 years on are still being felt, with more prosperity in what was West Germany than the former East Germany. However, there are some exceptions, notably General Motors, which has transformed Automobilwerke Eisenach, a former East German car manufacturer, into one of the most productive plants in Europe.

Force field analysis

According to Kurt Lewin (1951) change, whether planned or not, occurs when change drivers collectively overcome restraining forces.

Figure 7.5 Pressure build-up

Example

Pressure built up over a number of years in the United Kingdom to eventually outlaw the slave trade in 1807. Here the change drivers were people like William Wilberforce, the British politician, who pointed out the inherent injustices of the trade and campaigned to abolish it. The restraining forces were traders, ship owners and dock-related businesses, which had a great deal invested in the continuation of the industry.

Lewin (1951) suggested using **force field analysis** as a way of assessing the relevance of the particular change drivers and restraining forces associated with an impending change. This analysis, although subjective, can then be an indication of whether the benefits of a change outweigh the negatives associated with it.

KEY TERMS

Force field analysis is a technique for assessing the potential benefits of change and the restraining forces to change.

To give a flavour of the use of force field analysis, consider the choice faced by a student about to commence a university degree programme. There will be a number of reasons to attend (Change drivers) and a number of reasons not to (Restraining forces). The students would then assign a number student would use to gauge the change driver, or the restraining force to have, from 1 (weak) – 10 (strong).

In our example below, the student has rated 'Better long-term job prospects' strongly as a 9 and 'Expensive' not quite as strongly as an 8. Note that these are all personal to the student's particular situation. For example, a student could consider leaving home either as a change driver, or as a restraining force.

Change drivers (Reasons for the change)	Restraining forces (Reasons not to change)
Better long-term job prospects (9)	Expensive (8)
Interesting degree programme (8)	Leave home (5)
Independence (8)	Loneliness (7)
Opportunity to meet new friends (4)	Undecided about future career path (9)
Broaden life experience (5)	Length of time commitment (7)

Table 7.2   Force field analysis: Starting a three-year university degree programme

Once the analysis has been done the student should have an indication of whether the change would be beneficial or not. Of course, the weightings given to each driver or force are subjective and the student should be cautious about making any change if the total number of drivers is approximately the same as the total number of restraining forces. In our example, this is 34 and 38 respectively, suggesting that a university programme may not be the best thing for this person at the moment. However, note how this balance would change if the student had a clearer idea about their future career path.

ACTIVITY

Apply force field analysis to a particular career path that you may be considering for the future.

7.6 Managing change

Accepting the fact that organisations need to change has led to a well-established method for implementing change based on work by Kurt Lewin (1951).

Lewin's method is based on the following three-step process:

- unfreezing
- changing
- refreezing.

Unfreezing is the initial step when reasons for change are explained in an endeavour to convince people that change really is required for the benefit of the organisation. This is seen as a vital stage as employees will be reluctant to change the way they are currently working without what they see to be a valid reason.

Changing is the next step of the process, with the planned changes taking place. Here, new procedures are introduced, employees may need different skills that require training courses, new departments may need creating, and some departments may merge or even close. This is a time when people are interpreting and adapting to the changes taking place.

Refreezing consolidates the changes that have taken place and ensures that the previous way of doing things does not reoccur. It may be in this phase of the process that minor corrections and interventions are required to enforce the new processes.

Of course, the steps above may not be so distinctive in practice. However, the three-step process is a useful guide for organisations who are thinking of implementing major changes.

Lewin's guide is not now deemed appropriate for many organisations, due to the continually changing environment within which they operate. In particular, refreezing may be done so successfully that it becomes difficult in the future to unfreeze so this step may be detrimental to organisations who view change as continual and something to be embraced.

Managing resistance to change

Despite criticism, Lewin's guide is still a useful guide to organisations who wish to implement change. However, it does not help employees feel less worried about change.

We all do a lot of things quite naturally without much thought. For example you probably went into a routine this morning to get dressed without giving too much thought to it. You will probably have put on your shoes easily without stopping to think which shoe to put on first. Now try the following short experiment to try and understand how you might feel about a relatively easy change.

ACTIVITY

Clasp your hands together so that all your fingers are intertwined. Now notice which thumb is on top. Is it your left or right thumb? Repeat the exercise, but deliberately place your other thumb on top.

For many people there will be a slightly unnatural feel about the second clasp compared to the first. Even a slight change over which we have control can feel a bit uncomfortable. Generally, we do not like to change.

One of a manager's biggest challenges, and frustrations, is to implement change and overcome employees' fears and resistance to change. This natural reluctance means that managers who wish to implement change should try and understand and be aware of the main reasons people resist change. We consider some of these reasons below.

Self-interest

Employees are quite naturally going to resist any change that they think will take away some aspect of the job that they value. This could be a reduction in pay, a loss of status, shorter tea or lunch breaks, etc. So it is important for managers to take account of these concerns and address them early in the change process.

Uncertainty, misunderstanding and a lack of trust

There is often a lack of understanding, reinforced by a lack of trust, in employees about the reasons behind change. Rumours can swiftly circulate about reasons for change. Where communication from the management is unclear, rumours can become very difficult to correct, particularly if the workforce have little faith in the management team. Equally, if the management team has little trust in the workforce they are likely to give only partial information, which will help to fuel rumours and misinformation (see also Chapter 5.)

It should be clear from the above that communication is a vital part of the change process and indeed how change is introduced initially is a vital part of the successful implementation process

Kotter (1996) identified the following eight typical mistakes that managers make when trying to implement change.

- allowing too much complacency (no sense of urgency about the future)
- a failure to create a sufficiently powerful guiding coalition (getting a group of people together who are behind the change programme and who will help to drive it forward)
- a failure to understand the power of the vision (not reinforcing the objectives of the change and finding the strategy to achieve it)
- under-communicating the vision (failing to ensure that employees know where they are heading and what they need to do)

- permitting obstacles to stand in the way of the vision (failing to alter working practices for example, or not providing training if they are hindering the change process)
- a failure to create short-term wins (employees and the organisation need to feel that they are making some progress towards their goal)
- declaring victory too early (focusing too much on the short-term wins and losing momentum)
- a failure to cement the changes in the organisation's culture (Lewin's refreezing step).

 7.7 ## Summary

The chapter began with an introduction to culture and considered the way in which the visible and invisible artefacts help with our combined understanding of culture. It then considered how organisations viewed culture as something unique to them: in other words, the glue that holds an organisation together through a shared pattern of meaning and understanding.

Reasons for cultural change were then considered and the difficulties inherent in organisations attempting change were discussed. The chapter concluded with some well-established and useful tools to assist with the change process.

KEY IDEAS

Some of the main points covered in this chapter are listed below. If you feel unsure about any of them, then revisit the appropriate section. If you would like some additional reading on the topic, try the books listed below in recommended reading.

What is culture?
- Culture is the set of key values, beliefs and understandings shared by a group of people.
- Family and community expectations, educational experiences, religion and nationality are just some of the cultural influences we experience.
- Culture is difficult to classify and can be studied at a number of levels within different communities.
- Geert Hofstede's study identified four different dimensions of culture: power distance, uncertainty avoidance, individualism, and masculinity/femininity.

What do we understand as organisational culture?
- Organisational culture refers to the artefacts, visible and invisible, that relate to one organisation, which makes that organisation unique.
- Edgar Schein identified three levels of organisational culture within an organisation. These are the easily visible ones (artefacts) at the surface level of the organisation, the behavioural norms and values of the organisation, and finally the basic assumptions that everyone in the organisation relates to subconsciously.

continued . . . ▶

. . . continued

- Different organisations have differing types of culture. Charles Handy classified four different types of organisational cultures; power culture, role culture, task culture and person culture.

Cultural change

- Change in the culture of an organisation naturally makes people feel uneasy. The usual environment and their underlying assumptions about the organisation are about to change.
- There are two different important perspectives about cultural change. A managerial perspective, which views culture as something that can be managed by the organisation and a social science perspective, which sees the culture of an organisation as something that 'just is', which cannot be easily described.

Why we need change

- Organisations are naturally faced with a changing environment to which they must adapt in order to survive. These include; changing market conditions, international competition, government regulations and company growth.
- Force field analysis is a way of assessing the relevance of the particular change drivers (the reasons for change) and restraining forces (factors opposing change) associated with an impending change.

Managing change

- One of a manager's biggest challenges, and frustrations, is to implement change and overcome employee's fears and resistance to change.
- Resistance to change is mainly due to self-interest, uncertainty, misunderstanding and a lack of trust.
- A well-established method for implementing change is given by Kurt Lewin (1951). Lewin's method is based on a three-step process: unfreezing, changing and refreezing.

REFLECTIVE QUESTIONS

1 Imagine that you were born and educated in Russia. Do you think that you would have different cultural characteristics from those you have now? If so, what would they be?
2 Hofstede's original study was criticised for focusing on only one organisation, IBM. What do you think a common characteristic of an IBM employee might be, regardless of their nationality?
3 Can organisations manage culture?

RECOMMENDED READING

If you would like to learn more about some of the issues in the sections within this chapter you might like to consider the following books.

What is culture?
A book that really starts to consider culture at deeper levels, put in the context of three organisations which give a good grounding in what culture actually means, is the classic *Organisational Culture and Leadership* by Edgar Schein (1985).

What do we understand as organisational culture?
Most books by Charles Handy are well worth reading and as usual this one is no exception, *Understanding Organisations* (1993) is a must for anyone who is serious about the study of organisations.

Cultural change
A slightly more difficult book is *Images of Organisations* by Morgan (1986). Here, culture is considered as something that is always changing and too complex to manage.

Why we need change
A more difficult, although rewarding book that covers many of the more advanced issues around organisational change in general is Mary Jo Hatch's *Organisation Theory* (1997). It requires some serious study time but is worth the effort if you really want to study and understand organisational culture in some depth.

Managing change
The classic book to read about managing the change process is Lewin's *Field Theory in Social Science* (1951). However, an easier read, and just as important, is Kotter's *Leading Change* (1996), which emphasises the overall importance of communication in the change process.

USEFUL WEBSITES

www.culturalstudies.net/ A useful site that links to a host of other culture-related websites.
www.cia.gov/library/publications/the-world-factbook/ An excellent and frequently updated site where you can research lots of information about the world's countries.
www.thetimes100.co.uk/theory A good general site for facts about organisational culture.

REFERENCES

Handy, C.B. (1993) *Understanding Organisations*. 4th edn. London: Penguin.
Hatch, M.J. (1997) *Organisation Theory*. New York: Oxford University Press.
Hofstede, G. (1980) *Culture's Consequences: International Differences in Work-Related Values*. 2nd edn. Beverley Hills: Sage Publications.
Hofstede, G. (1993) *Culture's Consequence*. 2nd edn. Thousand Oaks: Sage Publications.

Kotter, J.P. (1996) *Leading Change.* Boston, MA: Harvard Business School Press.

Lewin, K. (1951) *Field Theory in Social Science.* New York: Harper and Row.

Morgan, G. (1986) *Images of Organisations.* London: Sage.

Ogburn, W.F. (1922) *Social Change: With Respect to Culture and Original Nature.* New York: B.W. Huebsch.

Peters, T.J. and Waterman, R.H. (1982) *In Search of Excellence: Lessons from America's Best-Run Companies.* New York: Harper and Row.

Jacques, E. (1952) *The Changing Culture of a Factory.* New York: Dryden Press.

Javidan, M. and House, R.J. (2001) 'Cultural Acumen for the Global Manager: Lessons from the Project GLOBE', *Organisational Dynamics,* vol. 29, no. 4, 289–305.

Pettigrew, A. (1979) 'On Studying Organisational Culture', *Administrative Science Quarterly*, vol. 24, 570–581.

Robbins, S. (1992) *Essentials of Organisational Behaviour.* 10th edn. New Jersey: Prentice Hall.

Schein, E.H. (1985) *Organisational Culture and Leadership.* San Francisco: Jossey-Bass.

Siehl, C. and Martin, J. (1984) 'The Role of Symbolic Management: How Can Managers Effectively Transmit Organisational Culture?' In: J. Hunt, D. Hosking, C. Schriesheim and R. Stewart, *Leaders and Managers: International Perspectives of Managerial Behavior and Leadership.* Elmsford, NY: Pergamon, 227–39.

Smircich, L. (1983) 'Concepts of Culture and Organizational Analysis', *Adminstrative Science Quarterly*, vol. 28, 339–58.

8 The External Micro Environment

'If we don't take care of our customers someone else will.'

(Unknown)

CHAPTER OUTLINE

8.1 Introduction
8.2 What do we mean by the external micro environment?
8.3 Industry and market structures
8.4 Analysing competition
8.5 International and ethical issues
8.6 Summary

CHAPTER OBJECTIVES

After carefully reading and engaging with the tasks and activities outlined in this chapter, you should have a better understanding of:
- the concept of the external micro environment
- industry and market structures and their impact on business
- how to use Porter's Five Forces model to analyse competition
- current and emerging ethical and international issues in the external micro environment.

8.1 Introduction

Like human beings, organisations interact and are affected by the immediate environment that surrounds them. This means that factors such as customers, suppliers and competitors have a direct impact on the organisation's operations and strategy.

CASE STUDY

The US clothes retailer Gap, which started operations more than 30 years ago, became a very successful company in the 1980s selling casual clothes, particularly basics such as jeans, t-shirts, sweatshirts, and jumpers. The business expanded rapidly and entered the UK market in 1987, reaching 134 stores in the British high street by 2007.

However, the organisation's immediate environment changed, and Gap now faces competition not only from other organisations that retail basics at lower prices but also from more up-market 'designer basics', particularly designer jeans. Retailers like Marks & Spencer and Next also made a dent in Gap's market, and even though officially Gap does not compete directly with the fast-moving fashion chains such as Zara, Topshop and H&M, this is a sector that has been growing.

Partly as a result of changes in the micro environment, Gap's sales have suffered and comparable store sales have decreased in 2006, 2007 and 2008 by 7, 4, and 12 per cent respectively (Doran, 2006; Rushe, 2007; Gap Inc. Annual Report 2008).

Like the opening quote and above case study suggest, organisations who fail to monitor and respond to the actors in their immediate environment will find themselves in trouble. In this chapter, we will be looking at key factors in the **external micro environment** and how they impact on organisations.

KEY TERMS

The **external micro environment** refers to external factors that have a direct and immediate impact on an organisation.

(8.2) What do we mean by the external micro environment?

The external micro environment, sometimes referred to as the operating environment, is the **industry** specific environment in which an organisation operates. It includes customers, competitors, suppliers, human and other resources. For example, for a restaurant, this would mean its customers, other restaurants, suppliers of produce and services, and the human resources available to work. Each organisation's micro environment is unique to them. For example, although Nike and Kurt Geiger are both shoe retailers they target and operate in different **market segment**s and thus have different micro environments.

The elements of the micro environment are not static. They are dynamic and interact directly with the organisation on a daily basis. They have an impact on the organisation's operations, and therefore it is necessary for organisations to continuously understand, analyse, and monitor their micro environment. Keeping an eye on what is happening in the external micro environment allows organisations to take advantage of opportunities, plan to reduce threats, and respond quickly to changes.

KEY TERMS

An **industry** is a group of organisations that operate in the same segment of the economy or are in a similar type of business. The three main industry sectors are the primary sector, which includes industries concerned with the extraction of raw materials, like mining and farming; the secondary sector, which includes manufacturing industries such as car manufacturing; and the tertiary sector, which includes service industries like the hospitality industry.
A **market segment** refers to a group of customers who share certain characteristics and have similar needs.

8.3 Industry and market structures

Market conditions are generally established by the **degree of market concentration** of the supply side, i.e. the number of sellers in a market determines its structure. It is said that market concentration is high if a small number of organisations control a large proportion of the market share, and it is low if a large number of organisations control a small proportion of the market share each.

Based on the above, market structures can be positioned along a continuum with perfect competition and monopoly at opposite ends, and oligopoly and monopolistic competition situated in between these two extremes (see Figure 8.1).

A monopoly exists when only one seller has the total share of a particular market. In the UK, many state-owned organisations providing public services were monopolies until the big deregulation and privatisation wave of the

KEY TERMS

The **degree of market concentration** refers to the number of organisations in a market and their respective market shares.

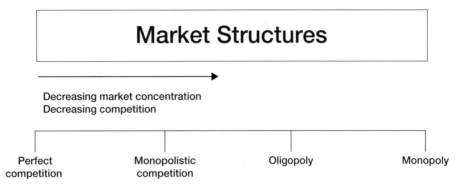

Figure 8.1 Market structures

1980s and 1990s. For example, BT used to have a monopoly as a telephone services provider until 1981 when a phased-up programme of liberalisation began opening up the market to competition. In 1982, Cable & Wireless were granted a license to operate a public telecommunications network (www.BT.com).

An oligopoly exists when a relatively small number of sellers control the majority of supply in a market. The soft drinks industry provides an example of an oligopoly. The main players in this industry – Coca Cola, Pepsi and Cadbury-Schweppes – control the UK and world markets through their brands.

Monopolistic competition exists when organisations have a monopolistic market share in a small segment of the total market. Clothes retailers in the UK high street, such as Next, Gap, and Marks & Spencer, for example, are in monopolistic competition. These organisations sell branded products that are not perfect substitutes for each other, i.e. the Gap brand is only available from that organisation and as such is different or perceived to be different from all other brands.

Perfect competition exists when there is a large number of sellers in a market, each of which only has a small market share. Although it is difficult to find real world cases of perfect competition: a market with all the stalls selling undifferentiated produce, e.g. apples, is often used to illustrate the concept of perfect competition as there are many potential buyers, numerous suppliers selling homogenous products, and low barriers to entry. More recently, eBay auctions can be said to share similar characteristics, and so would constitute another example of perfect competition.

Each market structure has different characteristics in terms of the amount and type of competition, who determines price, and how high or low barriers to entry are for that particular industry (see Table 8.1).

Figure 8.2 A market can be an example of perfect competition

Market structure	Characteristics
Monopoly	Only one seller in the market. Lack of competition. Seller has control over price.
Oligopoly	Small number of sellers control the market. Non-price competition, i.e. branding. Price interdependence.
Monopolistic competition	Numerous sellers and buyers in the market, but sellers have a 'monopoly' of their product, i.e consumers perceive this product to be unique in the market. Few barriers to entry. Non-price competition, i.e. product differentiation, branding.
Perfect competition	Numerous sellers and buyers in the market. Homogenous, non-differentiated goods. Perfect information about the prices charged by other sellers. Low barriers to entry.

Table 8.1   Market stuctures and their characteristics

Example

The soft drinks industry comprises only a few organisations that have a large share of the market. There tends to be price interdependence in this industry as organisations charge roughly the same for their products but compete in other areas, i.e. differentiating their products through branding by for example using pop stars or sports celebrities. The main players in the industry – Coca Cola, Pepsi and Cadbury Schweppes – compete on TV, fast-food restaurants, and supermarkets. This will ultimately have an impact on the organisations' profits.

ACTIVITY

1 Choose two organisations operating in two different types of market structures. Clearly identify what is the market structure for each one of them.
2 Compare the two organisations in terms of the characteristics of their particular market structure, who their competitors are, and how they compete (i.e. branding, pricing).

CASE STUDY

In 2004 Microsoft was fined approximately £331 million by the European Commission for allegedly breaking competition laws and abusing its position as market leader. Microsoft was also asked to share some of its technology with rival companies. Although the company appealed the verdict, Europe's competition authorities upheld their decision in 2007.

It has also been reported that smaller companies have complained about how Internet Explorer being built into the Windows Operating System disadvantages other web browsers. It is estimated that Microsoft controls approximately 80 per cent of the browser market compared to Firefox's 15 per cent.

(Blakely 2007; Blakely 2006; Charter 2007; Verdin 2004)

1 According to the information above, in what type of market structure does Microsoft operate? Justify your answer.

2 Discuss what could be the implications of the ruling for Microsoft.

Industry life cycle

In addition to considering the market structure of the industry where they operate, organisations need to consider the industry or product life cycle (see Figure 8.3). This refers to the key developmental stages in the life of an industry or product, each of which has unique characteristics in terms of market opportunities, growth, and profits. Awareness and analysis of a product's or industry's life cycles allows organisations to make decisions about entering new markets, or expanding into new segments of the same market. If an industry is in the decline stage for example, it may not be worth entering the market unless something innovative is offered to stimulate it.

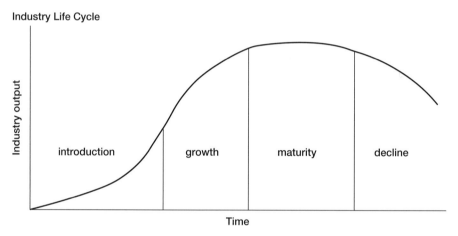

Figure 8.3 Industry/product life cycle
(Source: Adapted from Worthington and Britton, 1997 p. 247).

The first stage in the industry life cycle is the introductory stage when an industry is just starting. At this stage, products are just being launched into the marketplace, as for example iris-based personal identity cards. Sales and profits are at a low point as products are just beginning to be known and generate demand. There are relatively few buyers, and they are just starting to try the product. This is a crucial stage because organisations have probably borrowed capital or, in the case of established organisations, are using the profits generated by other products to subsidise the new product. At this stage promotion is crucial.

In the growth stage, sales rise dramatically as demand increases. Profits are probably still relatively low because of the need to invest heavily in advertising. However, market share is increasing. In this stage we find products such as smart phones (e.g. iPhones, Blackberries).

In the maturity stage, the dramatic increase in demand and sales slows down. This can be a very long or very short phase, depending on the type of industry. Jeans, DVDs, laptop computers, and cars are all examples of products that have reached the maturity stage. However, some of these products have been at this stage for longer than others. Maximum profits are achieved at this stage in many cases due to **economies of scale**. Promotion and advertising are aimed at retaining existing customers or getting customers from competitors. The overall aim is to remain at the peak of the maturity phase for as long as possible.

KEY TERMS

Economies of scale are the cost advantages an organisation can obtain by expanding the scale of its operation.

Finally, in the decline stage demand weakens. Products in the industry might be obsolete and organisations need to decide either to let the industry or product die out or to start a new life cycle, perhaps by investing in research and development. Through innovation, new technology and features, organisations can avoid reaching the decline stage. For example, the use of cheques has declined as they have largely been replaced by electronic debit cards.

It is important to note that there is no specific amount of time to be spent at any one stage and not all industries or products go through all stages. For example, disc cameras never became popular and went directly from the development stage to the decline stage.

Example

In August 2005 Dixons Group, the British-based electrical consumer goods retailer, announced it would no longer sell 35 mm cameras, signaling the end of an era. In 2005, digital cameras accounted for approximately 95 per cent of camera sales in Dixons stores, so, in tune with market trends the company does not need to worry about selling traditional cameras.

(Sources: BBC News, 2005; Ghose and Hanley, 2005).

Figure 8.4 Electronic debit cards have largely replaced cheques

Stage	Introduction	Growth	Maturity	Decline
Sales	Low.	Dramatic increase.	Stabilise.	Decrease. Need for a change of strategy or die out.
Profits	Low.	Relatively low.	High.	Decreasing.
Competition	Low.	Increasing as there are more organisations in the industry.	High.	Decreasing.
Costs	High.	Decreasing due to economies of scales.	Decreasing.	Depends on strategy.

Table 8.2   Stages in product life cycle

REFLECTIVE QUESTIONS

1 Choose an industry and think of examples of how different products in that industry have replaced each other as they move through the different phases of the life cycle. For example, 10 mm photographic cameras were replaced by 35 mm cameras, and these in turn have been replaced by digital cameras.

Markets

The term **market** has a number of meanings. It used to refer primarily to the place where goods were bought and sold. In some cases, it refers to the relationship between the demand and supply of a specific product. For example, when we ask what is the state of the oil market or the housing market, we are referring to the supply of and demand for these goods.

For the purpose of this chapter we will define a market in terms of customers, their need for a product and their ability to purchase or consume. For example, students are part of the market for textbooks and also part of the market for calculators, computers, papers, pens, etc. Individuals and organisations must have the desire and authority to purchase a product or service in order to be considered part of the market. For example, a 14-year-old boy might have the desire to buy beer but it is illegal for him to do so, therefore a brewer will not consider him part of the target market.

KEY TERMS

A **market** is made up of the individuals or organisations that require products or services and have the ability and willingness to purchase those products or services.

There are many different types of markets in an economy. Kotler and Armstrong (2000) classify markets as: consumer, business, reseller, government, and international markets.

Consumer markets

A consumer market consists of individuals who buy products for their own consumption or to be consumed by individuals within their household, not to make a profit. Each of us belongs to numerous consumer markets for products such as food, clothing, vehicles, services, etc. When we go to a supermarket to do our weekly shopping we are part of their consumer market. If we buy a train ticket from Liverpool to London we are part of a train company's consumer market.

Business markets

A business market consists of individuals or organisations that purchase products to be used either to produce other products, to provide a service or for use in their daily operations. These buyers actually make a profit of the goods they are purchasing. A hotel would be part of the business market for suppliers of bed linen or cleaning equipment. The hotel would also be a business market for example for telephone or internet providers.

Reseller markets

Reseller markets consist of wholesalers and retailers who act as intermediaries, buying products and reselling them to make a profit. In contrast to business markets, resellers do not change the physical characteristics of the products they handle (other than making perhaps minor alterations). For example, Boots and John Lewis would be reseller markets for cosmetic and fragrance companies such as Clinique, Benefit, Lancôme, Chanel, etc. Many products sold to consumer markets are sold first to reseller markets.

Figure 8.5 Department stores can be reseller markets for fragrance and cosmetic companies

Government markets

Government markets refer to the purchase of products and services by governments, either to be used in their daily operations or for the provision of public services such as education, water, road systems, healthcare, defence, etc. Because government agencies spend public funds to buy the products and services they require, they are accountable to the public and therefore usually have complex buying procedures. Some organisations, unwilling to deal with so much red tape, do not even attempt to sell to governments. For certain organisations, though, such as British Aerospace, the government may be one of only a few customers.

Example

In 2007, EDF Energy, the French utility company that bought London Energy in 1999, won a £1 billion four-year contract to supply renewable energy to 300 government department and civil service bodies. A spokesman for the organisation said that the contract provides them 'with long-term relationships with many public sector clients, creating the right atmosphere for a collaborative approach to finding solutions to their energy requirements. The public sector is looking [at] . . . buying renewable energy, accelerating their efforts to reducing energy consumption and installing low-carbon electricity generation in government buildings. (Colman, 2007)

International markets

International markets are those markets outside national boundaries and they can be classed as consumer, business, resell, or government markets.

Example

In January 2008, Ben Gordon, chief executive of Mothercare, announced that the organisation was looking to continue its international expansion and increase sales from its international operations. Mothercare already operated in 48 countries outside the UK, including Kazakhstan, New Zealand, Saudi Arabia, and China, and was considering opening 100 stores in India between 2006 and 2011. (Hawks, 2008; Jordan, 2008; Verjee, 2006)

ACTIVITY

Classify the following according to Kotler and Armstrong's (2000) types of customer markets:
- Claire, the manager of a private day nursery, purchased toys for the nursery from the Early Learning Centre.
- John ordered a special edition CD from an American online retailer.
- Starbucks bought Innocent Smoothies to be sold in their cafes.

Because individual needs and wants vary from one person to the next, in most cases it is inappropriate or impractical to aim the goods and services of an organisation to all **customers** and **consumers.** There are only a few markets where a single product or service is satisfactory for all. Therefore, it is necessary to identify groups who share similar buying needs or characteristics. This is called market segmentation. Having identified market segments, organisations must decide which markets to enter if any. For example, clothing sold through Top Shop is aimed at youthful female customers, whereas Hobbs aims at a more mature female customer. This difference in target market is reflected in each organisation's product styling, promotional campaign and price.

KEY TERMS

Customers are people or organisations who buy goods or services.
Consumers are people or organisations who use or consume goods or services.

The basic consumer characteristics used for market segmentation are:

- demographics, including age, gender, race, religion, family size, life stage (e.g. young, single, married, children, etc.), nationality
- socio-economics, including income, occupation, education, social class. To a certain extent, income determines consumer choices in terms of brands, housing, holidays, education, etc.
- geographic location, urban or rural location, type of housing
- personality and lifestyle. Holiday companies often use lifestyle to segment the market, e.g. Mark Warner focuses on families with young children.

The variables chosen to segment a market will depend on the type of product or service in question. For example, age and income can be relevant to a shoe retailer, but not necessarily religion, as the product will not be different or adapted to customers depending on their religious affiliation.

CASE STUDY

According to Robert Barnard, a director of hotel consultants PKF, there is now far more niche development and segmentation in London hotels as hoteliers target hotels at specific types of person. One Aldwych, near Covent Garden, attracts a media and theatre crowd; The Metropolitan is popular with fashion and TV customers; The Berkeley targets food lovers, and the London Hilton Park Lane has a women-only floor with women staff providing room service. Other hotels such as The Goring and Duke's target business travelers and recognise that security and discretion are high on the list of these customers' concerns (Urquhart, 2004).

CASE STUDY

At first glance, the funky advertisements plastered on billboards and admobiles around the Point Depot on the night of the Rolling Stones concert last September did not seem to be targeting the grey euro. A lyric from one of the band's songs was written in Day-Glo colours on the posters.

On closer examination, however, they parodied the lyrics. One, for example, screamed 'Get off my cloud' — but the subheading read '. . .without a stepladder'. The campaign, for Active 55, a cod-liver oil vitamin supplement from Seven Seas, won the grand prix in the 2003 Marketing Media awards organised by *Marketing* magazine.

'We saw it as a nice fit, the fact that the brand is called Active 55 and the Rolling Stones are almost the physical manifestation of the brand,' says Bill Kinlay, the chief executive of MindShare, which developed the campaign along with sister agency DDFH&B. 'The Rolling Stones are all over 55 and they are all active. The beauty of the campaign was that we spent very little but got the impact. A lot of people got the feeling that we sponsored the concert, and we didn't. We just placed posters strategically around the venue on the night.'

Marketing to the over-55s has gone beyond dreary advertising for stair lifts and support hose, with marketers starting to recognise that those in the age group are not parsimonious wrinklies but rather part of the 'SKI generation', those who are indulging in luxury by spending their children's inheritance money. 'There are a lot of 55-year-olds who have more in common with 35-year-olds,' says Kinlay. 'They have a hell of a lot of disposable income. In the traditional marketing sense they are not a massively sexy audience, but they are an extremely lucrative audience.'

John Lowe, the director of S&L Promotions, the publisher of the *Senior Times* and organiser of Dublin's annual 'Over 50s' show, agrees. 'By and large, this is a healthy, active group of people with no financial worries,' he says. 'They have paid off the mortgage, the kids have fled the nest and they have plenty of time on their hands. About 80 per cent of people from their late fifties into their mid-eighties in Ireland lead extremely active lives. A lot of marketers could do worse than address the grey euro.'

Not only is the mature market a wealthy segment of the population, but it is also growing. Amarach Consulting forecasts that the number of those between the ages of 45 and 65 in Ireland will grow by almost 25 per cent between 2001 and 2011. Likewise, the number of people over the age of 65 will grow by about 18 per cent in the same period and will at least double by 2031. Certain sectors have traditionally marketed to this age group. Hotels and holiday companies in particular recognise that older people can take up the slack in off-peak periods. 'It is an industry that is marketing very rigorously to older people, with "golden years" breaks and so on,' says Lowe.

Other sectors that traditionally have a strong showing at the 'Over 50s' show include financial companies, particularly those offering equity-release products, and healthcare firms.

'We had a consultant talking about Viagra for Pfizer and the place was packed out with people in their sixties and seventies,' says Lowe. 'It was very revealing and quite refreshing that people were talking frankly about sex issues.'

continued . . . ▶

◄ | *. . . continued*

Other sectors have, however, largely failed to consider this well-heeled market segment. Lowe cites IT and mobile phone companies in particular as slow to market to older people. 'It is a bit disappointing,' he says. 'All the interest is in the younger market. As we now know, the mobile phone market is reaching saturation point and I would have thought they would have addressed the older market, a potentially lucrative area waiting to be tapped.'

However, companies need to consider their strategies carefully. Campaigns that appeal to younger audiences might not cut the mustard with older consumers. 'Older people have the sense that most mainstream marketing and advertising is created by people who are much younger and who have little insight into what people who are over 50 want and do,' says Michael Cutbill, a marketing director of the UK firm Saga.

The company started off in 1951 by offering low-cost trips for older people to Folkestone, a seaside town in Kent. It is now a sprawling company dedicated to the over-50s market, selling everything from cruises on Saga ships to financial products and cars. Its magazine has a circulation of 1.2m and it also operates a number of regional and digital radio stations, one of which, PrimeTime radio, is available on NTL in Ireland.

Saga's marketing has been fine-tuned over the years. 'The first keynote for us is not to try to overhype things,' says Cutbill. 'If we give the customer a lot of information about our products and services in as dispassionate and objective a way as possible, that generally goes down very well.'

Personalisation and a strong customer service offering are also important factors in Saga's marketing strategy. 'If you stick to those general principles, then they will find favour with the audience rather than doing something flasher and brasher,' says Cutbill.

Millennium, a UK-based market research firm that targets the older market, came to much the same conclusion in its recent Mature Thinking report. Older people, it says, 'seek benefits, not brands; logic, not logos; information, not image'.

Millennium also emphasises that the senior market is not a homogenous group and divides it accordingly. The 'thrivers', for example, are those aged between 50 and 59 who are in the highest-earning period of their careers and have a penchant for sports cars. Following this group are the 'seniors', the 'elders' and the 'super elders' — each of which has different interests and spending habits.

Even within these sectors, segmentation is critical. As with any age group, people older than 55 have myriad interests and pursuits. Anglo Irish Bank, for example, targets different interest groups. 'We have a number of affinities on the deposit side with the likes of the UK Bowls Association and the Bridge Association of Ireland,' says Mary Nolan, the bank's group marketing manager.

Cutbill says Saga tries to acknowledge the diversity in the older groups in its marketing. 'We try to get as much information from the customers as they are happy to give us and then play those interests back to them,' he says. 'For example, we sell garden insurance and garden holidays, so we would tend to market those only to people who have expressed an interest in gardening.'

Older consumers are often happy to provide information on their interests, once they are satisfied that their privacy will be guaranteed. Anglo Irish Bank has found competitions a particularly successful marketing tool with this age group.

continued . . . ►

◄ *. . . continued*

'If they have retired early, they have more time to respond to direct marketing, phone lines or competitions,' says Nolan. 'They don't mind mailshots and they have time to fill out questionnaires.'

© *The Times* 2004/nisyndication.com
(Source: Foley, 2004)

1 What market segment do the organisations in the above example target?
2 What are the characteristics of this market segment?
3 How might organisations adapt their products or services to satisfy the needs of this market segment?

8.4 Analysing competition

Michael Porter's Five Forces model provides a framework to assess **competition** in an industry or sector by looking at five forces, which he identified as: supplier power, barriers to entry, threat of substitutes, buyer power, and degree of rivalry.

Porter's original research was designed to explain why some industries are more profitable than others, and why some organisations are more profitable than others within the same industry (Hitt, Black and Porter 2005).

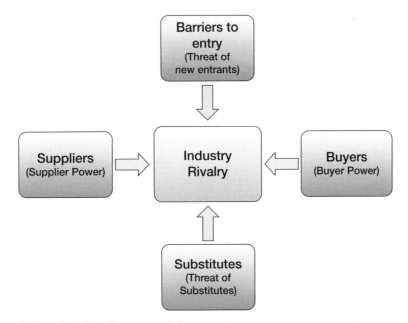

Figure 8.6 Porter's Five Forces model

KEY TERMS

Competition refers to other organisations that fight for or try to win an organisation's potential or actual customers.

We will now look at each one of the five forces in Porter's model.

Supplier power and buyer power

Supplier power and buyer power are in direct opposition to each other. The higher supplier power is the lower buyer power is and vice versa. Supplier power refers to how strong the position of suppliers is, and buyer power refers to the power buyers can exert on the organisation.

The number of suppliers and buyers in the market, how much access buyers have to information, the volume purchased by the buyer, availability of substitute products or services, and brand identity will all influence the degree of power buyers and suppliers have. For example, if there is one or very few suppliers for a product or service, or if there are a few or no substitutes available then suppliers will have a high bargaining power compared to buyers.

Barriers to entry

The extent to which industries are easy or difficult to enter for potential competitors varies depending on the **barriers to entry** that exist in a particular industry. Capital requirements, high set-up costs, economies of scale, expected retaliation, high switching costs, and brand loyalty to the existing players in the market are all barriers to entry. The harder these barriers are to overcome, the harder it is for potential competitors to enter the market.

For example, there are very low barriers to entry for anyone who wants to become a seller on eBay. Anyone can sell a product in the internet auction site provided they have some knowledge of computers and the internet. On the other hand, due to the extremely high capital requirements and set-up costs it is much more difficult for an organisation to go into oil exploration, for example.

KEY TERMS

Barriers to entry are the obstacles that make it difficult for potential entrants to get into a market.

Threat of substitutes

A substitute product can perform the same function or provide the same service as the product or service it substitutes. A substitute product or service provides an alternative way of satisfying customers' needs rather than being just the same product or service under a different brand. For example, Pepsi is not a substitute for Coca Cola as they are both carbonated soft drinks. However, other products that serve the function of satisfying thirst, such as fruit juices, smoothies, sports drinks, and bottled water are substitutes for carbonated drinks.

How easily a product or service can be substituted depends on factors such as switching costs, customer loyalty, and the availability of alternative products or services.

Degree of rivalry

This is the degree of competition amongst the existing players in an industry. The higher the degree of rivalry, the more difficult it will be for an organisation to compete in an industry.

The market structure (see Section 8.3) influences the degree of rivalry in an industry. Generally speaking, the more organisations competing in an industry the higher the intensity of their rivalry as they compete for the same number of customers.

If market growth is slow, stagnates or the market becomes saturated, the degree of rivalry will increase as organisations fight to maintain their market share in a shrinking market. Similarly, organisations operating in industries with high fixed costs face intense rivalry within the industry as they must attain high levels of production and sales in order to reduce unit costs. The less differentiated a product is the higher the levels of rivalry.

8.5 International and ethical Issues

International issues

Globalisation has eliminated many borders for organisations not only in terms of markets, but also of suppliers, manufacturing and human resources, thus totally shaking the micro environment of many industries.

KEY TERMS

The Organisation for Economic Cooperation and Development defines **globalisation** as 'the process through which markets and production become increasingly interdependent as a consequence of the dynamic of exchanging goods and services, and through the movement of capital and technology.'

CASE STUDY

The English football industry has seen a growth in overseas audiences and fans, with many of the players from countries other than the UK, and the clubs often owned by international investors.

Increasingly, the human resources (players and management) in English football are also sourced globally. In January 2001, Sven-Goran Eriksson became the first overseas manager of the English national team and Fabio Capello became the second in December 2007. The number of overseas players in Premier League reached 250 in August 2007, compared to 11 at the league's inception.

The English Premier League has revealed plans to stage an international round of competitive matches in overseas host cities starting in 2010. The matches will be screened live to the UK. This move is not unique to football, with the NFL already planning its second competitive game in Wembley.

The Premier League chief, Richard Scudamore has said that 'We are in a privileged position [as the world's most popular football league] but also a vulnerable position. There is a globalisation of sport we can't deny. And we are faced with a strategic decision. Do we seize the moment and seek to move forward, or do we batten down the hatches, stay domestic, sit there and watch other people do it, other leagues, other sports, other forms of entertainment?'

(Sources: Kelso, 2008; Nakrani, 2008; Oliver, 2008)

 What do you think are the implications of the globalisation of football for English football, in terms of markets, suppliers, competition, and availability of human resources?

Ethical issues

There is increasing concern regarding the power big buyers, such as the main supermarkets and other retailers have over their suppliers.

Food companies have been feeling the pressure as supermarket chains request they produce goods for promotional activities, demand upfront payments and 'contributions' to promotional costs, and require that certain types of carrier bags or packaging are used.

CASE STUDY

Pat O'Driscoll, the chief executive of Northern Foods, one of the UK's largest food producers with brands such as Fox's biscuits and Goodfella's pizzas, has announced a radical restructuring to try to stem losses at the group. About 75 per cent of Northern Foods' sales are accounted for by five customers – Tesco, J Sainsbury, Asda, Wm Morrison and Marks & Spencer. Their chilled-pastry business and cakes and speciality bread division made only £2 of operating profit for every £100 of sales, despite providing one of the most highly successful ranges to Marks & Spencer.

Even global organisations such as Procter & Gamble and Unilever, who used to be able to dictate conditions to the supermarkets, have seen a shift in the balance of power as the 'super' supermarkets influence and power increases.

(Sources: Fletcher, 2008; Rushe and Fletcher, 2005)

1 Analyse the reasons behind the increasing power of supermarkets when compared to their suppliers.
2 Discuss the implications of the increasing power of supermarkets over their suppliers.

1 Provide examples of the four different market structures: monopoly, oligopoly, monopolistic competition and perfect competition.
2 Explain which variables Tesco might use to segment the markets for its different products/stores, i.e. Tesco Value, Tesco Organics, Tesco Finest, Tesco Direct, Tesco Express stores, etc. Provide examples.
3 Use Porter's Five Forces model to analyse competition in an industry of your choice.
4 What are the implications of the internet (i.e. online sales) for Porter's model?

 ## 8.6 Summary

This chapter has looked at the external micro environment in which organisations operate. Factors such as customers, suppliers, competition and industry and market structures have been explained and their impact on organisations has been considered. As the elements of the micro environment are dynamic and continuously interact with the organisation, it is necessary for organisations to understand, analyse, and monitor their micro environment so that they can take advantage of opportunities, plan to reduce threats, and respond quickly to any relevant changes.

KEY IDEAS

Some of the main points covered in this chapter are listed below. If you feel unsure about any of them revisit the appropriate section. If you would like some additional reading on the topic try out the books listed below in recommended reading.

What do we mean by the external micro environment?
- The external micro environment is the industry-specific environment in which an organisation operates. It includes customers, competitors, suppliers, human and other resources.

Industry and market structures
- The degree of market concentration can be used to classify markets into monopolies, oligopolies, monopolistic competition or perfect competition markets.
- Industries and products are said to go through a life cycle that includes four different stages: development, growth, maturity and decline.
- Each stage in the life cycle has different characteristics and it is important for organisations to take into consideration the industry or product life cycle in order to make decisions about entering new markets, or expanding into new segments of the same market.
- There are many different types of markets in an economy. Kotler and Armstrong (2000) classify markets as: consumer, business, reseller, government, and international markets.
- Because customers' needs and wants vary, in most cases organisations need to aim their goods and services to specific segments of the market that share similar buying needs or characteristics.
- The basic consumer characteristics used for market segmentation are demographics, socio-economics, geographic location and lifestyle.

Analysing competition
- Michael Porter designed a model that provides a framework to assess competition in an industry or sector by looking at five forces which he identified: supplier power, barriers to entry, threat of substitutes, buyer power, and degree of rivalry.

International and ethical issues
- **Globalisation** has eliminated many borders for organisations not only in terms of markets, but also of suppliers, manufacturing and human resources, thus totally shaking the micro environment of many industries.
- There is increasing concern regarding the power big buyers have over their suppliers.

RECOMMENDED READING

If you would like to learn more about some of the issues in the sections within this chapter you might like to consider the following books.

Kotler, P. and Armstrong, G. (2000) *Principles of Marketing*. 9th edn. New Jersey: Prentice Hall.

Porter, M. (2004) *Competitive Strategy: Techniques for Analysing Industries and Competitors*. 1st export edn. New York: Free Press.

USEFUL WEBSITES

BBC – **www.bbc.co.uk**
The Guardian – **www.guardian.co.uk**
The Michael E. Porter homepage – **www.isc.hbs.edu**
Mintel – **www.mintel.com**
Tesco – **www.tesco.com**
The Times – **www.thetimesonline.co.uk**

REFERENCES

BBC News (2005) 'Dixons to End 35mm Camera Sales'. *BBC News*, (online) 8 August. Available at: http://news.bbc.co.uk/1/hi/business/4130620.stm (Accessed 1 December 2009).

Blakely, R. (2006) 'EU Ruling "Handicapped Microsoft in Perpetuity"'. *Time Online*, (online) 26 April. Available at: http://www.timesonline.co.uk/tol/news/world/europe/article709756.ece (Accessed 1 December 2009).

Blakely, R. (2007) 'Microsoft Faces New Competition Case'. *Times Online*, (online) 13 December. Available at: http://business.timesonline.co.uk/tol/business/industry_sectors/technology/article3048095.ece (Accessed 1 July 2008).

Capon, C. (2004) *Understanding Organisational Context.* 2nd edn. London: Prentice Hall.

Charter, D. (2007) 'Microsoft Loses Appeal Against £342 m EU Fine over Software Sharing'. *Times Online*, (online) 18 September. Available at: http://business.timesonline.co.uk/tol/business/industry_sectors/technology/article2472555.ece (Accessed 1 December 2009).

Colman, E. (2007) 'EDF Secures £1bn Government Green Energy Supply Deal'. *Times Online*, (online) 18 June. Available at: http://business.timesonline.co.uk/tol/business/industry_sectors/utilities/article1945805.ece (Accessed 1 July 2008).

Doran, J. (2006) 'Clothing Chain Plans to Plug Sales Gap'. *Times Online*, (online) 7 June. Available at: http://business.timesonline.co.uk/tol/business/industry_sectors/retailing/article672475.ece (Accessed 1 December 2009).

Fletcher R. (2008) 'Big Chains Surge As Suppliers Scrape By'. *Times Online*, (online) 4 June. Available at: http://business.timesonline.co.uk/tol/business/industry_sectors/consumer_goods/article671306.ece?token=null&offset=0 (Accessed 1 July 2008).

Foley, K. (2004) 'Marketing: Oldies Still Crave Satisfaction'. *Times Online*, (online) 16 May. Available at: http://business.timesonline.co.uk/tol/business/article424673.ece (Accessed 1 July 2008).

Gap Inc. (2008) *Annual Report 2008* (online). Available at: http://www.gapinc.com/public/documents/GPS_AR_08.pdf (Accessed 1 December 2009).

Ghose, P. and Hanley, B. (2005) 'Tune into the Big Consumer Picture'. *Times Online*, (online) 14 August. Available at: http://business.timesonline.co.uk/tol/business/industry_sectors/retailing/article554933.ece (Accessed 1 July 2008).

Hawkes, S. (2008) 'Mothercare Steps Up its Agenda for International Expansion'. *Times Online*, (online) 17 January. Available at: http://business.timesonline.co.uk/tol/business/industry_sectors/retailing/article3200732.ece (Accessed 1 July 2008).

Hitt, MA., Black, J.S. and Porter, L.W. (2005) *Management.* Upper Saddle River, NJ: Prentice Hall.

Jordan, D. (2008) 'Mothercare Bucks Gloom with 20.7 per cent Sales Rise'. *Times Online*, (online) 17 July. Available at: http://business.timesonline.co.uk/tol/business/industry_sectors/retailing/article4348773.ece (Accessed 1 December 2009).

Kelso, P. (2008) 'Premier League Prepares to Go Global'. *The Guardian*, (online) 8 February. Available at: www.guardian.co.uk/uk/2008/feb/08/football.newsstory (Accessed 1 July 2008).

Kotler, P. and Armstrong, G. (2000) *Principles of Marketing*. 9th edn. New Jersey: Prentice Hall.

Nakrani, S. (2008) 'Premier League vs. England Time-line'. *The Guardian*, (online) 11 June. Available at: http://www.guardian.co.uk/football/2008/jun/10/premierleague.englandfootballteam1 (Accessed 1 July 2008).

Naylor, J. (2004) *Management*. 2nd edn. London: Prentice Hall.

Oliver B. (2008) 'English Football Goes Global – and There is No Going Back'. *The Guardian*, (online) 9 February. Available at: http://www.guardian.co.uk/football/2008/feb/09/premierleague1 (Accessed 1 July 2008).

Rushe, D. (2007) 'Gap in Fashion Sales is Gaping'. *Times Online*, (online) 14 January. Available at: http://business.timesonline.co.uk/tol/business/article1292639.ece (Accessed 1 July 2008).

Rushe, D. and Fletcher, R. (2005) 'Gillette: The Best this Man Can Get'. *Times Online*, (online) 30 January. Available at: http://business.timesonline.co.uk/tol/business/industry_sectors/consumer_goods/article508113.ece (Accessed 1 December 2009).

The Times (2009) 'Donald Fisher: Co-founder of the Gap Clothing Chain'. *Times Online*, (online) 29 September. Available at: http://www.timesonline.co.uk/tol/comment/obituaries/article6852733.ece (Accessed 1 December 2009).

Urquhart, C. (2004) 'London Rooms Meet Needs of Niche Market'. *Times Online*, (online) 29 January. Available at: http://travel.timesonline.co.uk/tol/life_and_style/travel/business/article1004843.ece (Accessed 1 July 2008).

Verdin, M. (2004) 'Microsoft Fined Record £331m'. *Times Online*, (online) 24 March. Available at: http://business.timesonline.co.uk/tol/business/entrepreneur/article1051061.ece (Accessed 1 December 2009).

Verjee, N. (2006) 'Mothercare Steps Up India Expansion Plan'. *Times Online*, (online) 31 June. Available at: http://business.timesonline.co.uk/tol/business/industry_sectors/retailing/article620127.ece (Accessed 1 December 2009).

Worthington, I. and Britton, C. (1997) *The Business Environment*. Maidenhead, Berkshire: McGraw-Hill Education.

The Macro Environment – Political Influences

'We've learned that you have to stay the course. In Brazil we've survived seven economic reform plans, five presidents, two constitutions and 14 finance ministers.'

(Jim Cantalupo, CEO of McDonald's International, 1998)

CHAPTER OUTLINE

9.1 Introduction
9.2 What do we mean by the political environment?
9.3 Key political influences
9.4 Current and emerging ethical and international issues in the political environment
9.5 Analysing the effect of current and future political influences on organisations
9.6 Summary

CHAPTER OBJECTIVES

After carefully reading and engaging with the tasks and activities outlined in this chapter, you should have a better understanding of:
- the concept of the political environment
- key factors and trends in the political environment
- how the political environment affects organisations
- current and emerging ethical and international issues in the political environment.

9.1 Introduction

The political structures of a country have a significant effect on the success of any business. Factors like political stability, the political system of a country, government actions, and the cost of paying bribes have an impact on the level of risk an organisation faces and its ability to operate. Organisations manage this risk in different ways, but ultimately they need to decide whether the risks outweigh the opportunities, or vice versa.

For example, the opening quote indicates that McDonald's decided to take a long-term view of the political risk, and went on to become the unchallenged market leader in Brazil, partly due to the fact that they decided to remain in the country while there was political turmoil and dire economic prospects.

In another example, Shell managed political risk in Russia by signing up an agreement with a local company. Seven months after being forced by the Russian government to stop development work in the country, Shell signed an alliance to cooperate on oil and gas projects with Rosneft, one of Russia's leading energy companies. Malcolm Brinded, Shell's head of exploration and production, expressed his understanding of Russia's policy of seizing back control of its natural assets when he said: 'It's natural for governments to strike the appropriate balance between what is in the national interest and what needs to be done to stimulate international companies to bring in their development capabilities.' Industry analysts have said that the Shell-Rosneft alliance could lead to Shell playing a key role in the development of lucrative oil and gasfields in eastern Siberia (Hawkes, 2007).

9.2 What do we mean by the political environment?

The basic unit into which the world's people are divided is the nation-state. A state's institutions have the authority to rule the people within the specific territory it occupies and controls. The political environment is concerned with the processes by which power is exercised and the institutions by which laws are made and implemented within a state.

In every viable state there is a source of **legitimate authority**. In most modern states the source of legitimate authority is based on a **constitution,** which defines the fundamental political principles and rules on which a society is grounded.

The political environment includes the government and its institutions, the political philosophy and system of a state, and the political agreements to which a state has subscribed. Because governments are responsible for legislation and most economic decisions, there is overlap between the political, legal and economic environments. However, for the purposes of this book we have tried to maintain the distinction between these three elements of the macro environment.

KEY TERMS

An individual, institution or organisation is said to have **legitimate authority** when the power it exercises derives from some system of norms that is recognised by the law.

A **constitution** establishes the rules and principles from which government derives its powers.

9.3 Key political influences

There are many political elements in the external macro environment, so this chapter will focus on analysing the following key areas of political decision-making that impact on business:

● local government
● political ideology and political systems
● regional integration agreements.

We consider these in turn.

Local government

Local government is responsible for the provision of a wide range of services to individuals and organisations such as care for the elderly, leisure services, local planning, education, social services, and transport. Local government is also responsible for collecting business rates and making sure private businesses conform to trading and environmental standards. The local offices of national government like the Department of Social Security's Benefits, Inland Revenue, and the Department of Employment and Education also provide many services locally. As such local government has a considerable influence on organisations operating within its boundaries (Capon, 2006).

Figure 9.1 Local government services

ACTIVITY

Analyse the impact of the local government on the following organisations:

a) a hairdresser
b) a state school
c) a corner shop
d) a hotel.

CASE STUDY

Tesco and the people of Sheringham in Norfolk have been involved in a planning permission dispute for over a decade. To date there is no presence of any of the big four supermarkets in Sheringham.

Opinion in the town is divided, with people actively campaigning for and against the opening of a Tesco. Opponents argue, among other things, that the opening of the Tesco store would have a negative effect on local shops, with an estimated 10 per cent closing down within a year of the opening of the Tesco store. Another argument is that the road where the proposed store would be located would not be able to cope with the increase in traffic.

continued . . . ▶

◄ | *. . . continued*

On the other hand, a study by the council's retail consultant concluded that the negative impact on the town's local businesses could be offset by people who used to travel to do their shopping staying in Sheringham.

(Sources: Barkham, 2007; Engel, 2009; Stamp, 2007)

Political ideology and political system

A country's political ideology refers to the existing political philosophy regarding issues such as ownership of the means of production, the role of market forces, and government intervention.

The two main political ideologies, which sit at opposite ends of a spectrum, are **collectivism** and **individualism**.

In collectivist ideology, the good of the collective prevails over the good of the individual. In order to pursuit this goal, the state must control property and the distribution of wealth so that they can benefit society as a whole rather than individuals. This means that the state often owns the means of production. Politically there are two main positions within collectivism: those who believe collectivist ideology can only be achieved through revolution, communists, and those who believe collectivist ideology can be achieved through regulation by elected governments, the social democrats.

After the Second World War, and with the occupation of many countries by the Soviet Union, communism expanded throughout the world to include most of Eastern Europe, China and Cuba.

Individualism, on the other hand, promotes individual freedom to pursue individual goals without interference from the state. The role of the state is seen as protecting individual freedom and self-expression so they can achieve their goals.

KEY TERMS

Collectivism is a political ideology that sees the group or collective as the primary unit of political, social, and economic concern, therefore collective interests should supersede individual interests.

Individualism is a political ideology that advocates for allowing individuals, as far as possible, to make their own decisions without interference from the state.

A country's political system is concerned with the exercise of power (Morris and Willey, 1996). It includes the institutions and members of a state who are in power and make decisions. Depending on the concentration of power, political systems can be classified as democratic or totalitarian.

Democracy is a system of government by which political sovereignty is retained by the people. There are two basic types of democracy: direct and representative democracy.

In a direct democracy, all individuals vote on all issues and participate in making public decisions without the intermediation of public officials. However, the size and complexity of most modern states do not allow for all individuals in a society to vote directly on every issue. Therefore, most modern democratic nations have what is known as a representative democracy, in which people elect representatives to make decisions and legislate. Even though representatives are elected to act in the interest of the people who elect them, they retain the freedom to exercise their own judgment in making decisions.

Figure 9.2 Democracy

In a **totalitarian** system, political power is taken over and controlled by an individual or group of individuals representing a single political party. Totalitarian regimes do not allow opposition and attempt to control the private and public lives of society.

According to Hill (2007) there are four main forms of totalitarianism: communist, where control is in the hands of the communist party; theocratic, where political power resides with the religious leader(s); tribal, where the leaders of a tribe or ethnic group rule; and right wing totalitarianism where the military have political control. Since the collapse of the Soviet Union in the early 1990s, most communist and military totalitarian regimes have disappeared, however, theocratic and tribal totalitarianism continue to be present in some countries in Asia and Africa.

Even though there is usually a direct relationship between a country's political system and its political philosophy – with totalitarianism and democracy usually associated to collectivism and individualism respectively – this is not always the case. There are examples of democracies that support a collectivist philosophy or totalitarian regimes that encourage individualism. For example, China, even though still under a totalitarian regime, introduced market-based economic reforms that allow individuals to participate in private businesses.

KEY TERMS

Democracy is rule by the people.
Totalitarianism is rule by a single leader or a small group of individuals.

CASE STUDY

The United States foreign policy towards North Korea and Iran has been to use sanctions to cut off both countries from the international community should they persist with their nuclear programmes. However, perhaps due to China's role in the global economy, the United States approach towards China appears to be much more flexible despite the country's bad track record on political freedoms and restrictions on access to certain information.

The case of China seems to support the argument that the isolation of totalitarian states strengthens the power of dictatorships as people have limited access to information and are restricted from public discussions; whereas more openness can encourage political change. It appears that market policies, economic prosperity, and increasing access to the internet have combined to increase the expectation of political reform in China. The number of public demonstrations seems to have increased hand-in-hand with economic growth.

1 What type of political system is in place in China, Iran, and North Korea? Discuss what the implications are for business of having such a political system.

2 After reading the above case study, consider how a country's foreign policy and the use of sanctions could impact on the political system of another country.

ACTIVITY

Complete the following table:

Country	Political system
United Kingdom	
Venezuela	
Norway	
China	

Conduct research and provide examples of:

a) Communist totalitarianism
b) Right-wing totalitarianism
c) Theocratic totalitarianism
d) Tribal totalitarianism.

The exercise of power in the UK political system is through:

- Parliament
- central government and its departments
- local government
- the judiciary and criminal courts.

Parliament has the key role of passing legislation. It consists of the House of Commons, the House of Lords, and the Queen. At a general election the candidate who wins that most votes in each constituency becomes the Member of Parliament (MP) and the Queen invites the leader of the party with the most MPs in the House of Commons to become her Prime Minister.

The Prime Minister selects central government: this consists of the members of the Cabinet and Cabinet Ministers who have overall responsibility for the work of their government department. This element is called the executive and is responsible for putting laws and policies into effect.

The government departments and agencies are the administrative part of the state and include amongst others, the Home Office, the Department of Health, the Department for Transport, the Ministry of Defence, the Department for Children, Schools and Families, and the Foreign and Commonwealth Office.

They implement government policy, advise ministers, and provide goods and services that, arguably, could not be provided reliably or adequately by the private sector. These goods fall into two main groups:

● Public goods – which are provided for the population in general, i.e. defence, police, transport infrastructure
● Merit goods – which are to be used as and when the population has a need for them, i.e. health service, social security, education.

The Judiciary is the Judges and the Courts. They are formally separate from and independent from Parliament and Government. The head of the Judiciary is a member of the Government and the House of Lords. The role of the judiciary is to put into effect the laws enacted by Parliament and keep Government within its limits of its power. As a result of the UK's membership of the European Union, since 1973 the judiciary has been largely in charge of interpreting EU law.

Regional Integration Agreements

KEY TERMS

A **regional integration agreement** is when countries in a geographic region come together and agree to reduce or remove barriers to trade and to the free movement of the factors of production among the countries that have signed the agreement.

The following table shows different levels of regional integration.

Free Trade Area:	There are no barriers to trade among member countries. Each member state has individual trade policies with non-member states.
Customs Union:	There are no barriers to trade among member countries. A common external trade policy is agreed between member and non-member countries.
Common Market:	There are no barriers to trade among member countries. A common external trade policy is agreed between member and non-member countries. There are no restrictions to the movement of the factors of production between the member countries.

▶

Economic Union:	There are no barriers to trade among member countries. A common external trade policy is agreed between member and non-member countries. There are no restrictions to the movement of the factors of production between the member countries. Member countries share a common currency, tax rates, and monetary and fiscal policies.
Political Union:	This is the last step in integration where essentially different countries give up sovereignty and unite to form a single nation.
Source: Hill, C. (2007) *International Business: Competing in the Global Marketplace.* 6th international edn. London: McGraw-Hill.	

Table 9.1   Levels of Integration

1 At what level of integration is the European Union? Indicate what suggests this.

2 Discuss how further integration could impact on the different member countries of the European Union.

It is generally believed that if countries are economically and politically interdependent they are less likely to embark on war with each other and they also have more power to negotiate and deal with third countries. Following the Second World War, and with the Cold War going on, bringing European countries together not only reduced the potential for war between them but also gave them more independence from the two new emerging powers, the United States and the Soviet Union.

However, despite the benefits offered by integration there will always be groups within countries that will not gain and certain industries within countries might experience losses. There can also be concern about the implications integration has on a country's sovereignty. Giving too much control to the European Union is probably one of the reasons behind some countries deciding not to join the Euro as their currency (including the UK).

CASE STUDY

In 2006, Peugeot announced it would be closing its factory in Ryton in the West Midlands. The French manufacturer has set up operations in Slovakia where it benefits from government grants and lower labour costs which can be up to 85 per cent lower than in Western Europe.

Some people now refer to Eastern Europe as the New Detroit after many car manufacturers, not only from Europe but also from Korea, have relocated some of their operations to the region. Volkswagen has a factory in Slovakia, Toyota and Peugeot have a joint operation in the Czech Republic

continued . . . ▶

◀ . . . *continued*

and Hyundai has also opened a factory in that country. Ford has plans to manufacture the Ford Ka in Poland, both BMW and Audi assemble some of their cars in Hungary, and many Fiats are now manufactured in Poland and Turkey.

(Sources: Hutton, 2006; Smith, 2006)

1 Outline the opportunities and threats that regional integration brings to European car manufacturers.

Around the world, there are various examples of nations coming together under regional agreements to lift barriers to trade and achieve more openness. The main regional agreements include the following.

The Andean Community

Known as the Andean Pact until 1996. This agreement was originally signed in 1969 and has been renegotiated several times. The Andean Pact is a **customs union** that includes Colombia, Peru, Bolivia and until recently Venezuela (the country withdrew from the agreement in 2006). The Andean Community and Mercosur have now granted associate membership to each other.

Mercosur

MERCOSUR is a regional agreement originally signed in 1988 by Brazil and Argentina. In 1991 Paraguay and Uruguay joined the agreement.

The North American Free Trade Area (NAFTA)

This agreement includes Canada, the United States and Mexico. These countries came together in 1991 to form a free trade area.

The Association of Southeast Asian Nations (ASEAN)

ASEAN was originally signed by Indonesia, Malaysia, the Philippines, Singapore, and Thailand in 1967. Since then membership has expanded to include five more countries Brunei Darussalam, Vietnam, Lao PDR, Myanmar, and Cambodia which was the latest to join in 1999.

The European Union

The European Union now includes 25 countries, making it a market of more than 400 million people – the largest trading bloc in the world.

After the Second World War, Europe's position as the most powerful continent in the world had been suppressed by the emergence of the United States and the Soviet Union as world powers. After the war, France became the driving force behind the idea of strengthening links between Western European countries, and particularly between France and Germany, to reduce the potential of further wars in the region.

The Benelux customs union (Belgium, the Netherlands and Luxemburg) was formed in 1947, the Organisation for European Economic Co-operation (OEEC) was founded in 1948, the North Atlantic treaty Organisation (NATO) in 1949 and the European Coal and Steel Community in 1951. Its signatories France, West Germany, Italy and Benelux agreed to a supranational authority whose decisions would be binding on all members. This agreement laid the basis for today's European Union.

The European Union is an **economic union.** However, increasing harmonisation of fiscal and monetary policy, the adoption of a common currency, although not by all member countries, and the establishment of the European Parliament could be seen as indicators of further integration.

As a result of the UK's membership of the European Union, the distinction between the national and international political environment is becoming blurred. For example, on 15 March 2001, the Council of the European Union adopted a regulation 'listing the third countries whose nationals must be in possession of visas when crossing the external borders of member states and those whose nationals are exempt from that requirement', which had to be implemented by all member states including the ten new member states who adopted the regulation when they joined the EU on 1 May 2004 (Dutch Ministry of Foreign Affairs, 2008).

9.4 Current and emerging ethical and international issues in the political environment

Ethical issues

Organisations operating internationally face a series of ethical concerns relating to the political environment of their host countries. There is an ongoing debate over whether investing in countries where the government limits economic and political freedom perpetuates the situation or encourages change.

There is also debate about how far an organisation should go to protect its interests in countries where there is political turmoil or conflict.

CASE STUDY

Chiquita Brands, the American food multinational company and a leading banana producer in Latin America, has been accused of making illegal payments in Colombia to the left-wing National Liberation Army, (ELN) and the Revolutionary Armed Forces of Colombia (FARC). It has also been reported that the families of victims of Colombia's largest paramilitary group are suing Chiquita.

The company has admitted in court to paying rebel groups for protection after threats to the lives of its employees. However, Jeffrey Taylor, the US attorney said that 'funding a terrorist organisation can never be treated as a cost of doing business.'

Figure 9.3 Banana plantation
(Sources: BBC News, 2009; Mortished, 2007; Reid, 2007)

 Consider the ethical dilemmas that an organisation such as Chiquita Brands faces.

International issues

The political environment of a country has an impact on domestic and international organisations operating in that country. International organisations normally weigh benefits and risks before deciding to locate operations in or trade with a certain country. Although there is **political risk** in every country, the range of risk varies widely from country to country, and organisations generally aim to be in countries where there is a stable political environment.

KEY TERMS

Political risk is the likelihood that political forces will cause drastic changes in a country's business environment. These changes will generally hinder organisations from achieving their goals (Robock, 1971).

There are two main types of political risk that affect organisations: ownership risk, which poses a risk on property and life, and operating risk, which impacts on the daily operations of organisations.

Coups d'état generally bring about a radical change in government. Once in place, the new government's policies are frequently hostile to foreign organisations, as has happened in Cuba, Nicaragua and Iran, among other countries. **Expropriation** is an attractive action because it reinforces nationalism and transfers wealth and resources from foreign organisations to the country. Expropriation does not relieve the government from paying compensation to the former owners. However, compensation may take the form of local, non-transferable currency or may be based on the company's value in books.

KEY TERMS

A **coup d'état** is the sudden overthrow of a government, often illegally, by another faction of the state establishment, i.e the military.
Expropriation is the transfer of ownership by the host government to a domestic entity.

CASE STUDY

President Hugo Chávez of Venezuela's regime has targeted foreign oil companies. Approximately 32 service contracts with foreign oil companies in the Orinoco region have been converted into joint ventures with more than 50 per cent state ownership.

President Chávez has also introduced a steep increase in the rate of income tax foreign companies operating in Venezuela's Orinoco region have to pay, as well as in the royalties they pay to the Venezuelan government.

According to analysts these changes reflect Chávez's increasing power compared to the foreign oil companies. High oil prices have made the Venezuelan government less dependent on foreign investment and if foreign oil companies want to continue operating in Venezuela they will have to accept the new conditions.

continued . . . ▶

◄ . . . continued

Figure 9.4 Hugo Chávez
(Sources: Catán, 2007; Mortished, 2006; Mortished; 2005).

Another form of political risk may arise from **terrorism** and terrorist activities. Generally speaking, terrorist acts have a political objective; however, they are considered to be a criminal activity. Due to **globalisation**, terrorism trespasses national boundaries in terms of networks, activities, funding, organisation, management and membership. Since the terrorist attacks of September 11, 2001 on the World Trade Centre in New York, the threat of terrorist attacks has become a reality in many countries.

KEY TERMS

Terrorism refers to actions meant to inflict dramatic and deadly injury on civilians and create an atmosphere of fear, generally for a political or ideological (whether secular or religious) purpose. (UN Policy Working Group, 2002).
The Organisation for Economic Cooperation and Development defines **globalisation** as the process through which markets and production become increasingly interdependent as a consequence of the dynamic of exchanging goods and services, and through the movement of capital and technology.

ACTIVITY

Search the news and identify a case when the political environment of a foreign country has affected the operations of a UK organisation. Then complete the following table.

UK organisation	
Host country	
Key characteristics of host country's political environment	
Impact on organisation	
Actions taken by organisation if any	

CASE STUDY

Following the terrorist attacks of September 11, 2001, passengers within and outside the United States cancelled virtually all travel plans. This had terrible consequences for the airline industry.

Soon after the attacks a number of airlines collapsed or suffered severe financial losses. For example, Midway Airlines closed operations the next day although it later restarted limited operations. Continental, United, American Airlines, Northwest, US Airways and Delta all announced layoffs of thousands of employees. In the United Kingdom British Airways and Virgin also had significant cuts in staff numbers. Other international carriers both in Europe and in Asia faced restructuring, layoffs, and capacity cuts.

(Sources: Durmand and Armistead, 2005; Pratley, 2002; Ward, 2002)

 1 What has been the long-term impact of terrorism on the travel industry?

 ## 9.5 Analysing the effect of current and future political influences on organisations

In order to analyse the effect of political influences on a particular organisation, the first step is to consider the elements of the political environment and identify the relevant factors that apply to that organisation.

After the key factors have been identified, the next step is to analyse how each one of them impacts on the organisation, and decide whether it represents a threat that needs to be minimised or an opportunity that can be taken advantage of. When analysing political factors you will find that they have varying degrees of importance for different organisations. For some organisations it might be the level of political risk in a foreign country that is important, while for others it might be the impact of local government policies.

It is important not only to describe factors, but also to think through what they mean and how they affect the organisation in the present and how their impact might change in the future. Considering how and why the present is different from the past can be useful for your analysis.

Political element	What is the current status?	What seems to be the current trend and why – give reason/s	Likely current impact on organisation: • high • medium • low	Potential future impact on the organisation: • high • medium • low	Suggested action:
The local government					
Political system					
Political stability					
Political risk					
Membership of regional agreements	EU membership	Enlarged EU. Larger market. Potential low cost locations. Lower labour costs.	High	High	Research possibility of relocating. Conduct skills audit. Assess infrastructure. Risk assessment. Market research. See case study on page 202

Table 9.2   Template for analysing the effect of current and future key economic influences on organisations

ACTIVITY

Choose an organisation and, using the template in Table 9.2, analyse how the political environment impacts on your chosen organisation. ▶

Top tips:
- Make sure you systematically consider each of the elements.
- Then, carefully analyse how each in turn might affect the organisation now and in the future.
- Assess the likely impact as high, medium or low.
- In the light of your assessment, consider what action might be appropriate, for example, for any future trends that seem likely, you might wish to monitor events and/or prepare action plans for the organisation so it is ready to be able to exploit opportunities or minimise any threats.

The example given in the bottom row of the template above illustrates the potential impact of membership of regional agreements on a European car manufacturer. Please note that this is just one dimension and you must complete a full analysis.

Remember that it is essential to look at sources of information that will give exposure to new trends and possibilities. Your analysis will fail if the information it is based upon is superficial, inaccurate or even missing. Your first step is to understand where you can get relevant and current information from. Some of the secondary sources of information you can use in your research are: newspapers and periodicals, trade organisations, government agencies, and industry analysis.

 ## 9.6 Summary

The political environment includes a country's government and its institutions, its political philosophy and system, and the political agreements to which a State has subscribed. Organisations are affected by a country's political environment, but the type of influence that the political environment has on an organisation will vary from organisation to organisation and industry to industry.

It is important for organisations to identify the key trends in the political environment that could affect their present and future performance, and to analyse how each trend impacts on the organisation.

KEY IDEAS

Some of the main points covered in this chapter are listed below. If you feel unsure about any of them revisit the appropriate section. If you would like some additional reading on the topic try out the books listed below in recommended reading.

What do we mean by the political environment?

- The political environment refers to the processes by which power is exercised and the institutions by which laws are made and implemented within a State.

Key political influences

- Local government is responsible for regulating private businesses locally, has statutory responsibilities and provides a wide range of services to individuals and organisations.
- Local government influences the decisions and actions of organisations operating within its confines.
- Political philosophies and systems are categorised as collectivism/individualism and democracy/totalitarianism.
- Generally individualism and democracy, and totalitarianism and collectivism go hand in hand; however, this is not always the case. There are examples of totalitarian regimes supporting an individualist philosophy and democracies supporting a collectivist philosophy.
- The exercise of power in the United Kingdom's political system is through Parliament, central government and its departments, local government, the judiciary and criminal courts.
- Nations around the world are coming together under regional integration agreements that aim to reduce, and ultimately remove, barriers to trade.
- Some of the main integration agreements are the Andean Pact, the Association of Southeast Asian Nations, Mercosur, the North American Free Trade Agreement, and the European Union.

Current and emerging ethical and international issues

- The political environment of a country influences its attractiveness for doing business.
- It can also raise ethical concerns such as whether organisations should invest in countries where the government restricts political and/or economic freedom, and whether organisations should pay bribes or get involved in self-defence activities to protect their interests.

REFLECTIVE QUESTIONS

1 Explain the difference between a collectivist and an individualist political philosophy.
2 Conduct further research and identify which are the arguments against and for regional integration. Use examples wherever possible to illustrate your answer.

RECOMMENDED READING

If you would like to learn more about some of the issues in the sections within this chapter you might like to consider the following books.

Capon, C. (2006) *Understanding Organisational Context*. Great Britain: FT Prentice Hall.

Hill, C. (2007) *International Business: Competing in the Global Marketplace*. 6th international edn. London: McGraw-Hill.

Morrison, J. (2006) *The International Business Environment: Global and Local Marketplaces in a Changing World*. 2nd ed. New York: Palgrave.

Ravenhill, J. (2008) *Global Political Economy*. 2nd ed. Oxford: Oxford University Press.

USEFUL WEBSITES

BBC – **www.bbc.co.uk**

The Economist – **www.economist.com**

European Union – **www.europa.eu**

Financial Times – **www.ft.com**

Foreign and Commonwealth Office – **www.fco.gov.uk**

The Guardian – **www.guardian.co.uk**

Organisation for Economic Cooperation and Development – **www.oecd.org**

The Times – **www.thetimesonline.co.uk**

UK Parliament – **www.parliament.uk**

UK Government – **www.direct.gov.uk**

World Trade Organisation – **www.wto.org**

REFERENCES

Barkham, P. (2007) 'After 11 Years, Town Faces Defeat to Tesco'. *The Guardian*, (online) 2 November. Available at: http://www.guardian.co.uk/business/2007/nov/02/supermarkets (Accessed 21 November 2007).

BBC News, 'Chiquita Sued Over Colombia Role'. *BBC News*, (online) 7 June. Available at: http://news.bbc.co.uk/1/hi/business/6732739.stm (Accessed 12 November 2009).

Bremmer, I. (2006) 'If We Isolate Kim, He'll Get Stronger'. *Times Online*, (online) 15 October. Available at: http://www.timesonline.co.uk/tol/news (Accessed 18 November 2007).

Capon, C. (2006) *Understanding Organisational Context*. Harlow: FT Prentice Hall.

Catán, T. (2007) 'Chávez Seizes Oil Group's Control of $30bn Projects in May Day Raid'. *Times Online*, (online) 2 May. Available at: http://business.timesonline.co.uk/tol/business/industry_sectors/natural_resources/article1733837.ece (Accessed 12 November 2009).

Durman, P. and Armistead, L. (2005) 'The Markets Were in Freefall... It Was Mayhem'. *Times Online*, (online) 10 July. Available at: http://business.timesonline.co.uk/tol/business/industry_sectors/banking_and_finance/article542268.ece?token=null&offset=0&page=1 (Accessed 12 November 2009).

Dutch Ministry of Foreign Affairs (2008?) *Visa Policy*, (online). Available at: www.minbuza.nl/en/europeancooperation/EU,schen/Visa-Policy.html (Accessed 13 June 2008).

Engel, M. (2009) 'Dispatch from Sheringham'. *The Financial Times*, (online) 20 November. Available at: http://www.ft.com/cms/s/2/378012f8-d3e3-11de-8caf-00144feabdc0.html (Accessed 1 December 2009).

Hawkes, S. (2007). 'Shell Enters Alliance with Rosneft as Russia Acts to Lure Investment'. *Times Online*, (online) 10 July. Available at: http://business.timesonline.co.uk/tol/business/industry_sectors/natural_resources/article2051270.ece (Accessed 12 June 2008).

Hill, C. (2007) *International Business: Competing in the Global Marketplace*. 6th international edn. London: McGraw-Hill.

Hutton, R. (2006) 'Eastern Europe: The New Detroit'. *The Sunday Times*, 15 October.

Morris, H. and Willey, B. (1996) *The Corporate Environment: A Guide for Human Resource Managers*. Harlow: FT Prentice Hall.

Morrison, J. (2006) *The International Business Environment: Global and Local Marketplaces in a Changing World*. 2nd edn. London: Palgrave.

Mortished, C. (2005). 'Venezuela Squeezes Foreign Oil Groups'. *Times Online*, (online) 19 April. Available at: http://business.timesonline.co.uk/tol/business/economics/article382726.ece (Accessed 19 November 2007).

Mortished, C. (2006) 'Venezuela Doubles Tax on Oil Majors'. *Times Online*, (online) 9 May. Available at http://business.timesonline.co.uk/tol/business/industry_sectors/natural_resources/article714662.ece (Accessed 12 November 2009).

Mortished, C. (2007) 'US Banana Producer Made Payments to Colombian Terrorists'. *Times Online*, (online) 20 March. Available at: http://business.timesonline.co.uk/tol/business/markets/united_states (Accessed 19 November 2007).

Pratley, N. (2002) 'Review of 2002: The Year the Tide Went Out'. *Times Online*, (online) 29 December. Available at: http://business.timesonline.co.uk/tol/business/article806328.ece?token=null&offset=0&page=1 (Accessed 12 November 2009).

Reid, T. (2007) 'Banana Company, Chiquita, "Armed Guerrillas"'. *Times Online*, (online) 16 November. Available at: www.timesonline.co.uk/tol/news/world/us_and_americas/article2879864.ece (Accessed 12 November 2009).

Smith, E. and Nagley, J. (2006) 'The Name's Bond, Otto von Bond'. *Times Online*, (online) 21May. Available at: http://www.timesonline.co.uk/tol/driving/features/article721729.ece (Accessed 12 November 2009).

Stamp, G. (2007) 'Tesco Fuels Passions in Norfolk Town'. *BBC News*, (online) 16 April. Available at: http://news.bbc.co.uk/1/hi/business/6551629.stm (Accessed 1 December 2009).

Ward, R. (2002) 'September 11 and the Restructuring of the Airline Industry'. *Dollars and Sense* (online) May/June. Available at: http:// www.dollarsandsense.org/archives/2002/0502ward.html (Accessed 12 November 2009).

Whitell, G. (2009) 'President Obama Will Urge China to Join US in "World Leadership"'. *Times Online*, (online) 16 November. Available at: http://www.timesonline.co.uk/tol/news/world/us_and_americas/article6918071.ece (Accessed 1 December 2009).

10 The Macro Environment – Economic Influences

'It's the economy, stupid'

(Presidential candidate Bill Clinton's focused campaign message in 1992)

CHAPTER OUTLINE

10.1 Introduction
10.2 What do we mean by the economy?
10.3 Key economic influences
10.4 Emerging ethical and international issues around the economy
10.5 Analysing the effect of current and future key economic influences on organisations
10.6 Summary

CHAPTER OBJECTIVES

After carefully reading and engaging with the tasks and activities outlined in this chapter, you should have a better understanding of:
- the meaning of the term 'economy'
- the three types of economy
- the nature of the economic influences and their impact on organisations
- some of the ethical and international issues confronting organisations with regard to the economic environment.

10.1 Introduction

When Bill Clinton entered the race for the Presidency in the autumn of 1992, the American economy was just coming out of a two-year recession and a large number of Americans were anxious about their own economic prospects. The 1992 Clinton campaign was kept in focus with the simple message: '*It's the economy, stupid.*' This catchphrase, played repeatedly throughout the campaign, signalled the importance of the economy. Many political observers were of the view that this was a key factor that helped Bill Clinton win the US Presidential election (Feulner, 1996).

The economy remains a central issue for the USA. President Barack Obama faces what many view as an unprecedented economic challenge. As this chapter will demonstrate, the national economy is of great importance to individuals, organisations and countries across the world, i.e. *It's still the economy, stupid!*

Figure 10.1 Barack Obama faces an
unprecedented economic challenge

A growing economy will provide jobs and incomes for individuals; organisations (providing goods and services that are needed, or wanted) will have a greater opportunity to stay in business and grow. Thus, allowing the government of that growing economy to collect money from taxes to pay for various requirements, such as security, health and education for its citizens. A growing economy boosts confidence and optimism for the future among individuals, organisations and the nation. Conversely, the opposite happens if the economy shrinks (at certain levels, over a defined period of time, a shrinking economy is called a recession). Individuals may lose jobs and organisations may find it difficult to trade as individuals have less money to spend. Confidence is low. In essence – the economy can be used as a measure of the standard of living in a country.

The economic environment of an organisation consists of the macro economy of the country, plus the **microeconomic** environment of the organisation. Full coverage of economic theory and principles is neither possible nor the intention of this section. Here, we deal with the economic factors in the **macroeconomic** environment that are apt to be of interest to an organisation. In the dynamic and increasingly complex international environment in which businesses need to operate, organisations must understand how these factors affect, or have the potential to affect the achievement of their objectives, so that they can identify and respond to opportunities and threats (current and potential), maximising any opportunities and minimising any threats.

This chapter will explain the meaning of the widely used term economy, and discuss the main types used in the world today. It goes on to highlight the influence of the global economy, the role of trading blocks and bodies and those of financial institutions.

The national cycles of economies are examined in relation to their effect on unemployment, **economic growth,** inflation and level of imports. National income is presented as a method of assessing the economy and when comparing years, identifying trends in economic growth. We also point out that the state of the local and national economy can affect organisations. We go on to consider other key economic elements, such as inflation, interest rates, exchange rates and levels of employment. Government objectives and the economy are then briefly discussed.

KEY TERMS

Macroeconomic environment refers to economic influences in the external environment within which organisations exist and operate.
Microeconomic environment refers to economic influences, including prices and costs, of the economic decisions made by individuals and firms.
Economic growth can be defined as the rate of growth of national income, usually measured in terms of Gross National Product (GNP) or Gross Domestic Product (GDP) over a defined period of time – usually 12 months.

The GNP of a country is the amount of income produced by the domestic economy plus other factors, such as income earned abroad. These are taken into account over a defined period of time – usually 12 months. Income earned outside the country is added to the GDP, and conversely, income paid out abroad (for example, interest on loans) is taken away.

GDP in the UK provides a measure of the total economic activity in the UK. It is frequently referred to as one of the key gauges of economic activity. When the term 'growth in the economy' is used, this is with reference to the increase in GDP during the previous quarter. (Office for National Statistics, 2002)

 ## What do we mean by the economy?

Throughout the world resources are scarce and finite. Resources are needed to meet the needs and demands of people and organisations. This scarcity results in the need to make choices. Economics is concerned with the allocation of scarce resources: the **economy** is the system used within a community for the allocation of these scarce resources.

There was time in economics when it was considered that air and water were free goods and that their supply was infinite. However, with climate change and global warming, it is now thought that in the future water may become scarce, leading to potential conflict in certain parts of the world over supplies.

Choices over the allocation of resources relate to:

- what goods and services should be produced, in what quantities and by whom
- what goods and services will be purchased by customers and in what quantities.

KEY TERMS

A country's **economy** can be defined as how decisions about what to produce, for whom to produce and how to produce, are made.

Three major types of economy

Not every country operates the same type of economic system. Usually, though, we refer to three main economic systems (see Table 10.1).

It is generally the case that the politics of the country influences the chosen economic agenda. Traditionally, democracies are associated with free markets, for example, the USA is a country that works to the free market agenda, where demand and supply dictate how resources are used and distributed, with state

Economy	Major features of allocation/ownership of resources
Free market economy	Decisions are made by privately owned organisations and customers. Private ownership of the means of production Decisions as to what to buy and sell, quantities and place are all determined by private customers and organisations. Price acts as a signal and incentive for demand and supply of goods and services.
Centrally planned economy	Decisions made by the state. State control of the means of production. State control of the production and distribution of goods and services.
Mixed economy	A mixture of various combinations of centrally planned and free market economy.

Table 10.1   Features of the three main economic systems

involvement limited to defence and some state help in the provision of health and education.

Autocracies are associated with centrally planned economies. A traditional example of a centrally planned economy (often referred to as a socialist economy) was the former Union of Soviet Socialist Republics (USSR), where the model was one of centrally planning allocation of resources according to need. (This form of economy did not quite reap the benefits envisaged, due to a number of reasons). The model began to fall apart in the USSR in the 1980s, with the advent of Glasnost and liberalisation of the country. There are still countries today, such as Cuba, which operate a predominately centrally planned economic system, and there are examples of countries embarking on a centrally planned route at the beginning of the twenty-first century (see case study below).

KEY TERMS

An **autocracy** is a country that is ruled by a governmental institution where the political power is possessed by a single ruler (usually self appointed) who has unlimited power and authority.

Mikhail Gorbachev the Soviet ruler (1985–1991) introduced the term 'Glasnost', which literally means openness. Glasnost began a period of openness in the USSR. This liberal approach led to a fundamental change in the USSR. Information and government systems were challenged, which among other

Figure 10.2 Mikhail Gorbachev

things, ultimately led to the collapse of the former centrally planned economic system and the USSR itself. A result of this was the independence from Russia of many Eastern European states, which in turn, abandoned their centrally planned economies in favour of a more free market approach.

	Democracy	Autocracy
Power	Separation of power.	Power concentrated in one person (e.g. a dictator) or in one ruling body (e.g. USSR communist blocs).
Representation	Free and fair elections by individuals to choose who represents them in the governing body of the state.	No choice by individuals of who is to govern them – no elections or facility to remove these elements from power, except for revolution.
Individual freedom	Protection of liberties.	Very few or no personal liberties.

Table 10.2   Key characteristics of democratic and autocratic countries

CASE STUDY

After re-election at the beginning of 2007, Hugo Chávez began his second term in office as President of Venezuela. He outlined his nationalisation plans – to take over Venezuela's largest telecommunications company and electrical companies. He also made it very clear that he wanted the oil and natural gas industries to be subject to much greater state control. Hugo Chávez also called for the Central Bank's independence to be removed. Thousands of worker-managed businesses and co-operatives had already been established in his first term in office. These were all seen as part of Hugo Chávez's plan for Venezuela, which he referred to as '21st century socialism'.

(Sources: Catan, 2007; Forero, 2005; Glaister, 2007; Obiko Pearson, 2007)

1 What type of economic system did these actions seem to be taking Venezuela towards?
2 List the key features of this economic system.
3 Find out which other countries in the world have this type of economic system.

The majority of countries in Europe follow the mixed economy model i.e. their economies will contain both public and private sectors. However, the sizes of these sectors will vary. For example, Sweden has a larger state involvement in the provision of services than many other European countries.

Changes to a country's political system can change the economic structure, which can result sometimes in the opening up of markets and present organisations with new opportunities to expand and grow in these new markets.

The changing Eastern European economies in the 1980s and 1990s resulted in new markets and new labour pools for organisations to take advantage of in the areas of growth and cost savings respectively. Firms have relocated to Eastern Europe to save on costs (See Chapter 9), and at the same time, as new countries join the European Union, people from these countries (e.g. Poland) came to Britain, increasing the pool of labour in the UK.

In addition to changing Eastern European economies, developing economies such as Brazil, India and China offer organisational opportunities in growing markets.

Opportunities and threats posed by developing economies and differing political and economic systems for organisations need to be considered.

CASE STUDY

India and China are examples of emerging (growing) economies. UK companies have been eager to take advantage of these developing economies.

In 2006, the population of India was 1.1 billion – the second largest in the world, with approximately 300 million people leaving poverty and entering the more affluent middle classes. The economy at the time was the fourth largest in the world, and is still one of the most rapidly growing economies.

UK exports to India have been growing by 14 per cent per annum since 2002. UK companies have been keen to take advantage of these emerging markets – and this has been particularly evident where higher skills are required of manufactured goods, and also in the financial and business services. However, some analysts at the time reported that UK companies could do more to exploit trading opportunities in India as there was evidence that major competitors were getting ahead. One reason suggested was that perhaps India was being viewed by some UK companies as a place to take advantage of low cost labour, rather than as a growing market to trade with.

It is expected that both the Chinese and Indian economies will continue to expand rapidly – and by 2050, forecasts put them as being the first and third largest economies of the world. Not all UK companies however view this development as an opportunity. As India and China emerge into major economic players, there has been reported anxiety expressed by some UK companies that see India and China as potential competitors – a challenge to UK companies in terms of UK jobs and businesses.

(Sources: BERR, 2009; Trade and Industry Committee, 2006)

10.3 Key economic influences

In considering economic influences, it is useful to take a look at some different perspectives on the economy. Capon (2009) suggests that macroexternal environmental influences occur at three levels: global, national and local. We will look at these three levels of influence in turn.

Global economic influences

Countries do not function economically in isolation. External (international) factors affect domestic economies. These external factors include:

- the **global economy**
- **trading blocks**
- **trading bodies**
- international financial institutions.

KEY TERMS

The **global economy** refers to our world as an interconnected market place for goods and services.

By the end of June 2008, **stock markets** (e.g. The Dow Jones Index in New York and the London Stock Market) fell again because of fears over the effect of global economy. Prospects for the global economy at the time looked gloomy due to fears of inflation and increasing oil prices. At the time, many countries felt that they would not be too badly affected by the downturn. However, countries such as Germany discovered that this was simply not the case and it soon transpired that no country would be immune from a stock market slump in New York and London.

KEY TERMS

A **stock market** is the trading place for shares of (publicly quoted) companies.
A **trading block** is a defined geographic block consisting of a number of countries that have formally agreed to trade with one another, with agreed measures in place to facilitate this trade.

The European Union, commonly referred to as the EU, is an example of a trading block. Since 1993 there has been free movement of goods, services and labour across member countries. The ruling body of the EU is the European Parliament, which is based in Brussels (see Chapter 9).

Figure 10.3

In addition to trading blocks, countries will try and seek out trading advantages by establishing a **trading body** with partners who have similar aims.

KEY TERMS

A **trading body** consists of countries (not necessarily a geographical block) that formally agree to trade with another, with agreed measures and rules in place to facilitate this trade.

Following the post-war reconstruction of what was known as Western Europe, the Organisation for the Economic Co-operation and Development (OECD) was formed in 1961. It currently has 30 members who are all committed to a market economy and a democratic style of government.

One of the best-known trading bodies is the World Trade Organisation (WTO). This is a truly global organisation that deals with trading regulations between nations, which aims to decrease barriers to international trade. As you can imagine, negotiating and agreeing regulations that cross the boundaries of many countries, and getting them ratified in their respective parliaments is a major challenge.

One of the key roles of the WTO is to settle disputes among fellow WTO members. The priority is to settle the disputes, preferably by consultation, and not to pass judgement. The mechanism works by members agreeing to the WTO dispute settlement procedures and respecting the outcomes of any judgements made by the WTO (www.wto.org).

The WTO procedures are based on:

- clear and coherent rules
- schedules for completing cases
- rulings made by a panel, which the WTO's full membership then subsequently either approve or reject. (Appeals are possible.) (www.wto.org).

Another organisation that faces what many see as greater challenges than the WTO is the **World Bank**. This is an example of an International Financial Institution that gives financial and technical aid to developing countries around the world.

KEY TERMS

The **World Bank** is an international financial institution. One of its key goals is the reduction of global poverty. In addition to providing financial aid, it aims to improve the living standards of people in developing countries by, amongst other things, provision of knowledge and resources.

National economic influences

As already pointed out, the state of the **national economy** is crucial to individuals, organisations and countries, in terms of economic growth and standards of living. Although no nation works in isolation and all are affected by the global economic environment, the performance of the national economy is of concern to individuals and organisations. Politicians are often judged on the performance of their national economy. This section defines the national economy and examines the influences that affect it.

KEY TERMS

The **national economy** refers to the total activity in the country's economy over a defined period of time – usually 12 months, and is usually measured by using Gross Domestic Product (GDP).

National cycles

Over time, growth in an economy tends to fluctuate. For example, in some years a country may go through a period of high economic growth (called a boom) and at other times it may go through a slowdown of economic growth, or a high rate of economic shrinking (called a recession). This cycle of continual booms and recessions is referred to as the **business** or **trade** cycle.

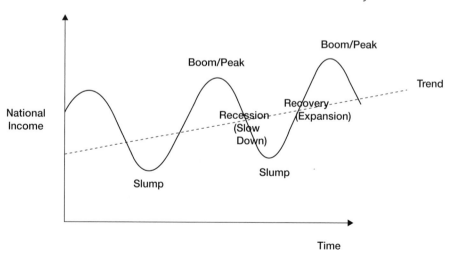

Figure 10.4 The business or trade cycle

The trade cycle affects unemployment levels, economic growth, inflation, exports and imports. There is also a psychological effect that economists are

KEY TERMS

Business or **trade cycle** refers to the variations of economic activity and the economic growth trend over the long term.

aware of that can reinforce a boom or a slump. In a boom, such as the housing boom that peaked in 2007, it started to be seen as normal for people to take out large loans and have an amount of credit that they would not consider having in 2009 when the UK was in recession. That is, people are generally much more cautious in a slump and less so in a boom.

Each stage is defined by certain characteristics: unemployment levels, economic growth, inflation and imports (as shown in Table 10.3 below).

Stage	Characterised by:
Recovery (expansion)	<ul><li>unemployment levels – begins and continues to fall</li><li>economic growth – begins and continues to grow as **national income** and output increases</li><li>inflation – may begin to increase</li><li>imports – begin to rise.</li></ul> Generally – confidence by workers and consumers begins to increase. Both consumption and investment increases.
Boom/Peak	<ul><li>unemployment levels – full employment (possible lack of sufficient number of workers to fuel the economy at its height)</li><li>economic growth – is strong and national income is high</li><li>inflation – continues to rise</li><li>imports – imports are high.</li></ul> Generally – confidence by businesses, workers and consumers is very high, which manifests in high imports and wages and profits increasing, leading to high tax revenue earnings by the Government. Both consumption and investment continue to be high.
Recession (slowdown)	<ul><li>unemployment levels – begin to increase</li><li>economic growth – decreases, as national income falls</li><li>inflation – begins to decrease</li><li>imports – begin to decline.</li></ul> Generally – confidence by businesses, workers and consumers decreases, which manifests in lower demand for imports. Tax revenues earned by the Government decrease. Added Government

►

Stage	Characterised by:
	expenditure on benefits for the unemployed increases. Both consumption and investment decreases.
Slump	• unemployment levels – high • economic growth – fall in economic activity and national income is low • inflation – decreases • imports – decrease. Generally – confidence by businesses, workers and consumers is very low, which manifests in lower levels of consumption, investment and imports.

Table 10.3   Characteristics of stages in the business or trade cycle

KEY TERMS

National income is the total income produced in one year by a country's economic activities. National income per head of population can then be calculated and compared between previous years in the same country, or between countries, as these may serve as useful indicators of a country's prosperity.

The graph in Figure 10.4 above is presented in a way that allows us to distinguish clearly between the different economic phases. However, in reality, trade cycles rarely occur as depicted. There can be variations in the degree of the phases, demonstrated by highs and lows of the curves (which can be extreme or mild) or variations in the length of phases – as some can be short (months) so some can be long (years).

Organisations are likely to be affected by the current and future position the country is/will be on the trade cycle in terms of their level of trade, access to labour and investment. So, it is necessary to identify where the nation currently stands in terms of the trade cycle, and what the trend of the trade cycle is most likely to be over the coming months and years.

ACTIVITY

Look at Figure 10.4 and answer the following questions:
a) Where do you think the UK is now in the trade cycle? Give reasons for your answer.
b) List the main characteristics of this stage giving examples.

1 Define and explain the term national income.
2 Define gross domestic product (GDP).
3 Define gross national product (GNP).
4 What is economic growth?
5 How can economic growth be measured?

Stock market

Generally, if the economy is located in a favourable position in the trade cycle and is health, with unemployment and inflation low, conditions for stock market trading are considered to be good, often referred to as a 'Bull market'. An overall rise in stock prices would be expected. Conversely, if the economy is located in a unfavourable position in the trade cycle, with increasing or high unemployment and inflation, conditions for stock market trading are considered to be poor, and would be reflected in an overall fall in stock prices, known as a 'Bear market'.

Stocks for companies are bought and sold daily in the stock market. Price is often dependent on actual or perceived future performance. If actual performance of a company is very good, for example, high profits are announced, the stock price for that company is likely to increase. Stock price movements can also move depending on perceived future performance.

CASE STUDY

Early in February 2007, shares in J Sainsbury, the UK's third biggest supermarket, rose by almost 14 per cent after it emerged that there had been talks of a takeover bid for the supermarket chain by private equity firms.

In mid February 2007, shares in J Sainsbury climbed again – nearly 2 per cent in one morning. With a number of interested parties already in pursuit of the supermarket, when the interest by a Qatari investment fund as a potential buyer became apparent, shares increased as shareholders held onto the shares in anticipation of a bidding war.

Both increases in share price were not due to any announcement of high performance by the company; the first was in response to the possibility of a takeover bid, and the second in anticipation of a bidding war by rival groups to acquire the company.

(Sources: BBC News, 2007; FTSE News, 2007 and Verjee, 2007).

Local economic influences

The local economy refers to the total economic activity in a particular region's economy over a defined period of time – usually 12 months.

It is generally the case the more economic growth in a particular region, the better, generally, for organisations. Conversely, the more depressed the local economy is, the worse it is for organisations in terms of level of trade.

One method to check the health of the local economy is by analysing the Regional Household income.

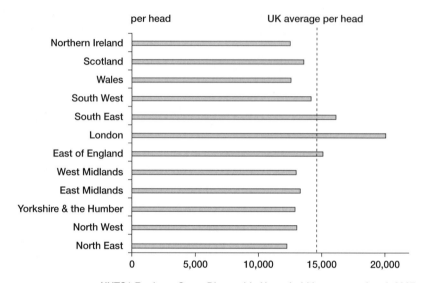

NUTS1 Regions: Gross Disposable Household Income per head, 2007

Figure 10.5 Regional Household Income Comparison, 2007
(Source: Office for National Statistics, 2007)

As shown in Figure 10.5, Inner London had the highest disposable household income (after tax) per head of population (£20,163) in 2007 and was 41 per cent above the UK average of £14,317.

Key economic factors

In addition to the economic influences identified, there are other economic factors that impact on organisations. We first need to consider *what* these elements are, and then secondly *how* they might influence organisations.

The key economic influences we need to consider are: inflation, interest rates and exchange rates.

Inflation

Inflation is an indicator of the general level of prices of both goods and wages. A key measure of the general rate of inflation is the consumer price index (CPI), which measures monthly percentage changes in the average level of prices of the goods and services bought by the majority of UK households. When there is a sustained rise in the general level of prices we term this as inflation.

If wages increase at the same rate, this is generally not a problem, as we can maintain our standard of living. However, if inflation (rise in prices) is higher than national wage rises, then our money in real terms, declines in value – that is, it will not be sufficient to buy the same amount of goods or services as prior to the inflation. Put simply, our money will not go as far as it did before.

Inflation can be affected by the increase in cost of:

- wages
- raw materials (e.g., an increase in cost of oil leads to increases in prices generally)
- land – if land is in short supply, e.g. in London and South East of England demand can exceed supply. This is then reflected in high land/property prices.
- capital (e.g. if interest rates increase at rates above inflation).

Inflation can also be caused by an increase in demand for goods and services in the economy, or by an increase in the amount of money in the economy (e.g. high consumer borrowing).

ACTIVITY

1 Using (reliable) statistics and/or current broadsheet newspapers, find out what the current rate of inflation is in the UK.
2 Using (reliable) statistics, find out what the figures for inflation in the UK have been over the last twelve months, the last two years and the last ten years.
3 Using (reliable) statistics and/or current broadsheet newspapers, find out the predicted figures for inflation in the UK in the future. Identify the reasons for any predictions found.
4 From the information you have gathered from parts a), b) and c), try to identify a trend. Give reasons to support your answer.

REFLECTIVE QUESTION

Consider your local region. How do you think the local economy affects organisations in the leisure sector?

Interest rates

Interest rates are set and considered monthly by The Bank of England, which has been independent of the Government in the UK since 1997.

The rise and fall in interest rates affects individuals and organisations. If interest rates are low, we can generally borrow more money. Our repayments for monies already borrowed may fall, so we can generally spend more money – affecting overall demand for goods and services. Organisations could benefit both from an increase in demand for goods and services and lower costs on any monies borrowed, which may contribute to increasing turnover and profits.

The opposite occurs if interest rates rise – individuals and organisations with monies borrowed (loans) are faced with increased payments, leaving less money available for individuals to spend, or for organisations to invest in the organisation, give to shareholders, use for wage rises, or to decrease prices.

ACTIVITY

1 Using (reliable) statistics and/or current broadsheet newspapers, find out what the current interest rate is in the UK.
2 Using statistics, websites and/or current broadsheet newspapers, find out what the predicted figures for interest rates in the UK are. Identify the reasons for any predictions found.
3 How will an increase in interest rates affect:
   ● a local hairdresser
   ● the supermarket chain Tesco
   ● the car manufacturer Vauxhall.

Give reasons and evidence to support your answers.

Exchange rates

Exchange rate is the value of *one* currency of a nation against the value of a currency of *another* (foreign) nation. It follows then that the countries that the UK trades with the most are the most important exchange rates. If a UK organisation trades with another foreign company, then their exchange rate will be of vital importance.

Governments try to make the environment conducive to export growth, while at the same time avoiding excessive growth in imports, because exporting brings money into the economy. They aim to provide an environment in which the earnings of foreign currency (through exporting for example) are at least equivalent to, or preferably surpass, the country's demand for foreign currency i.e. they endeavour to achieve a favourable **balance of payments.** In order to do this, one of the things they try to do is to control exchange rates.

For example, changes in exchange rates allow a country's goods and services to remain price competitive on international markets. A lower exchange rate (e.g. fewer dollars, yen, euros against the pound sterling) will make UK goods cheaper to overseas buyers, and therefore help to increase UK exports, thereby bringing money into the UK economy. If more money is coming into the UK economy, it will be stronger and therefore business in general will fare much better. A higher foreign exchange rate would achieve the opposite, making UK goods more expensive overseas and hence less competitive.

1 In February 2007, the exchange rate of the dollar was nearly $2 to one pound sterling. How do you think luxury exports to the US from the UK were affected?

2 In December 2009, the exchange rate of the dollar was $1.66 to one pound*. How do you think this exchange rate affected the sales of Jaguar cars in the US?

3 In December 2009, the exchange rate of the euro was €1.10 to one pound*. How do you think that would affect the UK as a tourist destination for people within the EU whose currency is the euro?

(*BBC News, 2009)

KEY TERMS

The **balance of payments** is a record of transactions (financial) between one nation and the other nation with which it trades. The imports and exports of a country, along with any inflows and outflows of capital and goods, will be recorded in the balance of payments.

Levels of employment

In the UK between 1945 and 1979 there was an all-party consensus on trying to minimise unemployment (to zero) as a government objective. However, with the increased rate of change of skills needed in the workplace (due to increasing globalisation and technological innovations), the accepted consensus is to keep unemployment low, and create an environment where the relevant skills the economy needs in order to be competitive can be acquired and developed.

Governments provide statistics on unemployment levels. It is the information on *trends* in employment and data on skills available that is considered to be important for organisations. By examining these trends, organisations can then gauge how unemployment and/or skills availability will impact on them.

Unemployment causes undesirable consequences in the economy. These are:

- Labour is available for organisations, but the required skills may still be in short supply.
- There is less money in the system for buying goods and services (i.e. potentially reduced demand).
- Tax revenue is reduced (fewer people paying income tax), compounded by increasing government spending on welfare payments.
- Resources are wasted.
- There are (well-documented) social problems associated with localities which have high unemployment.

Government and the economy

A key government objective is to manage the economy so that the environment is conducive to economic growth. In order to have any control over the economy, the government first needs to measure economic elements in the economy that gauge the state of the country's economic health.

Economic elements	Government objective
Employment	• Unemployment to be at an acceptable level. • Working population to acquire skills needed for organisations.
Inflation	• Maintain low inflation.
Imports and exports	• Maintain a balance between imports and exports.
Economic growth	• Pursue economic growth with a sustainable development agenda.

Table 10.4   Government objectives and the economy

10.4 Emerging ethical and international issues around the economy

As we are all aware, concerns are high about the level and use of the world's resources. We will now consider the ethical and international issues in terms of the economy.

Emerging ethical issues around the economy

The dwindling supplies of the world's oil, and other natural resources, plus the continuing use of coal and oil which contribute to climate change, particularly global warming, has led to calls from some economists to seek a new economic model, as they question the sustainability of the current model of economic growth.

There are concerns that the free market approach, with the allocation and use of resources decided by demand and supply, is not an effective way to deal with current issues in particular those such as carbon emissions – considered a main contributor to global warming (See Chapter 14).

It is likely that this fundamental debate over the allocation of resources within the current context will take on a number of ethical overtones, as the question is asked: Is the current model of economic growth sustainable?

REFLECTIVE QUESTION

Do you think global strategies of economic growth are sustainable?

Emerging international issues around the economy

A key concern between 2008 and 2010 has been the global recession. The promotion of international trade is seen by many as key to effective global economic growth. Concerns have been expressed about protectionist trends by some countries trying to protect jobs and their own economy, as this is viewed as detrimental to the idea of international trade.

10.5 Analysing the effect of current and future key economic influences on organisations

In order to analyse the effect of the economic influences on a particular organisation, we need to consider the economic elements and identify which are the relevant factors that apply to that organisation.

After the key factors have been identified, the next step is to analyse how each one of them impacts on that organisation and decide whether it represents a threat that needs to be minimised, or an opportunity that can be taken advantage of. When analysing economic influences you will find that they have varying degrees of importance for different organisations. For some organisations it might be the level of lending of the banks that is most important, while for other organisations it might be the impact of oil prices, or the state of the national economy. The impact of potential economic developments may also need to be considered.

It is important not only to describe factors, but also to think through what they mean and how they affect the organisation in the present and how their impact on the organisation might change in the future. Considering how and why the present is different from the past can be useful for your analysis.

ACTIVITY

Choose an organisation and, using the template below, analyse how the economic environment impacts on your chosen organisation.

Top tips:
- Make sure you systematically consider each of the elements.
- Then, carefully analyse how each in turn might affect the organisation now and in the future.
- Assess the likely impact as high, medium or low.
- In the light of your assessment, consider what action might be appropriate, for example, for any future impacts that seem likely, you might wish to monitor events and/or prepare action plans for the organisation so it is ready to be able to exploit opportunities or minimise any threats.

Macroeconomic element	What is the current status?	What seems to be the current trend and why – give reason/s	Likely current impact on organisation: • high • medium • low	Potential future impact on the organisation: • high • medium • low	Suggested action:
Examine political and economic systems of (current and potential) trading countries of the organisation					
Influence of trading blocks and bodies					
Stock markets • World • London					
UK position on the trade cycle					

▶

Macroeconomic element	What is the current status?	What seems to be the current trend and why – give reason/s	Likely current impact on organisation: • high • medium • low	Potential future impact on the organisation: • high • medium • low	Suggested action:
Economy • World • National • Local					
Inflation					
Interest rates					
Exchange rates					
Unemployment					
Emerging ethical issues					
Emerging international issues					
Other relevant economic factors					

Table 10.5 Template for analysing the effect of current and future key economic influences on organisations

10.6 Summary

The chapter began by outlining the importance of the economy to individual nations and the effect of the economy on individuals, organisations and governments. The term economy was explained and the three main types of economy were outlined. The focus of the chapter on the macroeconomic environmental factors was made clear. Key economic influences were introduced including international influences, national trade cycles and local economic effects. In addition to these, economic influences, key economic factors such as inflation, interest rates, exchange rates and levels of unemployment were examined in some detail. The chapter concluded by pointing out some emerging ethical and international issues around the macroeconomic environment.

KEY IDEAS

Some of the main points covered in this chapter are listed below. If you feel unsure about any of them, then revisit the appropriate section. If you would like some additional reading on the topic, try the books listed below in recommended reading.

What do we mean by the term economy?
- The economy is the system used within a community for the allocation of scarce resources.
- A nation's economy can be defined as the organisation within that country where decisions are made about what to produce, for whom to produce and how to produce.
- There are three main types of economy: free market, centrally planned and mixed.

Key economic influences
- International factors such as the global economy, trading blocs, trading bodies and international financial institutions can influence a domestic economy.
- The national economy is important to individuals, organisations and the government. For example, in terms of employment, income (individuals) opportunity to produce goods and services (organisations) and level of taxes collected, good standards of living for citizens (governments).
- The national economy refers to the total economic activity in the country's economy over a defined period of time – usually 12 months.
- Growth in the economy tends to fluctuate – going from high (boom) to low (recession). This cycle of booms and recessions is referred to as the business or trade cycle. The trade cycle affects: unemployment levels, economic growth, inflation and imports and exports.
- National income is used to measure the economic activity in the UK and can be used to measure economic growth.
- The local economy refers to the total economic activity in a particular region's economy over a defined period of time – usually 12 months.
- Key economic factors that influence organisations include inflation, interest rates, exchange rates and levels of employment.
- A key Government objective is to manage the economy so that the environment is conducive to economic growth.

Some emerging issues
- In light of current environmental concerns it is likely that the fundamental debate of the allocation of resources will take on a number of ethical overtones. The question being: Is the current model of economic growth sustainable?
- Will international trade be challenged by being the protectionist stances of some countries?

RECOMMENDED READING

Capon, C. (2009) *Understanding Organisational Context.* 3rd edn. London: Prentice Hall, pp. 38–48.
Sloman, J. and Sutcliffe, M. (2004) *Economics for Business.* 3rd edn. Harlow: Prentice Hall.
Worthington, I. and Britton, C. (2009) *The Business Environment.* 6th edn. Prentice Hall (Chapter 5).

USEFUL WEBSITES

European Union – **http://europa.eu/abc/panorama/index_en.htm.**
European Free Trade Area – **www.efta.int/.**
HM Treasury UK – **www.hm-treasury.gov.uk/.**
Organization for Economic Co-operation and Development – **www.oecd.org/.**
National Statistics – **www.statistics.gov.uk/.**
World Bank – **www.worldbank.org/.**
World Economic Forum – **www.weforum.org/en/index.htm.**
World Trade Organization – **www.wto.org/.**

REFERENCES

BBC News (2007) 'Bid Talk Lifts Sainsbury's Shares'. *BBC News*, (online) 2 February. Available at: http://news.bbc.co.uk/1/hi/business/6323371.stm (Accessed 28 November 2009).

BBC News (2009) 'Market Data'. *BBC News*, (online) 3 December. Available at: http://newsvote.bbc.co.uk/1/shared/fds/hi/business/market_data/overview/default.stm (Accessed 3 December 2009).

BERR (2009) *China and India: Opportunities and Challenges for UK Business* (BERR Economics Paper 5) London: BERR (Published February 2009) Available at: http://www.berr.gov.uk/files/file50349.pdf (Accessed 17 December 2009).

Capon, C. (2009) *Understanding the Business Environment*. 3rd edn. Harlow: FT Prentice Hall.

Catan, T. (2007) 'Chavez to Nationalize Telecoms and Power Companies'. *Times Online*, (online) 2 May. Available at: http://business.timesonline.co.uk/tol/business/industry_sectors/telecoms/article1290842.ece (Accessed 28 November 2009).

Feulner, E.J. (1996) *It's the Economy, Stupid* (online) ca. 16 May. Washington, DC: The Heritage Foundation. Available at http://www.heritage.org/Press/Commentary/ED051696b.cfm?RenderforPrint=1 (Accessed 4 December 2009).

Forero, J. (2005) 'Chávez Restyles Venezuela with "21st-Century Socialism"'. *The New York Times*, (online) 30 October. Available at: http://www.nytimes.com/2005/10/30/international/americas/30venezuela.html (Accessed 28 November 2009).

FTSE News (2007) 'UK Supermarkets Gain On UBS Upgrades'. *FTSE News*, (online) 6 February. Available at: http://www.ftse-news.com/172/uk-supermarkets-gain-on-ubs-upgrades/ (Accessed 4 December 2009).

Glaister, D. (2007) 'Chávez Wins Powers to Rule by Decree but Critics Cry "Heil, Hugo"'. *The Guardian*, (online) 1 February. Available at: http://www.guardian.co.uk/world/2007/feb/01/venezuela.danglaister (Accessed 4 December 2009).

Obiko Pearson, N. (2007) 'Analysts Hit Venezuela Nationalisation'. *The Washington Post*, (online) 9 January. Available at: http://www.washingtonpost.com/wp-dyn/content/article/2007/01/09/AR2007010901632.html (Accessed 28 November 2009).

Office for National Statistics (2002) *Guide to GDP: Measuring the UK's Economic Activity* (online) (12 August 2002). Available at: http://www.statistics.gov.uk/CCI/nugget.asp?ID=56 (Accessed 29 January 2007).

Office for National Statistics (2007) *Regional Household Income: Disposable Income per head highest in Inner London* (online) (Updated 2 April 2009). Available at: http://www.statistics.gov.uk/cci/nugget_print.asp?ID=1552 (Accessed 30 November 2009).

Trade and Industry Committee (2006) *Trade and Investment Opportunities with India. Third Report of Session 2005–6, Volume 1* (HC 881 of 2005–6) (online) London: HMSO. Available at: http://www.publications.parliament.uk/pa/cm200506/cmselect/cmtrdind/881/881i.pdf (Accessed 28 November 2009).

Verjee, N. (2007) 'Sainsbury's Shares Climb on Bid War Hopes'. *Times Online*, (online) 19 February. Available at: http://business.timesonline.co.uk/tol/business/industry_sectors/retailing/article1406380.ece (Accessed 19 February 2007).

http://www.wto.org/english/thewto_e/whatis_e/tif_e/disp1_e.htm (Accessed 3 December 2009).

11 The Macro Environment – Socio-cultural Influences

'*This time, like all times, is a very good one, if we but know what to do with it.*'

Ralph Waldo Emerson, 'The American Scholar' lecture at Harvard, 1837.

CHAPTER OUTLINE

11.1 Introduction
11.2 What do we mean by the socio-cultural environment?
11.3 Key socio-cultural influences
11.4 Current and emerging ethical and international issues in the socio-cultural environment
11.5 Analysing the effect of current and future socio-cultural influences on organisations
11.6 Summary

CHAPTER OBJECTIVES

After carefully reading and engaging with the tasks and activities outlined in this chapter, you should have a better understanding of:

- the socio-cultural environment
- key factors and trends in the socio-cultural environment
- how the socio-cultural environment affects organisations
- current and emerging ethical and international issues in the socio-cultural environment.

(11.1) Introduction

The world we live in today is very different from that of a generation ago and it appears to continue to change at an increasingly rapid pace. These changes pose **threats** and **opportunities** for organisations but, as in the case study above, it is the organisations that are able to anticipate trends and adapt to them that are the most successful.

KEY TERMS

Threats are obstacles an organisation encounters in its external environment. **Opportunities** arise from factors in the external environment that could potentially benefit the organisation.

The **socio-cultural environment** impacts on an organisation in terms of the type of products and services it offers, what markets it serves, where and how it produces, and how it sells its products and services.

In this chapter, we will be looking at key factors in the socio-cultural environment and how they impact on organisations. The analysis of the socio-cultural environment allows organisations to spot trends and determine whether they are a threat or an opportunity. What is an opportunity for one organisation might be a threat for another. However, as Emerson's quote implies, it is the organisation's response to the 'times' they live in and the changing needs and preferences of its customers that will determine its success or lack of it.

REFLECTIVE QUESTIONS

Consider how the 'times' you live in are different from the 'times' when your parents were the same age as you are now. For example, they would not have seen a mobile phone, except perhaps in the television series *Star Trek*.

11.2 What do we mean by the socio-cultural environment?

The socio-cultural environment refers to the **values**, attitudes, **norms** and lifestyle of the **population.** Therefore, socio-cultural influences on the organisation are directly related to people and to their preferences.

KEY TERMS

The socio-cultural environment refers to the values, attitudes, norms, and lifestyle of the population.
Values are the abstract ideas about what a group believes to be right or wrong (Hofstede, 2001).
Norms are the social rules and guidelines that prescribe appropriate behaviour in particular situations (Hofstede, 2001).
Population is the number of people that live in a particular geographic area.

But people change and so do their values, attitudes, norms and lifestyle. Some of these changes are relatively temporary and we can consider them to be mere **fashions**, while other changes show a longer-term decrease or increase in the population's preferences. These changes are called trends (Campbell, 1997). For the purposes of this chapter, we will focus on the analysis of socio-cultural **trends**.

KEY TERMS

A **fashion** is the result of a temporary change in the population's preferences.
Trends reflect long-term changes in the population's preferences.

Example

Since the 1980s there has been an increasing trend for people to exercise in order to keep fit. However, the popularity of different forms of exercise can be considered fashions: for example, aerobics in the 1980s was replaced relatively quickly in people's preferences by step, and spinning in the 1990s, which in turn have given way to other ways of keeping fit, such as yoga and Pilates.

Figure 11.1 Aerobics versus yoga

As we will see, some trends in the socio-cultural environment are directly related to other trends in the macro environment. For example, the rise in the 'weekend city break' as a leisure activity can be linked to the increase in spare income (economic environment), the advent of the internet (technological environment) and the increase in the number of people who are IT literate and who feel comfortable using the internet for business transactions (socio-cultural environment). The combination of these factors has created a market for the services of budget online operators such as easyJet, Ryanair and Thomsonfly. Other trends, such as people becoming more health conscious, cannot be so easily explained.

REFLECTIVE QUESTIONS

Suggest three products or services that have resulted from or whose demand has increased as a consequence of changes in the socio-cultural environment.

 11.3 ## Key socio-cultural influences

Below is a list of some of the key socio-cultural influences that might affect organisations and which we will be looking at in this chapter. These include:

- health
- education
- class structure and social mobility
- families
- leisure interest.

Health

In this section we will look at some of the key trends in health and how our attitudes to health have changed over the years, as we adjust to the continuous demands of leading a socially and economically productive life. As we will see throughout this section, these trends are not isolated and have been influenced by other changes in the external macroenvironment.

Attitudes towards smoking have experienced significant change in the last decades. Although more women smoke now than before, the overall number of regular smokers dropped from 35 per cent in 1982 to 21 per cent in 2007 (see Figure 11.2).

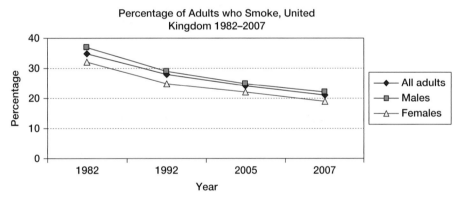

Figure 11.2 Percentage of adults who smoke, UK 1982–2007
(Source: Adapted from Office for National Statistics, 2007a)

Public opinion regarding smoking has also changed. Support for smoking restrictions at work increased from 81 per cent in 1996 to 86 per cent in 2003, while the proportion of people in favour of restrictions in restaurants moved up from 85 to 87 per cent over the same period.

CASE STUDY

Punch Taverns, Britain's largest pub company, experienced financial difficulties in 2008 as a series of events combined to keep customers away. These events include, among others, rising fuel costs, the economic downturn, the smoking ban (which came into force in July 2007) and low consumer confidence. (Ahmed, 2008; Andrews and Seib, 2008; Bawden 2009; Hassell, 2009).

CASE STUDY

There are indications that as a consequence of the smoking ban, the number of heart attack patients being admitted to emergency wards in England has decreased. Although rates of heart disease had been falling before the smoking ban, studies show that in the years following a smoking ban the number of people admitted to hospitals for heart disease decreases. According to studies conducted in Scotland and Ireland, which introduced the ban earlier, hospital admissions due to heart attacks fell by 17 per cent and 14 per cent respectively (Sources: Britton, 2009; Leake, 2009; Pavia, 2008).

Obesity is an issue that is currently the subject of intense debate. Some two thirds of men and almost 60 per cent of women are unhealthily overweight. In 1993, 13 per cent of men and 16 per cent of women in England were considered to be obese, but within just over a decade the number of obese men and women had already gone up to 23 per cent (see Figure 11.3). Almost 25 per cent of 4- to 5-year-olds and nearly a third of 10- to 11-year-olds were either obese or overweight. Experts predict that if this trend is not reversed, then by 2050, 60 per cent of men, 50 per cent of women, and 25 per cent of children will suffer from obesity (Rose, 2008).

KEY TERMS

Obesity is the presence of excess body fat, which frequently results in a significant harm to health.

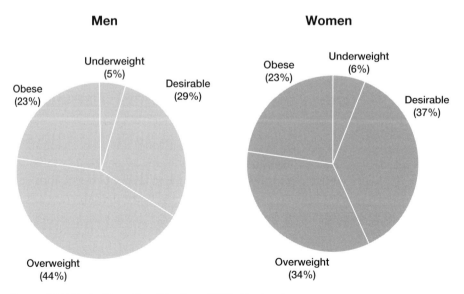

Figure 11.3 Body Mass Classification, 2004, England

Discuss what might be the causes for the increase in overweight and obese people in the UK. What changes in the socio-cultural environment do they reflect?

Since the mid-1970s, people in the UK have consumed less red meat in favour of more fish and poultry and have included what are considered to be healthier choices, such as organic food, in their diet.

An increase in real disposable income per capita has generated a demand for higher quality products. Research published by Mintel shows that one third of adults believe it is worth paying more for food that is organic, fairly traded or from local sources. The rise of celebrity chefs (notably Jamie Oliver and his campaign for better school meals) has also forced more information about nutrition into the public consciousness. The combination of these factors has brought about changes in the food supply industry. For example, Justin King, Sainsbury's chief executive, talks of 'a sea-change in customer attitudes' as customers opt for higher quality foods (Woods and Goodman, 2006).

The organisations listed in the left-hand column below are very different in size and scope. However, they are all affected by an increasing public concern regarding the consumption of healthy food. Consider the impact of these changes on each type of organisation.

Type of organisation	Impact of trend
A supermarket	
A primary school	
A fast-food restaurant	

Education

It is through education that we learn many of the skills, whether academic or practical, that set the ground for future learning or prepare us for working life. For increasing numbers of people, education does not simply mean compulsory education, as many more people participate in further and higher education (see Table 11.1).

United Kingdom								Thousands
	Men				Women			
	1970/71	1980/81	1990/91	2003/04	1970/71	1980/81	1990/91	2003/04
Further education[2]								
Full-time	116	154	219	532	95	196	261	548
Part-time	891	697	768	1,434	630	624	986	2,336
All further education	1,007	851	987	1,966	725	820	1,247	2,884
Higher education								
Undergraduate								
Full-time	241	277	345	543	173	196	319	664
Part-time	127	176	193	261	19	71	148	445
Postgraduate								
Full-time	33	41	50	110	10	21	34	111
Part-time	15	32	50	138	3	13	36	170
All higher education[3]	416	526	638	1,054	205	301	537	1,392
[1] *Home and overseas students. See Appendix, Part 3: Stages of education.*								
[2] *2003/04 includes 2002/03 data for further education institutions in Wales.*								
[3] *Figures for 2003/04 include a small number of higher education students for whom details are not available by level.*								
Source: Department for Education and Skills; National Assembly for Wales; Scottish Executive; Northern Ireland Department for Employment and Learning; Higher Education Statistics Agency								

Table 11.1   Students in further and higher education[1]: by type of course and sex

Although overall there has been an increase in the number of people enrolled in further and higher education, it is the number of female enrolments that shows the steepest increase. In the years between 1980/81 and 2003/04, female enrolments increased by more than four times.

This upward trend in enrolments in further and higher education indicates that the UK is becoming better educated and more highly skilled, which is a positive sign from a business point of view. However, a closer look at other education trends shows that there has been a decline in the number of applications to study science and engineering in higher education.

The availability of a pool of people with the right skills and qualifications has an impact on competitive advantage, not only at industry level but also at regional and national levels. The presence or absence of a large pool of educated people will influence an organisation's decision as to where to locate operations. The shortage of skilled workers in the UK has been, to some extent, one of the causes for organisations like Heinz and Kraft to move some of their operations to Russia, China and Eastern Europe (El Amin, 2007). On the other hand, India's relative abundance of English-speaking IT engineers has been one of the factors that have made the country the destination of choice for organisations looking to relocate or outsource information technology jobs.

Class structure and social mobility

A society's **class structure** ranks the population into social layers or classes according to factors such as family background, income and occupation. The main determinant of the categorisation by social class is the occupation of the main earner or breadwinner in a **household**. However, factors such as the increase in the number of double-income households and single-parent families make this classification more difficult. Social class provides a set category to group people, which allows us to make assumptions about the preferences of individuals within the same social class.

KEY TERMS

The General Household survey describes a **household** as a group of people who have the same address and share living accommodations and at least one meal a day.
Class structure refers to the way in which a society is organised in terms of the hierarchies in which a population is stratified according to status and social class.

Traditionally, British society has been divided into three main social classes:

- the upper class, which is composed of royalty, the aristocracy, and government officials, who in many cases have held wealth and/or power throughout generations, and business leaders who have made their money through work and achievement
- the middle class, which includes people in white-collar jobs. At the top end of the spectrum, we find people who are educated to a high level, i.e. professionals and managers, followed by skilled people such as nurses and teachers, and, at the bottom end of the spectrum, those in clerical jobs
- the working class, which is made up of individuals who perform manual work for a living.

The UK's class structure is said to allow less **social mobility** than that of other industrialised countries, for example Germany, France or Canada. Researchers from the London School of Economics found that in the UK children from poor backgrounds are more likely to continue the cycle of poverty. This means that it is more difficult for a person in the UK to change through work and achievements their social class and status than it would be for someone in other developed countries (Taylor, 2005).

KEY TERMS

Social mobility is the extent to which individuals within a given population can move out of the social class into which they are born.

Example

After starting his working life at the age of 16 as a metal worker in France, Pierre Bérégovoy became involved in politics and rose up the ranks of the socialist party to become Secretary General of the Presidency in 1981, Minister of Social Affairs in 1982, Minister of Economy and Finance from 1984–1986 and finally Prime Minister in 1992.

However, today's Britain is increasingly a classless society. The rapid expansion of further and higher education and the increased mobility of people for work, study and leisure has contributed to the breakdown of some of the traditional dissimilarities between people in different social classes and has led to more convergent preferences.

From a business perspective, social stratification affects business decisions such as which markets to target, and production location.

Families

Family life in the UK has changed considerably since the early 1970s. The number of marriages peaked in 1972, at 480,285 (see Figure 11.4). Since then, there has been an uninterrupted descending trend up to 2006 when there was a record low, of 275,140 marriages (Office for National Statistics, 2008c). According to the ONS this trend is likely to continue, with the proportion of married couples moving from 49 per cent in 2007 to a projected 41 per cent by 2031. (Office for National Statistics, 2009).

Overall, the number of divorces and cohabiting couples has showed an upward trend since the 1950s (see Figure 11.5). Between 1986 and 2005 the proportion of men and women under 60 who were cohabiting more than doubled from 11 per cent and 13 per cent respectively to 24 per cent.

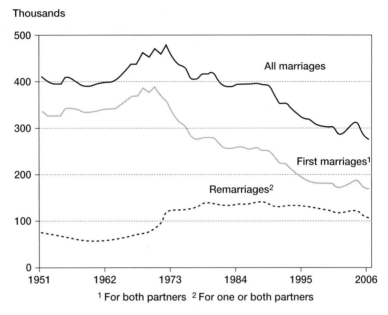

Figure 11.4 Marriages, United Kingdom, 1951–2006
(Source: Office for National Statistics, 2008c)

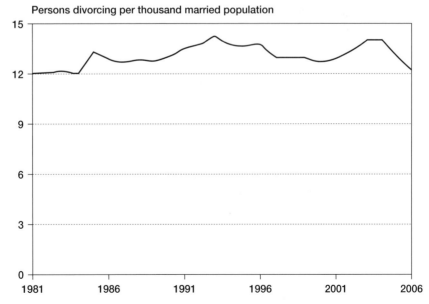

Figure 11.5 Divorce Rate England and Wales, 1981–2006
(Source: Office for National Statistics, 2008a)

Gender and age/year	1991	2001	2006
Men			
20 – 24	50	57	58
25 – 29	19	22	22
30 – 34	9	8	9
Women			
20 – 24	32	36	39
25 – 29	9	11	11
30 – 34	5	3	3
Source: Office for National Statistics, 2007b			

Table 11.2   Adults Living with their Parents by Sex and Age, England (percentages)

The number of divorces doubled between 1958 and 1968, and by 1972 this number had doubled again, peaking in 1993 at 180,000. The number of divorces dropped to 155,000 in 2000 but then increased from 2001 onwards to reach 167,000 in 2004. In 2005 and 2006 the divorce rate has fallen down to its lowest level since 1984 (Office for National Statistics, 2007b).

Although two-parent families still constitute the majority, they are no longer the norm and today children grow up in a wide range of families. Between 1971 and 2006 the proportion of children living with only one of their parents more than doubled from 3 per cent to 7 per cent (Office for National Statistics, 2007b).

Also there is an increased tendency for young men and women to continue living at home with their parents. Whereas in 1991 only 50 per cent of young men and 32 per cent of young women continued to live at home, by 2006 the figures had increased to 58 per cent and 39 per cent respectively (see Table 11.2).

Among the possible reasons for this trend are that more young adults stay at home while in education because of financial necessity, because they have difficulties entering the housing market, or because they are getting married at a later age. In 1971, the average age to get married for the first time was 25 for men and 23 for women. By 2005, the average age for first time marriages had moved to 32 for men and 29 for women.

Women are also waiting until later in life to have children, and when they do have them they are having fewer children. More women remain childless by the end of their fertile years, almost 20 per cent compared to 10 per cent of women born in the 1940s.

Leisure interests

People in the UK spend most of their time sleeping and working, and watching television, DVDs or videos, or listening to music. Men tend to watch TV or listen to the radio, practice sports or use a computer, while women tend to read or interact with others (Office for National Statistics, 2005).

Travelling abroad is a widespread leisure activity, with almost nine in ten air passengers at UK airports travelling internationally. Since the 1970s the number of foreign trips made by UK residents has shown an upward trend, and the figure has more than tripled since 1985 to a record 66.4 million foreign visits in 2005. These upward trends flattened most recently in 2001 following the 9/11 attacks and the foot-and-mouth crisis, but have since resumed. Two-thirds of these visits abroad were holidays, with Spain, France, and Greece remaining the most popular destinations for British tourists (Office for National Statistics, 2008b).

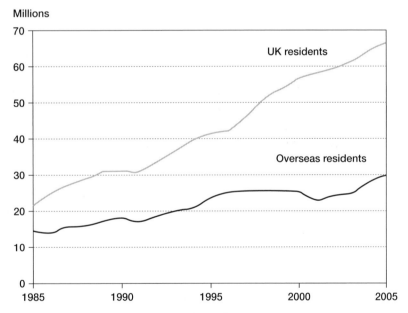

Figure 11.6 International visits to and from the UK, 1985–2005
(Source: Office for National Statistics, 2008b)

Current and emerging ethical and international issues in the socio-cultural environment.

Ethical issues

The new millennium has witnessed the rise of the ethical consumer. A growing number of people are increasingly concerned with causing less harm to the environment, and realise that their choices affect not only the environment but also other human beings. They not only demand to know where products are made, but also want to know how they are made, and who benefits in the process. All types of organisations, including banks, clothes retailers and supermarkets now need to provide for this new type of consumer.

CASE STUDY

The Cooperative Bank offers a wide range of ethical financial products. Both Topshop and Marks and Spencer have launched ethical clothing ranges. GAP, the American clothes retailer, has joined forces with U2's Bono and the Product Red Campaign to generate awareness and money to alleviate Aids/HIV in Africa. The Red campaign also includes other organisations such as American Express and Motorola. Sainsbury's sells fair trade bananas and Waitrose sustainable fish.

International airlines are replacing loyalty points with carbon points and charitable donations. With increasing concern about global warming, the airlines have decided to offer passengers carbon points based on the carbon dioxide emissions made by their flight and associated ground activities instead of loyalty miles.

These points can then be spent on green projects around the world, including forestry, energy efficiency and renewable energy programmes.

(Sources: Copping, 2007; Frary 2007; Leroux, 2009; Strimpel, 2007).

International issues

The liberalisation and deregulation of many national markets together with advances in information, communication and transportation technology are some of the factors that have led to globalisation. Globalisation has brought about increasingly convergent tastes, preferences and attitudes around the world. Worldwide, people wear branded or imitation sportswear, watch MTV and get fatter on fast food. However, even though some socio-cultural influences seem to follow global trends, deep cultural differences still remain across countries. Ignoring country differences in culture can lead to business failure.

CASE STUDY

Although increasingly many countries are embracing the material comforts of modern society and fast food is becoming more and more popular around the world, organisations need to make sure they respect and cater for cultural, including religious, differences. This was a lesson that McDonald's learned the hard way. Although the company had altered its burgers to vegetarian versions for the Indian market, it failed to reveal that animal fat was used to make its fries. When this information leaked to the public, it caused outrage amongst the Hindu community. The company had to apologise and change to a vegetable oil.

Differences in culture have an impact on an organisation's operations. Organisations need to have more **cross-cultural literacy** in order to respond and be able to adapt to the demands of international customers.

KEY TERMS

Cross-cultural literacy refers to an awareness and understanding of how cultural differences across and within nations can affect the way in which businesses operate.

CASE STUDY

Over the past decade Tesco has been enjoying international success, particularly in East European and Asian markets. The key has been to adapt to the market. The organisation spent years conducting thorough market research, which in some cases involved staff living with local families, in order to find out what customers want and how they shop. In Thailand's Tesco, although away from the heat of Bangkok's crowded markets, staff recreate the market experience by shouting out the prices of local fish and turtles. In China, shelves are stocked with a wide variety of rice and soya sauce, and at the opening of some stores staff gave away tissues – a luxury item in China.

Sir Terry Leahy, Tesco's CEO, said: 'The fact that we did not have a format we felt we could export overseas a decade ago has actually helped. We have had to be much more flexible.'

(Sources: Arlidge, 2008; Fletcher, 2006a; Fletcher, 2006b; Harlow, 2006; Macartney, 2007, Wighton, 2009).

Organisations need to determine to what extent their products and services need to adapt to international markets.

Example

IKEA furniture requires minimal adaptation between European markets. However, when the company entered the American market it found that perceptions of size and space were very different. Customers were buying vases to use them as drinking glasses!

ACTIVITY

Identify how much level of adaptation the following products/services might require for different international markets.

Product	Low level	Medium level	High level
Cars			
Sugar			
Personal computers			

Culture also has an impact on the values found in the workplace. Management processes and practices may need to vary according to culturally determined work-related values.

Probably the most famous study of how culture relates to values in the workplace was undertaken by Geert Hofstede (see Chapter 7). Hofstede's dimensions can have serious implications for management. Hospitals in America have experienced communication difficulties with Mexican nurses working in the country. Mexico scores high on Hofstede's power distance dimension, while the USA scores low. When an American doctor explains a procedure to a Mexican nurse, the nurse is more likely to say they have understood the instructions even if this is not the case because raising queries could be perceived as challenging the doctor's authority. On the other hand, coming from a culture with low power distance, the doctor will probably assume the nurse has understood the procedure.

11.5 Analysing the effect of current and future socio-cultural influences on organisations

In order to analyse the effect of socio-cultural influences on a particular organisation, the first step is to consider the elements of the socio-cultural environment and identify the relevant factors that apply to that organisation.

After the key factors have been identified, the next step is to analyse how each one of them impacts on the organisation, and decide whether it represents a threat that needs to be minimised or an opportunity that can be taken advantage of. When analysing socio-cultural factors you will find that they have varying degrees of importance for different organisations. For some organisations it might be education trends and work and career attitudes that are the most important, while for other organisations it might be health issues.

It is important not only to describe factors, but to think through what they mean and how they affect the organisation in the present and how their impact on the organisation might change in the future. Considering how and why the present is different from the past can be useful for your analysis.

ACTIVITY

Choose an organisation and, using the template below, analyse how the political environment impacts on your chosen organisation.

Top tips:
- Make sure you systematically consider each of the elements.
- Then, carefully analyse how each in turn might affect the organisation now and in the future.
- Assess the likely impact as high, medium or low.
- In light of your assessment, consider what action might be appropriate, for example, for any future trends that seem likely, you might wish to monitor the trend and/or prepare action plans for the organisation so it is ready to exploit opportunities or minimise any threats.

Factor	What is the current position?	What seems to be the current trend and why – give reason/s	Likely current impact on organisation: • high • medium • low	Potential future impact on the organisation: • high • medium • low	Suggested action:
Health					
Education					
Class structure and social mobility					
Families					
Leisure interests					
Any other relevant issues					

ACTIVITY

1 Identify which of the socio-cultural trends in the list below is most important for each organisation. Use arrows to indicate the connections.

Trend	Organisation
Composition of families	A hospital
Cigarette consumption	A wine importer
University enrolments by degree	A property developer

2 Write in each box which socio-cultural trends need to be considered by organisations providing the products or services listed below.

Product/service provided	Socio-cultural trend(s)
Higher education degrees	
Clothes retailing	
Food retailing	
Restaurants	

3 Conduct research and compare how education trends in the UK relate to those in other European countries.
4 Conduct research and provide examples of how different organisations have adapted their products or services to international markets.

(11.6) Summary

The socio-cultural environment affects organisations in different ways. By analysing the socio-cultural environment, organisations can spot trends and determine whether they are a threat or an opportunity for the organisation. The most successful organisations understand and adapt to socio-cultural trends.

The key socio-cultural influences studied in this chapter are health, education, class structure and social mobility, families, and leisure interests.

KEY IDEAS

Some of the main points covered in this chapter are listed below. If you feel unsure about any of them revisit the appropriate section. If you would like some additional reading on the topic try out the books listed below in recommended reading.

What do we mean by the socio-cultural environment?

- The socio-cultural environment refers to the values, attitudes, norms, and lifestyle of the population.

Key socio-cultural influences

- In the UK attitudes towards smoking have changed significantly in the past decades. The number of smokers has declined substantially, while the proportion of people in favour of smoking restrictions at work and in public places has increased.
- The number of overweight and obese children in the UK has increased over the last decades. However, the average diet now includes more healthy options and there is a demand for higher quality goods.
- There have been increases in the number of people, particularly women, participating in higher education.
- However, this increase is not spread evenly across subjects, and there has been a decline in the number of applications to study science and engineering.
- Traditionally, British society has been divided into three main social classes: the upper class, the middle class, and the working class. The UK's class structure is said to allow less social mobility than that of other developed nations.
- Family life in the UK has changed considerably since the early 1970s. There has been a continuous downward trend in the number of marriages, while the number of divorces and cohabiting couples has increased.
- People are getting married later in life, and women are waiting longer to have their first child. Although most children still live in a two-parent family, the number of those living with only one parent has increased over the past decades.
- Nowadays, people travel further and more often within the UK and abroad.

Current and emerging ethical and international issues

- Organisations need to take environmental and ethical issues into consideration. The new millennium has seen the rise of ethical consumers who demand products and services that are ethically produced and do not cause harm to the environment.
- Even though some socio-cultural influences seem to follow global trends, organisations operating in international markets need to be aware of the fact that deep cultural differences still remain across countries.

USEFUL WEBSITES

BBC – **www.bbc.co.uk**
Department of Health – **www.dh.gov.uk**
Department of Transport – **www.dft.gov.uk**
Geert Hofstede Cultural Dimensions for International Business – **www.geert-hofstede.com**

The Guardian – **www.guardian.co.uk**
Higher Education Statistics Agency – **www.hesa.ac.uk**
Mintel – **www.mintel.com**
Neighbourhood Statistics – **www.neighbourhood.statistics.gov.uk**
Office for National Statistics – **www.statistics.gov.uk**
The Times – **www.thetimesonline.co.uk**

REFERENCES

Ahmed, M. (2008) 'Smoking Ban Sends Punch Taverns Reeling'. *Times Online*, (online) 24 April. Available at: http://business.timesonline.co.uk/tol/business/industry_sectors/leisure/article3809693.ece.

Andrews, A. and Seib, C. (2009) 'Punch Taverns Delivers New Blow by Scrapping Dividend'. *Times Online*, (online) 4 September. Available at: http://business.timesonline.co.uk/tol/business/industry_sectors/leisure/article4670377.ece (Accessed 12 November 2009).

Arlidge, J. (2008) 'Tesco Express Rolls into China'. *Times Online*, (online) 13 April. Available at: http://business.timesonline.co.uk/tol/business/industry_sectors/retailing/article3671705.ece (Accessed 12 November 2009).

Bawden, T. (2009) 'Punch Taverns Offers Lessees the Opportunity to Buy Pubs'. *Times Online*, (online) 5 January. Available at: http://business.timesonline.co.uk/tol/business/industry_sectors/leisure/article5446972.ece (Accessed 12 November 2009).

Britton, J. (2009) 'Why Are Smoking Bans So Good at Cutting Heart Attack Rates? *Times Online*, (online) 27 September. Available at: http://www.timesonline.co.uk/tol/life_and_style/health/article6851189.ece (Accessed 12 November 2009).

Campbell, J. (1997) *Organisations and the Business Environment.* Oxford: Butterworth Heinemann.

Copping, N. (2007) 'All the Fun of the Fair Trade'. *Times Online*, (online) 8 January. Available at: http://women.timesonline.co.uk/tol/life_and_style/women/fashion/article1290007.ece (Accessed 12 February 2007).

El Amin, A. (2007) 'UK Skills and Employee Shortage Widens'. *Food navigator.com*, (online) http://www.foodnavigator.com/news/printNewsBis.asp?id=63181 (Accessed 12 February 2007).

Fletcher, R. (2006a) 'Inside the City: Tesco Ready for World Conquest', *Times Online*, (online) 5 March. Available at: http://business.timesonline.co.uk/tol/business/article737484.ece (Accessed 12 November 2009).

Fletcher, R. (2006b) 'Turtles and Toads Boost Tesco'. *Times Online*, (online) 5 March. Available at: http://business.timesonline.co.uk/tol/business/article737485.ece (Accessed 26 February 2007).

Frary, M. (2007) 'A Green Way to Get Rid of All Those Air Miles'. *The Times Business Travel*, 8 February, p.3.

Gaudoin, T. (2006) 'Mrs. Bono Saves the Day'. *Times Online*, (online) 2 December. Available at: http://women.timesonline.co.uk/tol/life_and_style/women/celebrity/article655140.ece (Accessed 12 February 2007).

Harlow, J. (2006) 'Tesco's Leahy is Wild about the West'. *Times Online*, (online) 3 September 2006. Available at: http://business.timesonline.co.uk/tol/business/industry_sectors/retailing/article626406.ece (Accessed 12 November 2009).

Hassell, N. (2009) 'Punch Drunk by Smoking Ban, Falling Sales and Soaring Costs'. *Times Online*, (online) 15 January. Available at: http://business.timesonline.co.uk/tol/business/markets/article5519631.ece (Accessed 12 November 2009).

Hill, C. (2006) *International Business: Competing in the Global Marketplace.* London: McGraw-Hill.

Hofstede, G. (2001) *Culture Consequences: Comparing Values, Behaviours, Institutions and Organisations across Nations.* London: Sage.

Leake, J. (2009) 'Heart Attacks Plummet After Smoking Ban'. *Times Online*, (online) 13 September. Available at: http://www.timesonline.co.uk/tol/life_and_style/health/article6832384.ece (Accessed 12 November 2009).

Leroux, M. (2009) 'Recession Fails to Dent Shoppers' Ethical Beliefs'. *Times Online*, (online) 13 October. Available at: http://business.timesonline.co.uk/tol/business/industry_sectors/retailing/article6872002.ece (Accessed 12 November 2009).

Macartney, J. (2007) 'Turtles Fill Trolleys as the Tesco Brand Enters China'. *Times Online*, (online) 27 January. Available at: http://business.timesonline.co.uk/tol/business/industry_sectors/retailing/article1265791.ece (Accessed 12 November 2009).

Office for National Statistics (2005) *Time Use Survey* (online). Available at: http://www.statistics.gov.uk/cci/nugget.asp?id=7 (Accessed 30 June 2008).

Office for National Statistics (2007a) *General Household Survey 2007: Smoking and Drinking Among Adults, 2007* (online) Newport: Office for National Statistics (Published 2007). Available at: http://www.statistics.gov.uk/downloads/theme_compendia/GHS07/GHSSmokingandDrinkingAmongAdults2007.pdf (Accessed 12 November 2009).

Office for National Statistics (2007b), *Social Trends* (online) Basingstoke: Palgrave Macmillan (Published 2007). Available at: http://www.statistics.gov.uk/downloads/theme_social/Social_Trends37/Social_Trends_37.pdf (Accessed 30 June 2008).

Office for National Statistics (2008a) *Divorces* (online). Available at: http://www.statistics.gov.uk/cci/nugget.asp?id=170 (Accessed 30 June 2008).

Office for National Statistics (2008b) *International Travel* (online). Available at: http://www.statistics.gov.uk/cci/nugget.asp?id=178 (Accessed 30 June 2008).

Office for National Statistics (2008c) *Marriages* (online). Available at: http://www.statistics.gov.uk/cci/nugget.asp?id=322 (Accessed 30 June 2007).

Office for National Statistics (2009) *Number of Cohabiting Couples Projected to Rise in England and Wales* (online) (Updated 31 March 2009). Available at http://www.statistics.gov.uk/pdfdir/marr0309.pdf (Accessed 12 November 2009).

Pavia, W. (2008) 'Heart Attack Admissions Fall by Up to 40 per cent since Smoking Ban'. *Times Online*, (online) 15 June. Available at: http://www.timesonline.co.uk/tol/news/uk/health/article4131177.ece (Accessed 30 June 2008).

Rose, D. (2008) 'One in Ten Children is Obese when Starting Primary School'. *Times Online*, (online) 24 June. Available at: http://www.timesonline.co.uk/tol/life_and_style/health/article4200903.ece (Accessed 30 June 2008).

Strimpel, Z. (2007) 'Are You an Ethical Consumer? *Times Online*, (online) 2 June. Available at: http://www.timesonline.co.uk/tol/money/consumer_affairs/article1867272.ece (Accessed 12 November 2009).

Taylor, M. (2005) 'UK Low in Social Mobility League, Says Charity'. *The Guardian*, (online) 25 April 2005. Available at: http://www.guardian.co.uk/britain/article/0,2763,1469685,00.html (Accessed 12 February 2007).

Western Union, www.westernunion.co.uk.

Wighton, D. (2009) 'Sir Terry Leahy Has Confounded His Critics Yet Again'. *Times Online*, (online) 7 October. Available at: http://business.timesonline.co.uk/tol/business/columnists/article6863857.ece (Accessed 12 November 2009).

Woods, R. and Goodman, M. (2006) 'Luxury Foods Fatten Up the Grocers' Profits'. *The Sunday Times*, 15 October, pp. 3–8.

12 The Macro Environment – Technological Influences

'Information technology and business are becoming inextricably interwoven. I don't think anybody can talk meaningfully about one without talking about the other.'

Bill Gates (1999)

CHAPTER OUTLINE

12.1 Introduction
12.2 What do we mean by the term 'technology'?
12.3 Key technological influences
12.4 Emerging ethical and international issues around the technological environment
12.5 Analysing the effect of current and future key technological influences on organisations
12.6 Summary

CHAPTER OBJECTIVES

After carefully reading and engaging with the tasks and activities outlined in this chapter, you should have a better understanding of:
- the term 'technology'
- key aspects of technological development
- the nature of the technological influences and their impact on organisations
- some of the ethical and international issues confronting organisations with regard to technology.

Introduction

The quotation at the beginning of the chapter refers to the way in which information technology (IT) and business are now linked. ICT facilitates easy and fast communication between organisations, their customers, employees, suppliers and other stakeholders. The internet allows us to access products and services offered by organisations '24/7'. However, it is not just businesses, but all organisations, such as the public sector and charities that have had their processes affected by IT. In the developed economies, new processes and products have evolved as a direct result of the use of IT.

Some refer to this way of working using IT and other new technologies as the third technological (or industrial) revolution, an acknowledgement of how today's ways of living and working are radically different from before their introduction.

REFLECTIVE QUESTIONS

1 What games does a 14-year-old play today? Ask your parents what games they played.
2 Where and how do you purchase things you need – food, clothes, DVDs and so on? Ask anyone over 50 years old how they used to acquire these things.
3 How are your university lectures and seminars conducted and how do you access information about your course? Compare this with the experiences of a student in a UK university in the1970s.

IT is just one form of technology, and although it may be the one that most people immediately think of when asked about technology, the term technology embraces other elements that will be identified and explored throughout the chapter.

The influence of technology is wide ranging in organisations and can influence all aspects, from developing/enhancing products and materials to administrative processes. Technology as an external influence has the potential to provide great opportunities or severely threaten organisations and industries. For example, a technological advance can simultaneously create the growth of one firm at the expense and decline of another.

Word processing led to the widespread use of personal computers (PCs), with companies such as, Dell computers, and PC World capitalising on this. At the same time, companies that produced electric typewriters saw their market decline significantly.

History tells us that if organisations do not keep up with technological advances they could find themselves overtaken by either or all of the following:

- competitors in the existing market
- new entrants to the market
- competitors taking the opportunity to enter a new market as the existing market declines
- new entrants taking the opportunity to enter a new market as the existing market declines.

CASE STUDY

Peter Wood, the founder of Direct Line insurance, caused a radical shake-up of the insurance industry. In 1985, Wood set up Direct Line insurance company, where for the first time in the insurance industry, the telephone was used to sell car insurance directly to customers. This was only made possible by the advent of IT. In fact, Wood had a background in IT, not the insurance industry. This mode of operation saved Wood paying for major overheads, such as offices. There was also no need for insurance brokers. These savings were passed on to the customer, with the added bonus of speed and simplicity. The strategy was successful, with Direct Line gaining 10 per cent of the insurance market within ten years. Direct Line is now the UK's number one direct car insurer, and has expanded its portfolio to include, among other things, travel, pet and home insurance.

(Sources: Bolton and Thompson, 2004; http://www.directline.com/about_us/history.htm, n.d.)

ACTIVITY

1 Find out what company Peter Wood started up in 2000.
2 Identify the changes in technology that have enabled this new type of operation to develop.

The two examples given demonstrated how technology, more specifically IT, could be both a strategic opportunity (for example the insurance industry) and also an organisational threat (for example, for companies making electric typewriters). To examine technological influences in more detail, this chapter will first of all explain what we mean by the term 'technology'. We will then examine the key technological developments, providing a historical context to the technological dimension, and go on to identify the key technological influences of concern for organisations. The impact of technology on organisations is considered, followed by an examination of technology in relation to: organisations and change, research and development (R&D) and employment. The chapter concludes by outlining some of the key ethical and international dimensions with regard to the technological environment.

 ## What do we mean by the term 'technology'?

We often refer to a product itself as a piece of technology. Technology is a broad term that refers to the application of science and/or knowledge for a specific purpose. In a business context that specific purpose might be the development and production of a product or service.

This expands the (perhaps popular, but misinformed) view that technology is just a reference to modern technology, and, in particular, information and communications technology. We can see that this widens the scientific input and application of knowledge to all kinds of fields – not just electronics – in creating products and processes.

So, we can see that taking our explanation 'application of science and/or knowledge' in the full sense of the meaning, that technology is concerned with the development of:

- materials
- products
- processes.

Any such developments, e.g. innovative product features of existing products/materials or new products/materials, will lead to technological change. This type of change is closely linked to the key relationship between technology and research and development. Process technological change concerns innovations in how products/materials are made and how organisations are managed. It is important to point out the nature of transferability in the 'application of science and/or knowledge' to materials, products and processes, so that innovations or progress in one field can affect another, for example:

- improvements in materials can shape product development
- improvements in products can shape process development.

Key technological developments

The concept of technology in terms of materials, products and processes has been around for a long time. When we think of technology today, the more contemporary developments such as PCs, the internet, microchips, robots and biotechnologies may spring to mind. If we look back, we can see technology, in terms of materials, products and processes, has evolved over time. It could be said that there are three key technological (or industrial) revolutions that can be identified.

Era	Impact
Late 1700s	*First technological revolution:* • the steam engine revolutionises production methods • human labour replaced by machinery in production processes • significant changes in the textile industry, with machinery involved in the production of cotton.
Mid 1800s	• railroads • steel production.
Beginning in the 1900s (developed throughout the century).	*Second technological revolution:* • use and development of chemicals • combustion engine • electricity powers machines giving rise to assembly lines and the continuous flow of production.
Beginning in the mid- 1900s (developed throughout the century and continuing development in the 21st century).	*Third technological revolution:* • computing and information technologies revolutionise work patterns and transform tasks • lasers • microchips • biotechnology, e.g. genetics • robots • the internet • electronic-based computing and information technologies revolutionise work patterns by transformation of tasks • optic fibres • nanotechnology • renewable energy • artificial intelligence.

Table 12.1   The three key technological revolutions

REFLECTIVE QUESTIONS

1 How can individuals or organisations gather information about any new technological innovations?

Key technological influences

Some of the key technological influences on organisations are those that were developed in the latter half of the twentieth century, some of which are continuing to be developed (e.g. IT) and those more recently developed (e.g. nanotechnology, currently at early stages of development).

We will now identify and examine some of these key technological influences and look at how they impact on organisations.

Technology and the impact on organisations

Technology and innovation go together hand in hand. As a direct result of any form of technological innovation relating to product, process or material, organisational processes such as research, design, production, marketing, management systems, personnel requirements and administration will require changes.

Technology and change

Technological advances have led to new products and processes, such as:

- creation of a new product, e.g. developments in motion and gravity sensors made it possible for the Nintendo Wii
- enhancement of an existing product (added or improved features, improved quality), e.g. developments in laser technology made it possible for Blu-Ray enhanced photo and audio quality
- changes in methods of production, e.g. developments in robotic technologies made possible robotic assembly lines for car manufacturing
- changes in distribution methods (see Table 12.2)
- changes in the storage and dissemination of information (see Table 12.2)
- changes in administrative processes (see Figure 12.1).

Technological change can offer a new strategic direction for an organisation, or involve changes to operational procedures.

It is useful then to consider the main sources of technology change.

Figure 12.1a Early steam engine

Figure 12.1b Car assembly line, mid-twentieth Century

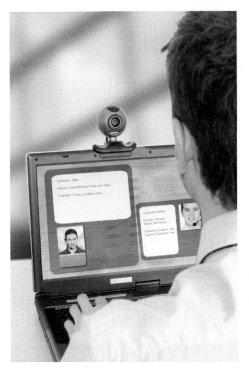

Figure 12.1c Staff in different geographical locations can communicate via webcam

A main source of technology change – IT

The field of IT includes products such as: mobile phones, faxes, internet and world wide web, personal computers (PC), video conferencing and email.

The most recent wave of this type of technology has had an ever increasing and dramatic effect on the way we work and indeed in our personal lives. Developments have transformed the industrial landscape, where some products are in severe decline as result of technological change, e.g. DVD has largely replaced the production of the video. On the other hand, there have been enormous opportunities allowing for the introduction of new types of industries, i.e. the creation, development, production and sale of electronic games such as PlayStation 3 and Xbox 360. IT has made possible almost instant communications globally – a key feature of the rapid rate of globalisation over the last 25 years. At times, technology developed for one purpose can end up being used for a different one. If we take the example of Facebook, this phenomenon has occurred more than once.

It is unlikely that Mark Zuckerberg imagined when he started his networking site that it would develop into the global phenomenon we know as Facebook. Creative uses of the site were probably not considered when Facebook was

CASE STUDY

Facebook, established in 2004 by Mark Zuckerberg and his fellow students while still at Harvard University, is a worldwide social networking site. Originally, the website was set up for and used by Harvard University students. It later expanded its membership to other Ivy League universities in the USA. As Facebook developed and its reputation grew, membership extended to University students across the world. Currently, anyone aged 13 or over can join.

At its inception, Facebook was competing with the already established MySpace and Bebo, which at the time were growing social networking sites. By 2009, however, a survey by Compete.com placed Facebook firmly as the number one most popular global social networking site, having the most users worldwide. Social networking is now an integral part of many people's daily lives.

Facebook is now being used by some organisations for somewhat different purposes other than *social* networking. Some colleges in the UK are using social networking sites such as Facebook to keep students informed about courses and help keep them in touch with the staff. As a result, one college feels that student retention rates have improved, with fewer students dropping out. Other colleges have piloted the use of Facebook as a way of letting students know about deadlines for their work. Is this just the beginning of alternative uses for social networking sites – what lies ahead?

(Sources: Bunz, 2009; Coughlan, 2009; Kazeniac, 2009)

first established, either. As we will see later, Facebook is also being used in the services sector as well as by colleges.

IT developments can impact on organisations in many ways. Table 12.2 highlights some of the key areas.

CASE STUDY

IT – the impact on the services sector
Experience of IT in the hotel sector

Initially, two key developments transformed activities in hotels – Electronic Point of Sales (EPOS) and Universal Registration system (Global Booking Systems). Other technological developments continue to change the hotel industry in terms of organisational and customer behaviour.

Electronic Point of Sales (EPOS)

Developments such as EPOS have allowed guests' purchases in hotels to be logged in real time to their accounts automatically. Originally in hotels, data was collected manually from all individual service points – reception, restaurant and bars – and recorded on guests' accounts. The advent of the computer and software systems allowed for developments such as EPOS to replace the electro-mechanical till systems with an efficient, reliable, comprehensive integrated till system in the hotel reception, bars and restaurant, for sales, stock control and purchases. This is used to manage resources and to assist

continued . . .

◀ *. . . continued*

in the smooth flow of accurate information, from a guest checking into the hotel, to using the facilities right through to checking out.

Universal Registration system (Global Booking Systems)

The telephone and fax used to be the main technological tools for booking hotel bedrooms, conferences and banquets. Over time, a sophisticated system evolved.

The advent of the computer initially allowed for a Computerised Booking and Billing system – which only recorded the guest's arrival, length of stay and personal details. Then there were three notable advances in technology, which significantly altered the way hotels marketed and organised bookings and how customers accessed information about hotel rooms and services and made bookings. These were:

- First, the connection of the Computerised Booking and Billing to a billing platform via a small in-house telephone exchange, to record and charge to the room any telephone calls made by the guest.
- Second, this was further developed and connected into the hotel's EPOS system.
- Third, the internet revolutionised modes of operations. In 1998, globally five per cent of total hotel bedroom bookings were online – the majority of these within the USA. The prediction at the time was that within ten years, 95 per cent of all hotel bookings – bedrooms, conferences and banquets – would be online. Four systems developed worldwide, into what was then known as a central booking and reservation system. Booking systems were connected to the internet. The major hotel chains operated via a global distribution system (GDS). Smaller hotel companies could link into the GDS. This resulted in individuals being able to access the hotel site via the internet directly and make a booking online from anywhere in the world.

Recent developments

Hotels now use e-marketing (e.g. via email) to inform people about their offers and services. Since 2008, as a further development to hotels' integrated websites, pages have been opened on Facebook and Twitter as a marketing tool. The aims include: to assist in the flow of information, to advertise special offers, target special interest groups (e.g. student alumni) and generate loyalty. There are early indications that this type of marketing is effective in generating new business. It also allows smaller independent groups to compete globally with the major players.

The effect of this technology has made operations easier and more efficient, providing more secure and accurate information. Although staff need training to use the equipment (and constant updating) this is normally straightforward and supplied by the software suppliers. The costs incurred have not been significant when measured against the benefits achieved.

(Source: Interview with a director of an independent hotel in the UK)

1 In what ways has technology allowed small independent hotel groups to compete globally with major hotel chains?
2 In what way do you think video conferencing could impact on the hotel industry? (You might want to consider other external PESTLED elements here, and identify if any developments in any of those elements might influence any increase in the need to use video conferencing).

Area of impact	Effect on organisations:
Administration	• computer systems led • electronic offices • administrators require IT skills.
Storage and Distribution of physical goods (e.g. stock)	• computerised stock control • just-in-time methods • electronic point of sale (EPOS) links to stock control.
Storage and Distribution of information	• data storage largely electronic, moving towards the paperless office • information sent electronically (email) • information given/retrieved on the internet • generation of sales electronically to an increasing global market, decreasing need for the traditional physical store to display goods for sale.
Communication	• email allows for quick communication, all across the world (time differences not a problem as emails are asynchronous) • faxes can be sent and received instantly, and can be used as legally binding documents, speeding up many organisational processes • video conferencing allows people in different geographic locations to meet up and see each other on screen to conduct meetings • webcams • social networking sites used for sales marketing.
Production	• Computer Aided Design (CAD) allows for speedy and accurate design and redesigning of products.
Electronic Funds Transfer at Point of Sale	• credit or debit cards can be used in most retailers, whereby funds from the bank are transferred directly to the retailer.
Management	• Management Information Systems (MIS) can be used to track stock on a hourly basis, so management are aware of which products are selling and which are not. This can assist management in deciding stock levels (making sure that revenue is not lost because of over-stocking or under-stocking of an item).
(Source: Adapted from Worthington and Britton, 2006)	

Table 12.2   Key impacts of IT on organisations

The case study highlights the transformation in one sector due to technology – in terms of how services are operated, and how as customers we book and find out about services.

REFLECTIVE QUESTIONS

The experiences highlighted in the hotel sector with the advances of IT are similar to that in many sectors.

1 Think about a holiday or short trip that you have been on. How did you find out about it?
2 How did you book it? Did you travel by rail or by plane? If so, how did you make that booking?

ACTIVITY

Consider the following technological innovations and list all applications for their use that you can think of:

a) bar coding – use in retailing and in industry
b) Robotics – use in industry
c) video conferencing – use in industry and in academia.

Artificial intelligence

Artificial Intelligence (AI) refers to a branch of computer science that aims to create intelligent machines or, as referred to in layman terms, a computer that can think for itself.

You have probably seen pictures or clips on television of robot assembly plants manufacturing cars – but as sophisticated as the technology of these robots is on these assembly plants, the robots are only performing a narrow range of tasks. To even begin to try and simulate something as complex as the human brain in order to create intelligent machines involves a highly complex array of different types of systems and programming. For this reason, this area of technology is in the early stages of development. One of the key aims for future development is the creation of a humanoid robot – to turn into reality the intelligent machines featured so often in many of our science fiction books and films.

It is likely that there is a long road ahead for artificial intelligence. Should this technology become available, professional and organisational life may change radically.

1 Identify two industry sectors that you think will undergo significant changes with the introduction of 'humanoid' robots.
2 List operational changes you think will occur in these two sectors. Give reasons for your answers.
3 List new strategic opportunities for organisations and potential threats.

REFLECTIVE QUESTION

What do you think the world would be like if 'humanoid' robots became a part of everyday life?

Biotechnology

The OECD in 2005 offered a provisional single definition of biotechnology as:

'The application of science and technology to living organisms, as well as parts, products and models thereof, to alter living or non-living materials for the production of knowledge, goods and services' (OECD, 2005).

The applications of biotechnology are broad – including uses in medicines, agriculture and food science – and will change over time. Table 12.3 gives some examples of the applications of biotechnology. This list is certainly not exhaustive, it merely identifies some biotechnological applications to provide some examples.

The importance of the biotechnology sector in the UK is reflected both in terms of the research and development undertaken and of the high levels of investment currently made in that sector.

Nanotechnology

Nanotechnology is concerned with the scientific study of structures and materials that are extremely small. For example, they would usually have at least one dimension that was less than 100 nanometres (nm). To put this small size into context, a strand of your hair is about 80,000 nm wide. In simple terms, nanotechnology is the process whereby materials and machines are created that operate at the nanoscale. Because of its potential, nanotechnology attracts more state funding than all other areas of technology.

Figure 12.2 Robot serving drinks

Biotechnology	Use
Genetic engineering	For example, genetically modified (GM) crops may help increase food production, by decreasing the susceptibility of the crops to disease and harm from pests.
Gene therapy	Identification and replacement of defective genes in humans, plants and animals.
Bioinformatics	Construction of databases on genomes Modelling complex biological processes.
Nanobiotechnology	Applies processes of biotechnology at the nano level (See section on nanotechnology, below.) (OECD, 2005)

Table 12.3   Example of applications of biotechnology

KEY TERMS

Nanotechnology involves the creation of new methods of manufacturing, controlling matter at an atomic scale. It is often referred to as the field of nanotechnologies because of the wide variety of different materials and technologies involved. The potential for application of nanotechnologies is in a variety of fields, including IT, electronics and medicine.

This form of technology creates totally new ways of thinking and making products, referred to as **disruptive** solutions.

The term **disruptive** is used to describe a process when previous methods of production have been made obsolete by newer more advanced methods.

Nanotechnology is one of the most recent technologies and is in the early stages of development. Nanotechnologies offer great potential to:

- benefit society, industry, environment and health
- create much faster computer systems
- improve the quality of life by better diagnosis and treatment of disease
- reduce air, water and land pollution
- respond to key issues of the day such as climate change by possibly contributing to energy efficiency and storage.

It is acknowledged that at this early stage in the development, research needs to be conducted into nanotechnologies in order to fully understand both the potential benefits and potential harms. (Department for Innovation, Universities and Skills, 2008).

1 Define the term 'technology'.
2 Explain what we mean by technology.
3 Outline the key technological developments.
4 Highlight some of the key applications of IT in organisations.
5 Distinguish between biotechnology and nano technology.

Technology and research and development (R&D)

We can ask the question 'how has much of this technological change come about?' One answer is via **research** and **development**.

KEY TERMS

Research can either be applied or theoretical (pure).
When research conducted is used in a production process, we refer to this as **development.**

R&D is undertaken in different institutions, and can be differentiated by the method of funding and by end use criteria (theoretical or applied).

	R&D
Universities	● most of the pure (theoretical) research undertaken in the UK ● funded by the public sector
Private Sector	● mostly applied R&D undertaken ● design of new product/feature and new production process which will enhance profitability ● funded by the companies themselves

As technological innovation can lead not only to an organisation's economic growth, but also a nation's, the amount of R&D undertaken is crucial.

In the EU:

● Total R&D expenditure for 2002 was almost 2 per cent of GDP for the EU member states
● In the Business and Enterprise sector in 2001, at least 55 per cent of R&D expenditure was funded by the sector itself in most of the EU member states. (European Commission, 2005)

Technology and employment

Technology can offer both opportunities and threats in terms of employment.

Opportunities:

- in new industries, for example, electronic gaming industry
- in designing, updating and maintaining technological systems for products and services
- training, due to possible shortages in the labour supply of sufficiently skilled employees.

Threats/challenges

- job losses in declining industries (old technologies being replaced by new ones)
- in changes to the type and level of skills requirement of employees (leading to training and potential additional cost).

Figure 12.3 Staff are trained to use new technologies

Emerging ethical and international issues around the technological environment

There are both costs and benefits to technological development. Often, the perspective taken is from an individual viewpoint.

REFLECTIVE QUESTIONS

1 Do you view technological developments as being good for humankind?
2 Do you take the view that technological progress is causing problems for humankind?
3 Or, is the answer to the above questions dependent on specific technological developments? If so, what are they?

Emerging ethical issues around the technological environment

Ethical issues can be weighed in terms of costs against the (perceived) benefits of technology. It is likely that both biotechnology and nanotechnology could impact positively on our lives – but can anyone really say at what cost? Any risk analysis or cost-benefit assessment may be made with business interests underpinning them. Is it possible to produce purely objective assessments? It may be that strong independent bodies are needed to advise the policy and regulator makers (Government bodies) to ensure due process.

The five main ethical concerns relating to technology are discussed next in terms of costs and perceived benefits.

1 The potential effects on the environment – via polluting technological processes and products, and concern about waste disposal.

The development, process, use and disposal of technology often contributes to environmental degradation, such as use of non-renewable resources, pollution and global warming. Although these negative environmental impacts are generally considered to be a threat to the balance of our ecosystems and to humankind in general, they can also present opportunities for organisations in the field of technological innovations to overcome these problems, for example, in renewable energies such as wind, solar and water power. There are added opportunities for organisations to contribute to more sustainable methods of production (for more about this, see Chapter 14).

Costs:	(perceived) Benefits:
• pollution • global warming • waste disposal e.g. plastics, nuclear, toxic waste.	• economic growth • increased living standards • technology may have been the cause, but technology (with sufficient R&D and investment) can contribute to the 'cure'.

2 Contributing to the diminishing stock of natural resources – with particular concern for the world's stocks of fossil fuels (for more about this see Chapter 14).

Costs:	(perceived) Benefits:
• decreasing natural resources.	• economic growth • increased living standards • contribution to creation of renewable energy.

3 Contributing to unemployment levels and potentially creating a monotonous and/or stressful working environment (as discussed above in the section on Technology and employment).

4 Potential for harmful unknown/side effects of developing technologies such as, the bio- or nano-technologies.

Costs:	(perceived) Benefits:
• GM products could possibly affect other non GM crops, • and/or lead to health problems which have not yet been identified • fear that some side effects may be as yet unknown.	• food technology may help provide abundant quantities of reasonably priced food, needed for the world's growing population • many potential benefits for humankind.

5 Technology – overload and change.

Costs:	(perceived) Benefits:
• information overload • identity fraud • exploitation of vulnerable groups on the internet • surveillance technology threatening civil liberties creating 'Big Brother' syndrome	• allows for global communications 24/7 • allows flexible employment patterns • surveillance technology protecting civil liberties

Costs:	(perceived) Benefits:
● technology creating constant change referred to as 'waves of change' that employers and employees are finding difficult to cope with.	● improved technological processes and communications.

While there are no clear-cut answers to some of the above ethical debates, some of the fear lies in 'fear of the unknown', the fact that the outcomes of using some of these technologies long term are not yet fully understood. The pragmatic approach is to carefully assess the risks and the benefits, and in light of the absence of full scientific knowledge, proceed with caution (i.e. do not introduce any new science and/or technology if there is a *possibility* that the costs outweigh the benefits, even if there is no scientific evidence yet available to demonstrate that this is so).

Emerging international issues around the technological environment

The increase in globalisation has been in part due to the benefits of IT. Organisations can now be in constant contact with their employees, customers, suppliers and other stakeholders, and vice versa, they can all be in contact with the organisation.

Technology has been a major feature of economic growth – and hence increase in living standards – as characterised by countries such as USA, Japan and some countries in Western Europe. The relationship between the two is such that the more that economic growth occurs the more technological development there is.

The technology gap between developed and developing economies is one of concern. Some envisage that this divide will decrease between nations, although it must be pointed out that to close the technological gap, a combination of 'low tech' and 'high tech' solutions are needed.

Technology:	Developing countries:
New technologies/ 'high tech'	● need to adapt to new technology (do not have to be world leaders, can be followers) ● potential to wait for new discoveries to become less expensive.
'low tech', e.g. simple farming tool	● incremental development to help people out of poverty, particularly in agriculture.
(Source: Adapted from Wetherly and Otter, 2008)	

Creating conditions for advances in technology to occur in developing countries is generally agreed as the way to narrow the gap between 'rich' and 'poor' nations.

REFLECTIVE QUESTIONS

1 What is the role of research and development in technology?
2 What is the relationship between technological advancement and employment?
3 In what way does technology impact on the environment?
4 In what way can technology play a role in reducing world poverty?

12.5 Analysing the effect of current and future key technological influences on organisations

In order to analyse the effect of the technological influences on a particular organisation, we need to consider the technological elements and identify which are the relevant factors that apply to that organisation.

After the key factors have been identified, the next step is to analyse how each one of them impacts on that organisation and decide whether it represents a threat that needs to be minimised, or an opportunity that can be taken advantage of. When analysing technological influences you will find that they have varying degrees of importance for different organisations. For some organisations it might be the level of IT developments that is most important, while for other organisations it might be the impact of developing technologies, such as nanotechnology or artificial intelligence. The impact of potential technological developments also may need to be considered.

It is important not only to describe factors, but also to think through what they mean and how they affect the organisation in the present as well as how their impact might change in the future. Considering how and why the present is different from the past can be useful for your analysis.

ACTIVITY

Choose an organisation and, using the template below, analyse how the technological environment impacts on your chosen organisation.

Top tips:
● Make sure you systematically consider each of the elements.
● Then, carefully analyse how each in turn might affect the organisation now and in the future.

- Assess the likely impact as high, medium or low.
- In light of your assessment, consider what action might be appropriate, for example, for any future trends that seem likely, you might wish to monitor the trend and/or prepare action plans for the organisation so it is ready to exploit opportunities or minimise any threats.

Technological element	What is the current position?	What seems to be the current trend and why – give reason/s	Likely current impact on organisation: ● high ● medium ● low	Potential future impact on the organisation: ● high ● medium ● low	Suggested action:
IT					
IT – Communications					
IT – MIS					
Artificial Intelligence					
Biotechnology					
Nanotechnology					
Low-carbon technologies					
Renewable energy					
Emerging ethical issues					
Emerging international issues					
Other relevant technological developments or issues					

Table 12.4 Template for analysing the effect of current and future key technological influences on organisations

12.6 Summary

The chapter began by outlining the importance of technology to organisations. The quote at the beginning of the chapter highlighted the inextricable link between business and information technology, where it was acknowledged that information technology was just one form of technology, and that technology embraced many other forms. Not only businesses, but all forms of organisation such as public sector and charities, that have been affected by IT.

The term technology was explained and the key technological developments highlighted. The chapter went on identify key technological influences and their impact on organisations. The key technological influences on organisations were examined and the need for organisations to respond to these influences highlighted. In addition to strategic opportunities and threats, the implications of technology in terms of organisational change, research and development, employment and the environment were briefly examined. The chapter concluded by pointing out some emerging ethical and international issues around the technological environment.

KEY IDEAS

Some of the main points covered in this chapter are listed below. If you feel unsure about any of them, then revisit the appropriate section. If you would like some additional reading on the topic, try the books listed below in recommended reading.

What do we mean by the term 'technology'?
- The term technology is explained as basically, the application of science and/or knowledge to the development and production of a product or service.
- Technology is concerned with the development of materials, products and processes.

Key technological developments
- The word technology is sometimes interpreted to mean contemporary technology such as IT, PCs and world wide web. However, this is a misconception as there have been significant technological developments in the past.
- Three key technological (industrial) revolutions were identified: first one in the late 1700s, the second one in the beginning of the 1900s and the third one beginning in the mid-1900s and continuing development in the twenty-first century.

Key technological influences
- Technology impacts on organisational change in terms of potential changes to products, methods of production, distribution methods and administrative processes.
- Change can be strategic or operational.
- Main sources of current and potential future technological change:
  - IT in terms of administration, stock controls, communication, production, sales information and MIS
  - Biotechnology, in terms of genetic engineering, gene therapy bioinformatics and nanobiotechnology
  - Nanotechnology ('engineering at a very small scale') is one of the more recent technological innovations. It is considered to offer great potential to benefit society, industry and health.
  - Artificial Intelligence a term we associate with 'robots'. Rather than go into detail about AI, the chapter asks you to think about what the shape of the world might be if AI was developed and there were 'humanoid' robots as part of our normal every day life..

continued . . . ▶

◀ | *. . . continued*

- The majority of technological change arises from research and development undertaken.
- Research can be applied or pure (theoretical).
- Development is the application of research in the production process.
- Technology can pose both opportunities (such as new industries) and threats (such as job losses) to employment.

Some emerging issues

- There are both costs and benefits to technological development. Often, the perspective taken is one from an individual viewpoint.
- The main ethical issues with regard to technology concern matters such as the environment, patterns of employment, constant change, potential for unknown/harmful side effects and information overload.
- There are no clear cut answers to these issues, but much of the fear lies in 'fear of the unknown'.
- A pragmatic approach is to carefully assess the risks and benefits, and in the absence of scientific knowledge, proceed with caution.
- Technology plays a significant role in economic growth and helping to raise people's living standards.
- Technology is needed by developing countries to narrow the gap between 'rich and 'poor' nations.
- 'High tech' refers to new technologies, whereas 'low tech' refers to a simple form of technology, such as a simple farming tool. People in developing countries can use 'low tech' for incremental development to help lift them out of poverty.

RECOMMENDED READING

You might like to consider the following title.
Worthington, I. and Britton, C. (2009) *The Business Environment*. 6th edn. Harlow: FT Prentice Hall, Chapter 7, pp.171 – 185.

USEFUL WEBSITES

Health and Safety website on nanotechnology: **www.hse.gov.uk/horizons/nanotech.htm**

REFERENCES

Bolton, B. and Thompson, J. (2004) *Entrepreneurs: Talent, Temperament, Technique*. 2nd edn. London: Butterworth Heinemann.
Bunz, M. (2009) 'After Social Networks, What Next?' *The Guardian*, (online) 24 November. Available at: http://www.guardian.co.uk/media/pda/2009/nov/24/future-of-social-networks-twitter-linkedin-mobile-application-next (Accessed 25 November 2009).

Coughlan, S. (2009) 'Facebook "cuts student drop-outs"' *BBC News*, (online) 13 October. Available at: http://news.bbc.co.uk/1/hi/education/8299050.stm (Accessed 25 November 2009).

Department for Innovation, Universities and Skills (2008) *Policy Document: Summary Statement Nanotechnologies* (online) Department for Innovation, Universities and Skills. Available at: http://www.di us.gov.uk/~/media/publications/S/summary-statement-nanotechnologies.pdf (Accessed 26 November 2009).

European Commission (2005) *Research Headlines: Sustained Growth in R & D Expenditure in Most EU 25 Nations* (online) 14 March. Available at: http://ec.europa.eu/research/headlines/news/article 05 03 14 en.html (Accessed 26 November 2009).

Gates, B.(1999) *Business at the Speed of Thought* (e-book). Available at: http://www.freewebs.com/net-ebooks/New per cent20Book/BusinesstheSpeedof per cent20ThoughtSucceedingintheDigitalEconomy muya.pdf (Accessed 19 November 2009).

Kazeniac, A. (2009) *Social Networks: Facebook Takes over Top Spot, Twitter Climbs* (online) 2 February. Available at: http://blog.compete.com/2009/02/09/facebook-myspace-twitter-social-network/ (Accessed 30 November 2009).

OECD (2005) *Directorate for Science, Technology and Industry* (Statistical definition of Biotechnology) (online) (Updated 2005). Available at: http://www.oecd.org/document/42/0,3343, en 2649 34537 1933994 1 1 1 1,00.html (Accessed 19 May 2008).

Wetherly, P. and Otter, D. (2008) *The Business Environment: Themes and Issues*. Oxford: Oxford University Press.

Worthington, I. and Britton, C. (2006) *The Business Environment*. 5th edn. Harlow: FT Prentice Hall.

http://www.directline.com/about us/history.htm (n.d.) (Accessed 26 November 2009).

13 The Macro Environment – Legal Influences

'*Obedience of the law is demanded; not asked as a favour*'.

by Theodore Roosevelt (26th President of USA from 1901–1909)

CHAPTER OUTLINE

13.1 Introduction
13.2 What do we mean by the term 'legal'?
13.3 Key legal influences
13.4 Emerging ethical and international issues around the legal environment
13.5 Analysing the effect of current and future key legal influences on organisations
13.6 Summary

CHAPTER OBJECTIVES

After carefully reading and engaging with the tasks and activities outlined in this chapter, you should have a better understanding of:

- the two main sources of law
- the nature of the English legal process
- the nature of the legal environment and its impact on organisations
- some of the ethical and international issues in the legal environment that confront organisations.

 ## 13.1 Introduction

The quotation at the beginning of the chapter tells us very firmly what our relationship is to the Law – we must obey the law. If we do not, a penalty for not doing so will be imposed. This is via the nation's legal processes – in the UK for example, that might be a warning, fine, community service or a custodial sentence, depending on the severity of the breach of law. There are laws that affect individuals, organisations and nations.

For organisations, the quotation at the beginning of the chapter indicates that laws must be obeyed and, again, failure to comply with laws will result in sanctions against the organisation such as fines and in extreme cases, custodial sentences for individuals within organisations. In that sense, it is important to be fully aware of existing laws affecting organisations, and to be fully compliant.

Example

In 2007, a UK broadcasting company was fined £1 million by the broadcasting regulator. This was over phone-in competitions in which potential winners were found to have been chosen before the lines were closed (ofcom, 2007).

Laws can constrain organisational activity by enforcing standards, for example, Health and Safety, or by demanding compliance to ever increasing environmental issues, for example, Environmental and Climate Change Laws. It can also provide a framework for existence. In addition to which, the legal environment provides organisations a framework within which they can achieve their objectives.

The influence of the legal environment on organisations is extensive and it would be an impossibility to identify and examine all legal influences on organisations here. Rather than attempting to give a comprehensive description of UK legislation in all its forms, this chapter focuses on some of the implications of the legal environment that impact on business.

The chapter also raises awareness of the legal environment in terms of the opportunity and threats posed to organisations in general terms, as it would be unhelpful to even attempt to provide specialised legal information, which might mislead or be inadequate. We must emphasise here that law is a highly specialised field. In fact, for specific legal data and advice, organisations themselves either have their own law departments or subcontract certain legal areas to law specialists.

What do we mean by the term 'legal'?

The term refers to those aspects of life that falls under the jurisdiction of the law. The law can be said to be rules and morals of a society codified into regulation. Laws differ from country to country.

Example

An Act passed in 1984 in the USA required all states to increase the minimum age at which you could purchase alcohol to 21. In the UK, however, currently you have to be 18 years old to purchase alcohol. (See The Licensing Act 2003, which applies to England and Wales, and the National Minimum Drinking Act of 1984, USA).

Figure 13.1

The law affects all areas of human activity. As business is a part of human activity, business is affected by laws, which can offer opportunities or constraints just like the rest of the macro external elements.

Competition law (see also Section 13.3) can act as a framework that enhances competition and also one that could constrain large organisations thought to be abusing their market position. If an organisation is found by the Office of Fair Trading (OFT) to be guilty of abusing market power, the OFT can impose fines on the organisation.

KEY TERMS

Competition law ensures that large companies cannot abuse their market power, thereby protecting the free market and competition.

Deregulation of an industry occurs when the industry becomes free from government power or controls. The rationale behind this concept is that the market should regulate businesses and industries rather than Government. Hence deregulation is a mechanism to create more competition in the market place.

The example below shows an opportunity for the banking industry brought about by financial **deregulation**.

Example

In 1986, financial deregulation, which had been a key aim for the Thatcher government, allowed banks to offer a wide variety of financial services that had previously been the domain of other industries, such as building societies and insurance firms. Financial deregulation allowed banks to sell mortgages, life assurances and pensions. By the same token, the financial deregulation meant that building societies could offer banking services.

The law is closely linked to the political and economic environment of a country. It is generally agreed that the more economically developed a country is, the more laws pervade every aspect of society – hence, in a business context, there will be more laws regulating business activity than in less economically developed nations.

Closely linked to the political environment is the legal environment. The legal environment can be considered within the political environmental element, and is done so in many academic textbooks. In the UK however, the legal system is highly developed with the legal framework enveloping much of human activity. Business is one of the many human activities regulated by the law. Thus, organisations of all sizes in all sectors are both constrained by the law and also able to achieve their goals via operations conducted within that legal framework. As such, the legal environment can have a major impact on organisations and their ability to achieve their objectives. Hence, we consider that it warrants inclusion as a full macro environmental element, rather than an inclusion in the political element – to which it is closely linked.

Before identifying types of legal influences, we need to understand:

- the meaning of the term **law**
- the two main sources of law.

Then we will go on to identify the key areas in which the law affects organisations.

The meaning of the term 'law'

The development of law in a nation is dependent on the historical, economic and cultural (including religious) contexts of that nation. From the time humans began living in groups, social rules governed behaviour. Over time, more complex communication patterns and language developed. As groups of humans living together became larger, and more complex, more and more social rules governed behaviour. As societies developed many accepted social norms and values became codified into law.

KEY TERMS

In England, we could say that **law** is a set of rules laid down either by custom, practice or statute, which enforces standards of behaviour.

Rules of law need to be formulated (the role of the Executive, part of which is the Government of the day), passed (the role of Parliament) and enforced (the role of the judiciary). The law is not static and changes in response to societal expectations, world events, environmental developments as well as political influences, such as pressure groups.

The two main sources of law

The two main sources of law are **common law** and **statute law**, outlined in Table 13.1.

Source of law:	Derivation:	Referred to/also termed:
Common law	Is largely based upon judgements made in court. A decision/ judgement in a case can then set a precedent for future decisions in that area/context.	May be referred to as judicial precedent.
Statute law	Is largely derived from **Acts of Parliament**	Is also termed 'legislation'.

Table 13.1   Outline of common and statute law

New laws

There is usually a time lag of the accepted issues of the day being codified into regulations and law. There are two key reasons for this:

- society generally takes time to come to some agreement and thereby to instigate the legal process to formulate new laws
- the legal process itself can be lengthy.

Legal process in England

Common law and statute law are derived from the Courts and Parliament respectively. It is useful, therefore, to have some knowledge of these processes. (Further reading is recommended at the end of the chapter if you would like to explore this further.)

Acts of Parliament

Parliament undertakes many roles, but a key role in England is the debating and passing of statute law, which we can refer to as legislation. The majority of new laws (or changes to existing laws) are introduced by the government (however, there are exceptions where an MP or Lord can introduce a law, e.g. Private Member's Bill). Before a draft law (known as a **Bill**) is introduced (see Figure 13.2) there would have been much preliminary consultation, discussion and debate with interested parties (e.g. environmental pressure groups interested in any forthcoming environmental laws, or charity organisations interested in social justice laws).

KEY TERMS

An **Act of Parliament** is a bill that:

- has been enacted by Parliament
- has received Royal Assent
- represents the highest law of the land (except in cases where it is overridden by the EU).

A **Bill** is a proposal for a new law, which if passed becomes an Act of Parliament and a new law.

Bills may apply to:

- England (only)
- one or more parts of the UK, for example England and Wales
- the whole of the UK.

A forum for introducing proposed Laws is via the Monarch's Speech in the **State Opening of Parliament**. The speech is read annually by the monarch, seated on the Throne, in the House of Lords.

Although the speech is delivered by the reigning monarch, the Government of the day draws it up. The content is, in essence, an outline of the Government's proposed legislative programme – and is therefore linked to the prevailing political influence of the day. It also contains the Government's proposed policies for the forthcoming parliamentary session. Proposed changes to existing legislation and proposed introduction of new laws undergo set Parliamentary procedures.

Figure 13.2 The Queen addressing the State Opening of Parliament

KEY TERMS

State Opening of Parliament signals the beginning of a new Parliamentary session (generally one year – November to November). The ceremony is elaborate (dating from 1852) and contains the Monarch's Speech (a tradition that dates back to the sixteenth century).

Example

In November 2007, the Queen unveiled the Government's proposed legislative programme (Bills) for the forthcoming programme. The key areas of legislation were in the areas of anti-terrorism, measures on climate change, healthcare, nuclear power, education and training and housing (29 bills and draft bills in all).

Paper	Roles
Green paper	• consultation paper • outlines draft versions of Government proposals (i.e. not fully formed) • asks for public comment before finalised version is formed.
White Paper	• the proposed legislation.

Table 13.2   Changes to existing legislation and proposed new legislation

Bills for consideration may well include the updating of legislation already in existence, which has been found through practice and interpretation to be less effective than required.

A Bill is published to allow consultation and thorough examination before formal introduction to the Parliament (either House of Lords or House of Commons)

It is usually considered by specialised committees to allow MPs or Members of the Lords to contribute or influence the Bill (this is known as pre-legislative scrutiny).

1 If a statute is passed by Parliament, which party's political ideology of the time is likely to triumph? Give reasons for your answer.

We must also consider **Statutory Instruments**.

KEY TERMS

Statutory Instrument (or secondary legislation) is legislation that:

• can be put into place quicker than statute law
• can be drawn up by a Member of Parliament
• has a role in EU directives finding themselves in UK Law via Statutory Instrument.

CASE STUDY

The long-delayed EC directive on Waste Electrical and Electronic Equipment (WEEE) regulations came into force in the UK in 2007. This requires distributors and producers to make arrangements for disposing of appliances and gadgets. By re-using and recycling equipment, these regulations aim to decrease the amount of these products ending up in landfill sites.

These regulations make producers responsible for:

- collection
- treatment
- recovery of old/waste electrical equipment.

The regulations also make distributors of electrical equipment allow consumers to return their old/ waste equipment, with no charge for the service (Source: Adapted from http://www.berr.gov.uk (n.d.)).

In addition to knowledge of existing laws and their likely impact on organisations, new legislation that could affect the organisation needs to be closely watched and developments followed. It follows that the Parliamentary system must be understood and closely monitored. All impending legislation needs to be known and those with potential impact on organisations identified. Then a thorough analysis of the likely impact of these on the organisation in question should be conducted.

ACTIVITY

Using the website www.parliament.uk:
- Read the content of the latest Queen's Speech.
- From the proposed draft Bills, choose two that are likely to have an organisational impact.
- Analyse the organisational impact.

The courts

Law is enforced through the courts system. In England, there are several courts of law, with differing functions and tasks. (see Table 13.3 below).

KEY TERMS

Civil matters refer to issues such as those dealing with **contract** (an agreement between two parties) and **tort** (which concerns laws for compensation: these are as a result of any harm committed where one party either threatens to or actually causes harm to the interests of another party, such as negligence, or trespass). This can be contrasted with criminal law which deals with any harm committed against society, for example murder or theft.

Name of court	Roles
House of Lords	• Highest Court of Appeal for Domestic Matters (note the influence of the European Court of Justice). • Decisions are binding in all the other courts (judicial precedent). • Appeals from the Divisional Courts, the Court of Appeal and (under certain circumstances) directly from the High Court.
Court of Appeal – civil	• Second highest Court of Appeal. • Bound by decisions of the House of Lords. • Decisions bind lower courts. • Hears appeals from defendants against decisions of the County Court and the High Court. • Could also hear appeals against decisions made in tribunals, for example Employment tribunals.
Court of Appeal – criminal	• Second highest Court of Appeal. • Bound by decisions of the House of Lords. • Decisions bind lower courts. • Hears appeals from defendants against decisions of criminal cases of the Crown Court (there are exceptions). • Sentences or convictions could be reviewed.
High court – Queens Bench division – Chancery Division – Family Division (Chancery and Family divisions hear appeals of cases from the Magistrates' Court and (to a lesser extent) the Crown Court as appropriate to their division)	• Divided into three parts. • Deals with **Tort** and **Contract** law. • Contains courts to deal with commercial matters (amongst others). • Judicial review. • Deals with Equity matters. • Contains courts to deal with Patents and Appeals from the commissioner of the Inland Revenue (among others). • Deals with matrimonial matters. • Matters involving children.

▶

Name of court	Roles
County court	<ul><li>First line approach for **civil matters.**</li><li>Established to provide an inexpensive way of settling smaller civil disputes.</li><li>Covers areas such as company insolvency, bankruptcy, divorce, contested wills, tort, contract, trusts, mortgages and partnerships.</li><li>For cases of claims less than £25,000.</li><li>Claims of £25,000–£50,000 may be heard or sent to the High Court.</li><li>Higher amounts are heard in the High Court</li></ul>
County Court – Small Claims division	<ul><li>Hears cases of claims for less than £3,000 (costs are generally not expensive and are usually linked to sums in the case in question).</li></ul>
Crown court	<ul><li>Found mainly in boroughs and county towns.</li><li>Is primarily a criminal court (with some civil jurisdiction).</li><li>Deals with more serious cases – such as homicide.</li><li>Hears sentence or conviction appeals made by the Magistrates Court from defendants found guilty.</li></ul>
Magistrates court	<ul><li>In the area of general criminal matters, where they deal with approximately 95 per cent of criminal cases. (However, serious criminal matters are passed to the Crown Court for trial.)</li><li>Covers minor offences.</li><li>Decides on verdict and sentence.</li><li>Deals with contraventions of either Consumer Protection or Trade Descriptions laws.</li></ul>

Table 13.3   Summary of the key English courts

In addition to the court system there are **tribunals** and further governmental bodies created to give legal access in order to either address disputes between parties (for example, employment tribunals), or give increasing protection to consumers such as trading standards and environmental health departments.

KEY TERMS

Tribunals have been established by various Acts of Parliament to hear particular types of cases. They can exercise a judicial role, in which case they behave very similarly to a court. In an organisational context, the Employment tribunals and the Employment Appeal Tribunal are most significant.

Tribunals normally consist of three people, one of whom is legally qualified – the chairperson.

Advantages:	Disadvantages:
• waiting time to hear a case at a tribunal is likely to be shorter than would be a court case	• lack of court procedure and processes
• tribunal costs are likely to be lower than court costs (self representation is possible here)	• lack of legal representation
• generally there are no court fees	• lack of legal aid, may prevent some claimants finding appropriate representation should they so desire
• losers of cases do not usually have to pay costs to the winners of the case	• courts and Council of Tribunals control tribunals
• tribunal proceedings are informal – which allows for self representation	• courts have the power to reverse decisions of tribunals in certain circumstances (i.e. if the law has been applied incorrectly).
• tribunals will have technical expertise, for example the chairperson of an employment tribunal will be a lawyer whose expertise lies in employment law.	

Table 13.4   Advantages and disadvantages of tribunals

It is generally put forward that tribunals offer some advantages and disadvantages, shown in Table 13.4.

CASE STUDY

Outlined below are the key points of a tribunal outcome of the sacking of a journalist with a newspaper, who lost a claim for unfair dismissal.

Key features of the case:

Points of view: the journalist	Points of view: the newspaper
• was dismissed abruptly after 13 years' service to the newspaper • initially found about the sacking via email	• acknowledged that in view of the journalist's length of service, the decision should have been better handled and communicated

continued . . . ▶

◄ *. . . continued*

Points of view: the journalist	Points of view: the newspaper
• received a formal letter from the newspaper a few days after the email • was left distressed by the heartless manner of the dismissal • had worked hard for many years • although a freelance journalist, had been constantly available for the newspaper over the years.	• had regarded the journalist as self-employed – not a staff member of the paper.

The outcome:

- The claimant was unsuccessful and the case was dismissed. The reason given was that the claimant was a self-employed freelance journalist, not an employee of the paper.
- Hence, due to the nature of the contract – irrespective of the way the claimant was dismissed – the paper had the right to terminate the contract and inform the journalist that services were no longer required.

(Sources: Milmo, 2001; Harding, 2001 and The Guardian By Agencies, 2001.)

As can be seen in the case study, the nature of the contract was the key to the outcome of the case, regardless of the perception of the claimant of the terms of employment over the years.

Environmental health departments are run by Local Authorities and deal with matters affecting health including food (for example, food considered unfit for consumption), hygiene standards in shops restaurants and catering establishments.

Consumer complaints reported to **environmental health** departments, such as food poisoning thought to be contracted from the consumption of food at a restaurant, are investigated. Any similar complaints will be considered and a portfolio of evidence may be gathered in order to lead to a prosecution, or even close down the offending catering premises.

1 Access the website of the environmental health department in your local authority.
2 List at least five key areas the department provides services for.
3 Examine in detail the sections identified, looking at environmental health practices (look at jurisdiction, inspection and complaints procedures and any others you can find).

4 Assess the likely impact of an environmental health department (high, medium or low) on the following, giving reasons for your answer:
- a 150-bed hotel with conference and banqueting facilities for 300 people
- a small biosciences laboratory.

Trading standards departments are run by County Councils. They have the authority to investigate complaints made by consumers including:

- inaccurate weights and measures
- false or misleading prices
- consumer credit
- safety of consumer legislation to trading standards.

Trading standards officials visit businesses in the hospitality industry to check weights and measures.

CASE STUDY

In autumn 2008, officials from the trading standards came to the premises of a UK hotel. It had been reported that large quantities of unbranded gin and vodka were being sold in the area as premium-branded products. Not only were the offenders deceiving the public, but as the alcohol by volume ratio of the unbranded product was reported to be up to 25 per cent lower in some cases, the HM Revenue and Customs was also being deceived. In this case, tests conducted on all the bars at the hotel proved that the premises had only the original branded products, which therefore contained the correct alcohol by volume ratio. Anyone caught offending the trading standards in a case like this would face severe penalties.

(Source: Interview with a director of an independent hotel in the UK)

The national law, plus any supra-national laws which supersede laws of the land, can affect organisations in different ways. Key areas of interest for organisations are identified in Section 13.3. Various sources can be used to access information:

- case and statute legislation
- consultations with specialist law firms
- trade magazines
- trade conferences
- legal, business and finance sections in broadsheet newspapers
- websites such as www.personneltoday.com; www.parliament.uk; www.parliament.uk/commons/index.cfm; www.acas.org.uk.

In addition to dealing with current laws, organisations need to be aware of impending legislation and of recent case law. The website www.personneltoday. com or the press, e.g. *The Times* legal section are useful resources for monitoring the progress of potential legislation. Keeping up to date with this area of the external environment enables organisations to take advantage of any opportunities presented, or to minimise the likely impact of any threats posed by future legislation.

 ## 13.3 Key legal influences

There are a number of areas within which business is influenced by the legal environment. Organisations' relationships include those with customers, suppliers, employees and competitors. These relationships are to some degree influenced by the current laws of the land. Organisations are also presented with regulatory frameworks with respect to their environmental impact (as discussed in Chapter 14). It would be impossible to address all the regulations and laws that do, or could impact on organisations in this chapter. Some are highlighted as examples.

The key legal influences on organisations include those in the areas of employment, health and safety, consumer rights, copyright and patents, the increasing number of environmental laws and regulations and competition. We highlight some of the key features of each of these here, to give a flavour of what the laws and regulations cover, and where appropriate, the penalties that can be applied for non-compliance.

Employment

The relationship between employer and employee is governed by **Law of Contract.**

The employer has a duty of care to his/her employees. If the employer breaks this duty of care, then the employee can sue the employer for negligence (termed 'tort of negligence').

The employer is also held accountable for the action of his/her employees – hence, in the course of duty, negligence by an employee which results in a member of the public suffering harm or injury, can result in the injured party making a claim against the employee and also against the employer (this may be termed 'vicarious liability').

In addition to the Laws of Contract are employment laws that govern various areas of employment practice and offer employees protection against unfair dismissal and poor employment practices (such as during recruitment).

Disciplinary and Grievance procedures have elements of both statutes (see Table 13.7, page 306) and **Statutory Instruments,** for example the Dispute Resolution Regulation 2004.

Protection against all kinds of discrimination is offered via anti-discrimination laws, for example, the Disability Discrimination Act 1995. (For further examples see Table 13.7.)

KEY TERMS

Law of Contract is in essence an agreement between two (or more) parties, which can be verbal or written. A contract consists of the following key elements: offer, acceptance, consideration, intention to create legal relations and capacity (see Figure 13.6) and can be legally enforceable.

CASE STUDY

To comply with the minimum requirements of the Disability Discrimination Act 1995, an independent 54-bedroom hotel, banqueting and conference centre in the UK was required to install a number of ramped areas to avoid stairs and steps. Where it would have been impractical to install a ramp or lift, it installed new facilities in more accessible parts of the complex. The cost to the company was around £30,000.

(Source: Interview with a director of an independent hotel in the UK)

Law of contract

An organisation conducting day-to-day operations will have contracts with various groups, such as suppliers, customers and employees. The contract is likely to be an agreement where one party agrees to do something in exchange for money (or payment of some kind, not necessarily financial). In this context a contract of agreement could be to:

- buy (or supply) goods or services
- propose employment
- supply finance.

A relationship between the organisation and parties does not represent a legal relationship unless it is evident, or can be proven, that a contract between the two parties exists, as shown in Table 13.6.

Some key aspects with regard to contracts need to be considered. A contract must be legal and reached voluntarily in order to be enforceable by law. Additionally, there must be a genuine agreement. Hence, any contracts with mistakes or misrepresentation of facts may, depending on the circumstances, be voidable.

Figure 13.3 An organisation will have contracts with suppliers, customers and employees

Elements required for contract status:	Key points:
Offer*:	<ul><li>declaration by one party (termed 'the offeror') that they intend to be legally bound to terms stated in the contract (offer) if it is accepted by the other party (termed 'the offeree')</li><li>the declaration can be verbal or written</li><li>the declaration must be clear and unambiguous.</li></ul>
Acceptance:	<ul><li>must be made by the party to whom the offer was made (offeree)</li><li>must be clearly and resolutely communicated.</li><li>must be on the original offer and cannot have any new terms or conditions added.</li><li>a contract exists as soon as an offer is accepted (see all elements in this table to ensure criteria is met): both sides are then legally bound.</li></ul>
Consideration:	<ul><li>essential in most contracts</li><li>used in a legal sense of benefit</li><li>in essence, parties agree to do something in the future</li></ul>

▶

Elements required for contract status:	Key points:
	• in an organisational context this will most likely take the form of a cash payment in return for any provision of goods or services
Intention to create legal relations:	• offer and acceptance must be made in a situation which clearly show the parties involved intended the relations to be legal • in many organisational agreements there is, generally, a presumption that both parties intended to make a legally binding contract • a party (offeror or offeree), who wishes to refute this presumption, has the onus to disprove it and produce evidence accordingly.
Capacity:	• adults (individuals and organisations) generally have the capacity to make contracts between them • contractual capacity is not accorded to minors or those with mental disorders (here, the law is offering protection to vulnerable people).

Table 13.6 Elements required for contract status

(*Offers are different to 'invitation to treat', which is in essence, as the name suggests, an invitation to make an offer. This includes advertisements and goods on display. It also covers auctions.)

KEY TERMS

Consideration can be defined as 'some right, interest, profit or benefit accruing to one party or some forbearance, detriment, loss or responsibility given, suffered or undertaken by another', as in Currie v Misa (1875) LR IO E x 153. So consideration is the exchange of promises – for example, 'I promise to give you £4,500 and you promise to give me that car'.

1 What legal instrument governs the relationship between employers and employees?
2 An employer owes a duty of care to their employees. What could the employee do if this duty of care by the employer (to their employees) was broken?
3 Is an employer held accountable for the action of their employees?

4 What key areas do Employment Laws govern?
5 Define the term contract law.
6 What six elements need to be present in a contract?

Health and safety

Laws and regulations relating to health and safety are wide ranging. They chiefly govern the employer's duty to provide a healthy and safe working environment.

The Health and Safety at Work Act 1974 provides the basis for the majority of the health and safety Laws and regulations. The Health and Safety (Offences) Act 2008 amends part of the Health and Safety at Work Act 1974 to give tougher penalties – from increased fines to custodial sentences – for breaches of health and safety.

ACTIVITY

Do you know of any companies that have breached Health and Safety Laws? Conduct some research and find out about the various types of cases – you can do this by typing in 'Health and Safety Breaches' into a reliable search engine.

Consumer rights

Since the latter half of the twentieth century there has been increasing legislation that gives protection to the consumer. Legislation is there to give protection to the consumer (where the consumer is seen as the weaker party and thus in need of protection, as opposed to business to business relationships, which are viewed as a more equal partnership). Legislation includes trade descriptions of goods and services, statement of price, sales of goods and consumer protection.

The UK Government requirement to implement an EU directive resulted in enactment of The Consumer Protection Act 1987, which gives the consumer who suffers harm to themselves or their property, as a direct result of the goods or services purchased being defective, the right to claim damages.

Copyright and patent

Organisational assets are measured both in terms of tangible (land, building and finance) but also the intangible (brand, research and development in new and innovative areas). Legal protection is provided so these intangible assets cannot be copied. Protection is provided in the area of **patents** and **trademarks.**

REFLECTIVE QUESTIONS

1 Think of the opportunities that increasing Health and Safety legislation might have for organisations.
2 List the consumer rights you think you have. Conduct some research and find out more (e.g. try the site www.consumerdirect.gov.uk/).

KEY TERMS

A **patent** of a product, usually applied for by the inventor, gives the owner of that patent the exclusive right, over a particular period in time, to reap any benefits accorded to the product.
A **trademark** is any reproducible sign – such as a logo or a brand name – that clearly enables distinction of one product (good or service) from another.

ACTIVITY

We live in a world where even young children are aware of brands. Think of your day so far. What did you eat and drink? What are you wearing? What type of phone are you using? The list is endless. . . In just the course of one normal day, how many different brands and trademarks can you identify?

Environmental impact of organisational operations and strategies

This is an expanding area of UK legislation. Legislation is provided to combat pollution and toxic waste disposal. Increasing global attention to aspects such as climate change, are driving further legislation in environmental areas.

1 Identify the proposed environmental legislation in the Queen's Speech.
2 Identify proposed environmental regulations and directives.
3 Assess how these, if brought into force, could impact on the strategies and operations of organisations in:
- the retail sector
- the manufacturing sector
- the health sector.

Competition

In many Western economies, such as the UK and USA, there is an assumption that the free market is the most efficient way in which to conduct economic affairs, where society will be best served in the tasks of allocation of scarce resources (i.e. decisions of what to produce, how and to whom should it be distributed – as discussed in Chapter 10). Laws exist to foster competitive and free markets. They are there to prevent non-competitive practices.

The Competition Act 1998 (which came into force on March 1st 2000) contains two main elements, which forbid organisations to:

- abuse a dominant market position
- have any form of anti-competitive agreements.

Any organisations found to be in breach of these laws:

- can have financial penalties applied. These could be up to 10 per cent of turnover (UK) for up to 3 years' trading
- can be sued for damages by both customers and competitors.

In addition to which, there is an aim to prevent anti-competitive behaviour. The Director General of Fair Trading has been awarded new powers to intervene and prevent anti-competitive behaviour at the outset. (BERR, 2008).

ACTIVITY

Visit the Office of Fair Trading website (www.oft.gov.uk) and make a note of the organisations that have been investigated and ultimately sanctioned for breach of competition law.

Key Acts

The aim of the following section is not to list all the Acts that can affect organisations: this would be impossible to do within the confines of this chapter. The aim is to raise awareness of some of the key areas where existing legislation impacts and, hence, where forthcoming legislation needs to be monitored in particular.

Some sector specific examples are also provided, including those involved in the Provision of Food and in the Financial Sector.

Business and Management area	Existing Key Statutes
Employment Law	<ul><li>Employment Rights Act 1996 (This act contains most of the law on individual employment rights)</li><li>National Minimum Wage Act 1998</li><li>Data Protection Act 1998</li><li>Public Interest Disclosure Act 1998</li><li>Employment Act 2002 (includes Disciplinary and Grievance)</li><li>Employment Act 2008</li></ul>
Discrimination	<ul><li>Sex Discrimination Act 1975</li><li>Sex Discrimination Act 1986</li><li>Equal Pay Act 1970</li><li>Race Relations Act 1976</li><li>Race Relations (Amendment) Act 2002</li><li>Disability Discrimination Act 1995</li><li>Disability Discrimination Act 2005 (see elements of The Human Rights Act 2000)</li><li>Equality Act 2006</li></ul>
Trade Union (right to representation)	<ul><li>Trade Union and Labour Relations (Consolidation) Act 1992 (This act contains most of the law on collective employment rights)</li><li>Trade Union Reform and Employment Rights Act 1993</li><li>Employment Relations Act 1999, and 2004</li></ul>
Health and Safety	<ul><li>Health and Safety at Work Act 1975</li><li>Control of Major Accident Hazards Regulation 1999</li><li>Health and Safety (Offences) Act 2008</li></ul>
Consumer Rights	<ul><li>Trades Description Act 1968</li><li>Consumer Credit Act 1974</li><li>Sale of Goods Act 1979</li><li>Consumer Protection Act 1987</li></ul>
Copyright and patent	<ul><li>Copyright, Designs and Patents Act 1988</li><li>Patents Act 1997</li><li>Trade Marks Act 1994</li></ul>
Environmental impact of organisational operations and strategies	<ul><li>Environment Act 1990</li><li>Environmental Protection Act 1995</li><li>Climate Change and Sustainable Energy Act 2006</li></ul>
Competition	<ul><li>Competition Act 1998</li></ul>
Food Sector	<ul><li>Food Safety Act 1990</li></ul>
Financial Sector	<ul><li>Financial Services Act 1986</li></ul>

Table 13.7

13.4 Emerging ethical and international issues around the legal environment

Ethical issues arise from the fact that different countries have different laws.

Ethical issues

As a result of the different laws in different countries, the question and dilemma posed to organisations is: How does an organisation operate across countries that have differing standards and laws in key areas, such as the environment, employment practices, health and safety standards, copyright and patent laws and competition?

For example, a UK-based company could operate in a country that has fewer environmental laws and regulations than in the UK. The company must decide whether to comply with these lower environmental standards only, or operate within the same environment standards (higher and, most likely, more costly) that apply to the UK.

Countries sometimes differ in their approach to organisational issues due to different historical, economic, religious and cultural contexts or different regulatory contexts.

For example, in the case of staff selection, equal opportunity underpins employment practice in the USA, UK and other western economies. However, working with friends and family is often the favoured option in China, India and other eastern economies. Regulations concerning child labour vary hugely.

Despite differences, there are universal values that are shared by all countries. There have been attempts to codify such shared values and publish them in a universal guide. (The Universal Declaration of Human Rights 1948). (See www. un.org/geninfo/faq/humanrights/hr2.htm)

The different ethical standards and values in different countries raise difficulties in the area of international business ethics. The implications are principally the concerns of organisations trading across nations, such as multinational companies.

There are two key main approaches to international business ethics:

● ethical universalism (there is only one set of moral principles determining right and wrong, which can and should be universally applied)
● ethical relativism (there are no universal rights and wrongs, but different moral judgements, made by more than one set of individuals, or culture, and that they may all have right on their side). (McEwan, 2001.)

Figure 13.4 Countries have laws and regulations in place to prevent child exploitation

Some argue that if there are no universal codes, then if country A has poor pay and working conditions, or low health and safety or environmental standards, then what is to stop multinational companies relocating there and exploiting country A? On the other hand, critics of universalism, point to the danger of 'ethical imperialism', where one set of values is imposed on a society.

REFLECTIVE QUESTIONS

International Business Ethics arises from differences in laws and standards, as well as different values and beliefs, between countries. Think about the advantages and disadvantages of:
- ethical universalism
- ethical relativism.

International issues

If the laws are the same in nations across the world, another problem in the international arena is the differing levels of law enforcement in different countries. For example, a lack of law enforcement in some countries has contributed to the growing trade in piracy of goods.

(13.5) Analysing the effect of current and future key legal influences on organisations

In order to analyse the effect of the legal influences on a particular organisation, we need to consider the legal elements and identify the relevant factors that apply to that organisation.

After the key factors have been identified, the next step is to analyse how each one of them impacts on the organisation, and decide whether it represents a threat that needs to be minimised, or an opportunity that can be taken advantage of. When analysing legal influences you will find that they have varying degrees of importance for different organisations. For some organisations it might be the level of environmental legislation and regulation that is most important, while for other organisations it might be the impact of judicial precedent. The impact of potential future legislation also may need to be considered.

It is important not only to describe factors, but also to think through what they mean and how they affect the organisation in the present and how their impact might change in the future. Considering how and why the present is different from the past can be useful for your analysis.

ACTIVITY

Choose an organisation and, using the template in Table 13.8 below, analyse how the legal environment impacts on your chosen organisation.

Top tips:
- Make sure you systematically consider each of the elements.
- Carefully analyse how each in turn might affect the organisation now and in the future.
- Assess the likely impact as high, medium or low.
- In the light of your assessment, consider what action might be appropriate. For example, for any future trends that seem likely, you might wish to monitor events and/or prepare action plans for the organisation so it is ready to be able to exploit opportunities or minimise any threats.

Legal element	What is the current status?	What seems to be the trend? Why – give reason/s	Likely current impact on organisation: ● high ● medium ● low	Potential future impact on the organisation: ● high ● medium ● low	Suggested action:
Green paper					
White paper					
Bills					
EU Directives					
Regulations					
Recent tribunal judgements					
Emerging ethical issues					
Emerging international issues					
Other relevant legal issues					

Table 13.8 Template for analysing how the legal environment impacts on an organisation

 ## Summary

The chapter began by outlining the relationship between organisations and the law. It was pointed out that the law must be obeyed by organisations and that laws present organisations with constraints and opportunities.

The term 'legal' was clarified. The chapter then considered the meaning of the term 'law', identifying common law and statute law as the two main sources of law. It went on to describe the legal process in England. The key legal influences on organisations were examined, with examples given on the impact they have had on organisations and the need for organisations to respond to these influences highlighted. Finally, the chapter presented the complexity of these issues, pointing out some emerging ethical and international issues around the legal environment.

KEY IDEAS

Some of the main points covered in this chapter are listed below. If you feel unsure about any of them revisit the appropriate section. If you would like some additional reading on the topic, try the books listed below in recommended reading.

What do we mean by the term 'legal'?
- All aspects of life that fall under the jurisdiction of the law are referred to as 'legal'.
- The codification of society's rules and morals into regulation could be said to be the law, hence the variance in laws between countries.

The meaning of the term law:
- Development of law in a particular country is dependent on the historical, economic and cultural (including religious) contexts of an individual nation.
- It could be said that law is a set of rules laid down by either custom or practice or statute, which enforces standards of behaviour.
- Rules need to be formulated (role of Parliament) and enforced (role of the judiciary).
- There are two main sources of law: Common law and Statute law.
- Common law is largely based upon judgements made in court and may be referred to as judicial precedent.
- Statute law is largely derived from Acts of Parliament and is also termed 'legislation'.

Legal process in England:
- Parliament undertakes many roles, but a key role is the debating and passing of statute law.
- A Bill is a proposed new law. Should this be passed by Parliament, it becomes an Act of Parliament and a new law.
- Proposed laws are outlined via the Monarch's Speech in the State Opening of Parliament. Although read by the Monarch, the contents are devised by the Government of the day. Additionally, the Monarch's speech contains the Government's proposed policies for that forthcoming Parliamentary session.
- Both proposed changes to existing legislation and proposed introduction of new laws undergo set Parliamentary procedures.
- Laws are enforced through the courts system. There are a number of courts in England, with differing functions, performing differing tasks.
- Civil matters centre on issues of contract (an agreement between two parties) and tort (which concerns laws for compensation).
- Tribunals, established by various Acts of Parliament, hear particular types of cases. In an organisational context, employment tribunals and employment appeal tribunals are most significant. They exercise a judicial role, and in that sense, behave very similarly to a court.
- Trading standards investigate complaints by consumers, including inaccurate weights and measures, false pricing, safety of consumer legislation to trading standards.

Key legal influences:
- Some of the key legal influences on organisations were identified in the following areas: Employment, Health and Safety, Consumer Rights, Copyright and patent, Environmental impact of organisational operations and strategies, and Competition. Acts of Parliament and Law of Contract govern many of the aspects in the areas identified.

continued . . . ▶

◄ ... *continued*

Some emerging issues:

● One of the key ethical issues arises for global organisations is the fact that different countries have different laws. The dilemma posed is: How does an organisation operate across countries that have differing standards and laws in key areas such as the environment, employment practices, health and safety standards, competition, copyright and patent laws?

● There are two main approaches to international business ethics – ethical universalism and ethical relativism.

● Another key issue around international issues in the legal environment is the differing levels of law enforcement in different countries.

1 Name the two main sources of law.

2 With regard to law, list items contained in the Queen's speech.

3 Differentiate between courts and tribunals.

4 Identify five areas within which organisations are influenced by the legal environment. Give examples for each.

RECOMMENDED READING

If you would like to learn more about some of the issues in the sections within this chapter you might like to consider the following books.

Adams, A. (2006) *Law for Business Students*. 4th edn. London: Longman.

Elliott, C. and Quinn, F. (2005) *English Legal System*. 6th edn. London: Longman.

MacIntyre, E. (2007) *Business Law*. 3rd edn. Harlow: Pearson.

USEFUL WEBSITES

Advisory and Conciliatory Service – **www.acas.org.uk/**

BBC website – **www.bbc.co.uk**

Business Enterprise and Regulatory Reform – **www.berr.gov.uk**

Consumer Direct – **www.consumerdirect.gov.uk/**

Health and Safety Executive – **www.hse.gov.uk/**

Office of Fair Trading – **www.oft.gov.uk**

Parliament website – **www.parliament.uk**

Personnelltoday.com – **www.personneltoday.com**

REFERENCES

BERR (2008) *Competition Act 1998* (online). Available at: www.berr.gov.uk/bbf/competition/law/competition-act/index.html (Accessed 23 June 2008).

The Guardian By Agencies (2001) 'Times Chef Tells Court of Sacking'. *The Guardian*, (online) 9 January. Available at: www.guardian.co.uk/media/2001/jan/09/pressandpublishing.thetimes (Accessed 15 October 2009).

Harding, T. (2001) 'Cookery Writer for *The Times* Sacked by Email'. *The Telegraph*, (online) 9 January. Available at: www.telegraph.co.uk/news/uknews/1313891/Cookery-writer-for-The-Times-sacked-by-email.html (Accessed 15 October 2009).

McEwan, T. (2001) *Managing Values and Beliefs in Organisations*. Harlow: Prentice Hall.

Milmo, C. (2001) 'Times' Cookery Writer Tells of "Callous Sacking"'. *The Independent*, (online) 9 January. Available at: www.independent.co.uk/news/media/times-cookery-writer-tells-of-callous-sacking-703763.html (Accessed 29 November 2007).

Ofcom (2007) *Content Sanctions Committee* (online). Available at: www.ofcom.org.uk/tv/obb/ocsc adjud/yswp.pdf (Accessed 23 November 2009).

http://www.berr.gov.uk/whatwedo/sectors/sustainability/weee/page30269.html# (n.d.) (Accessed 22 October 2009).

14 The Macro Environment – Environmental Influences

'We do not inherit the earth from our ancestors, we borrow it from our children'

Native American proverb

CHAPTER OUTLINE

14.1 Introduction
14.2 What do we mean by the environment?
14.3 Key environmental influences
14.4 Emerging ethical and international issues around the environment
14.5 Analysing the effect of current and future key environmental influences on organisations
14.6 Summary

CHAPTER OBJECTIVES

After carefully reading and engaging with the tasks and activities outlined in this chapter, you should have a better understanding of:

- the causes of key environmental issues
- the consequences of environmental issues on individuals, organisations and governments
- the nature of the environmental influences and their impact on organisations
- key world initiatives combating climate change
- some of the ethical and international issues confronting organisations with regard to the environment.

Introduction

In the 1960s Joni Mitchell's popular song 'Big Yellow Taxi' highlighted the adverse effect human activity could have on the planet. The opening line indicates that the environment is being swallowed up by man-made constructions. The song goes on to demand that products, such as insecticides with potentially harmful animal and human side effects no longer be used. A chilling line in the song further suggests that trees would end up in a museum, where people would be charged to see them. This realisation that human activity could have a potentially adverse affect on the planet is not a new phenomenon. Below is a quotation from the late nineteenth century that despairs about man's treatment of the environment.

'Man has been endowed with reason, with the power to create, so that he can add to what he's been given. But up to now he hasn't been a creator, only a destroyer. Forests keep disappearing, rivers dry up, wild life's become extinct, the climate's ruined and the land grows poorer and uglier every day.'

(Russian playwright Anton Chekhov, in *Uncle Vanya*, 1897)

However, the beginning of what is now known as the environmental movement did not begin until the 1960s. At that time there was a growing realisation by individuals, organisations and governments that the environment was being affected adversely by human activity, by increasing population and by the industrial and technological processes across the world. As a result of this, there has been a growing demand from varied parties across the world for economic growth to occur without damaging the environment. We refer to this as **sustainable development**.

KEY TERMS

Sustainable development is referred to by the Report of the World Commission on Environment and Development as: '. . .sustainable development. . . implies meeting the needs of the present without compromising the ability of future generations to meet their own needs.' (UN, 1987)

This has become the most widely accepted definition of sustainable development.

Sustainable development is widely accepted to include three elements: economic, social and environmental. This chapter's focus is on the environmental aspect of sustainable development. However, we acknowledge that this is just one part of the tripod of elements underpinning the concept of sustainable development.

Organisational responses to environmental influences in action: the retail sector

Many organisations have Corporate Social Responsibility (CSR) policies that outline their organisation's social and environmental policies. Jones et al. (2005) note that retailers have taken on board issues relating to the social, environmental and economic impacts of their actions due to a number of reasons, such as growing awareness by consumers, new laws, pressure from investors, media interest, governmental pressures and the development of information technologies. There are some well-known environmental policies in the retail sector. In the case study below, we consider two examples: Marks and Spencer and John Lewis partnership, both known for their commitment to environmental policies.

CASE STUDY

Marks and Spencer (M&S)

Plan A, a wide ranging environmental plan containing 100 points to be achieved over 5 years, was launched early in 2007, at a planned cost of £200 million. Plan A, over a time frame, had commitments to, among other things: combat climate change, increase energy efficiency, use more renewable energy, reduce waste, use sustainable raw materials, use more recyclable products and promote healthy lifestyles to their customers. Plan A was acknowledged to have a very large impact on M&S, transforming its operations, as it aimed, over time, to become carbon neutral.

John Lewis Partnership

The John Lewis Partnership has a Corporate Social Responsibility policy, in which their key environmental initiatives are outlined. In addition to strategies such as the reduction of its carbon emissions and sourcing materials in a sustainable manner, John Lewis is also embarking on other innovative initiatives. In 2007, one of its new Distribution Centres – due to open in 2009 – was located in a park with leading-edge environmentally sustainable features, such as use of renewable energy, leading to an overall reduction of carbon dioxide by about 40 per cent, with energy savings of around £250,000. Their other environmental initiatives include:

- ethical sourcing standards, and selling sustainable and responsibly sourced products
- designing and building shops and warehouses to operate sustainably
- combating climate change by: improving energy efficiency, reducing carbon dioxide emissions, sourcing electricity from green sources and reducing carbon dioxide emissions caused by transportation of store deliveries

continued . . . ▶

◄ *. . . continued*

- reducing waste and increasing the amount of recycling
- working with and help improve their suppliers' environmental sustainability

(Sources: Bowers, 2007; John Lewis, 2008; The Crown Estate, 2007; http://plana.marksandspencer.com/about (n.d.)).

1 Why do you think many organisations in the retail sector, for example M&S and John Lewis, have environmental policies?

2 The case study highlights some of the environmental initiatives M&S and John Lewis partnership undertake. Choose one of the organisations, then:
- access their website (M&S Plan A or John Lewis CSR Report 2008) and research their environmental strategies in more detail, listing the main initiatives
- identify the different types departments and operations in the organisation that will be affected by the environmental initiatives highlighted above, and give some explanation as to how they will be affected.

3 Conduct desk research to ascertain the level of environmental policy statements on organisational web pages. Randomly select five from each of the following types of organisation:
- public sector
- voluntary sector
- social enterprise sector
- large plc organisations
- SMEs.

4 From the activity conducted in 3, how would you currently assess the level of environmental concern as stated in organisational policies researched?

In addition to assessing the current level of environmental concern as outlined in organisational policies, the case study considered the impact on the different departments and operational processes affected by responses made to environmental influences. Many organisations, not just those in the retail sector, are outlining their environmental policies in their organisational material, and are changing their strategies and transforming their operations to environmentally more acceptable and sustainable methods. (We have to acknowledge, however, that policy statements do not always translate into action.)

First, let's consider some environmental issues and how they impact on organisations. Oil, coal and gas are natural resources and are used to make energy. Oil is additionally a component of products, for example plastics.

REFLECTIVE QUESTIONS

Think about how much energy you use in a day. For example, do you drive a car, or take the bus? You may charge your mobile phone and watch a DVD. Maybe you do some supermarket shopping or buy a takeaway?

All these actions require energy and materials. Oil, coal and gas have fuelled the economies in both domestic and industrial terms. Our dependence on these resources is high. The question must be posed – how much stock do we have of these resources?

There is general agreement that world oil reserves will run out someday (with some predictions ranging from between 25 and 100 years), although there is some dispute as to when that time exactly will be. It is also widely acknowledged that before that point is reached, when oil production has peaked, oil will become more difficult (and hence more costly) to extract.

The implications for individuals, organisations and governments are enormous. Oil is one of a number of key natural resources that underpins the developed and developing economies' economic growth. The following key areas could affect organisations:

- energy requirements, where cost effective alternative energy sources will be needed
- replacement of oil as a component of products.

Is this all bad news for organisations, or does it create opportunities for organisations? Some organisations have built up their success by providing biofuels – an alternative fuel to oil.

Example

Brazil is one of the world's largest producers of sugar cane and **ethanol**. Ethanol has been a fuel, termed biofuel, for motor vehicles in Brazil for just over 20 years. In fact, in Brazil you will find a choice of three types of fuel at the vast majority of filling stations: ethanol; petrol and 20 per cent ethanol blend; and petrol.

In 2007, over 80 per cent of cars were modified so that they could run on ethanol/ blend or petrol. Brazilians could be said to have the most environmentally friendly cars in the world.

(Sources: Lynch, 2007; and Turton, 2007)

KEY TERMS

Ethanol is the term given to the chemical ethyl alcohol, commonly called alcohol, a reference to its use in alcoholic beverages. When processed appropriately, ethanol can be used as a fuel. An efficient way to produce this biofuel is by the fermentation of sugar cane.

As can be seen from the above example, there are opportunities for organisations in the energy sector. Brazilian companies are currently investing billions of dollars in the industry in order to increase ethanol production, with the ultimate aim of increasing global exports of ethanol. However, some critics suggest that ethanol production cannot be undertaken on a very large scale, as the earth does not have the capacity to replace oil with biofuels. This is because not enough crops could be grown to service global demand without impacting on deforestation and on people's reliance on these crops as food.

Even where oil, coal and gas supplies are abundant (e.g. currently China has large coal stocks and Russia has large oil reserves) a vexing question to consider is should supplies be used at current, or even at increasing rates? They cause pollution and contribute to our major pollution problem **global warming** (which will be considered in more detail throughout the chapter). Consequences of global warming include heat waves, flooding, rising sea levels and melting glaciers.

KEY TERMS

Global warming is the term given to the increasing temperature of the Earth's surface. This occurs when gases such as carbon dioxide, termed 'greenhouse gases', are released into the atmosphere. This causes heat to be trapped and the planet to warm up.

CASE STUDY

In July 2007, England experienced the worst flooding for 60 years, with large parts of Gloucestershire under water and no power supplies to approximately 250,000 homes in the area. There were also some parts of Oxfordshire under water. This followed severe flooding in Yorkshire. where parts of Sheffield city centre were under six feet of water. Thousands of homes and businesses have been destroyed in these two major floods, with the cost put at billions of pounds.

At the same time, parts of southern Europe had experienced severe heat waves, with over 500 hundred deaths (the majority in Hungary) attributed to the intense heat. The temperature across southern Europe at times reached over 40°C. The increasing numbers of fires across Greece, lead key figures in the Greek Government to be concerned about the impact of these high temperatures on the tourist industry.

(Sources: BBC News, 2007; Smith et al, 2007)

Figure 14.1 Floods

Figure 14.2 A forest fire

In 2007, the wet weather in the UK affected organisations in different ways. The services such as police, fire and rescue teams in the flooded areas found themselves overstretched. UK holiday bookings decreased in the month of the flooding. General retail sales in England declined in the months of June and July. This was attributed to the wet weather. However, some products had increased sales:

- pizza restaurants and takeaways
- umbrellas
- raincoats
- overseas holidays.

In addition to global warming, another major concern is pollution. Industrial processes can lead to chemical pollution. This can occur in the air, land or sea. Pollution is not necessarily confined to the place it occurs. For example, chemicals dumped into a river will often end up in the sea.

Organisations can be affected by environmental influences in many ways. As with all the external influences considered in the second part of this book, these environmental influences can present both opportunities and threats.

CASE STUDY

Barclays plc has invested substantial sums of money in order to achieve its goal of becoming carbon neutral. In 2007, at the Business in the Community Environmental Impact awards, it was awarded the Environmental Leadership Award. Barclays had led the way in offering new environmental products and services. Additionally, in 2006, in its own operations, had managed to reduce office waste and energy used in its offices and buildings, and they reported a saving of £500,000 by the use of energy efficient investments (Business in the Community, 2007).

As can be seen in the case study above, Barclays plc responded to environmental influences and by doing so have saved money in some departments, reduced energy use, cut down waste and possibly gained a business advantage by being one of the first companies to implement these steps. More and more organisations are beginning to respond to these environmental issues.

Issues such as dwindling oil resources, industrial pollution and global warming are just a few examples given of the types of environmental issues shaping the world we live in today. The authors acknowledge that very few texts to date will have included the environment as a key external influence. Most texts include the environment as part of the sociocultural (S) element of a PEST analysis; as a stakeholder, or as an ethical issue. We argue that the inclusion of the environment as an element in an external analysis is a firm acknowledgement of the fact that the environment is now a key external influence affecting organisations. As such, it needs to be incorporated into any macro external analysis conducted by organisations.

Accordingly, this chapter aims to introduce you to some of the complexities for organisations that arise from the key environmental influences.

14.2 What do we mean by the environment?

The term 'environment' for the purpose of this chapter, refers to the physical environment of the planet. This includes land, sea, air and fresh water. It is the reliance and treatment by humans of the environment over years and the consequences of this human activity that is the dominant theme in this chapter, rather than any of the natural occurrences that may alter the environmental status quo.

So our use of the term here must not be confused with the more general term of 'business environment' or 'environment of business' which is usually a reference to the:

- internal business environment, addressing issues such as those in the first part of the book
- the micro external business environment (see Chapter 8)
- the entire macro – external business environment, all the PESTLED elements.

Although it is acknowledged that there are naturally occurring environmental changes that organisations need to respond to, there is a concern that human activity is increasing the rate and pace of some environmental changes, for example, global warming. Hence, much of the focus of the chapter is on the contributions of human activity to environmental problems. It is these activities that we have a chance to address as society. Before we consider the causes and consequences of human activity on the environment it is useful to have an understanding of a brief history of environmental issues.

Historical perspectives on environmental issues

Historically, the first communities throughout the world lived as hunter-gatherers. A significant development was in the Neolithic era, when the transition from hunter-gatherer to nomadic herding and eventually to small agricultural populations occurred. From these small agricultural populations grew communities – small rural communities at first; then came towns and eventually the city states, which first brought in the pollution era (Markham, 1994). As towns and cities developed over the decades, so did the problems in terms of water and air pollution, waste management and population growth.

The industrial revolution began in the UK in the 1770s. With the advent of the steam engine and various new technological advances coupled with a new entrepreneurial culture, a new era brought in the factory as a method of production. This brought about social and economic changes and transformed the way people lived and worked. Many people moved away from rural areas to newly developing or expanding towns and cities in order to work in these factories in the new industries: paper, textiles, steel works, ship building, chemical and engineering plants. This move from rural areas to towns and cities, and increasing concentrations of people in these towns and cities, is referred to as urbanisation.

This trend of urbanisation and industrialisation then spread across the globe. New methods of transport and scientific discoveries such as electricity revolutionised the way individuals lived and worked, creating more new industries: e.g. car manufacturing, aviation, plastics. These industries were fuelled by coal (to make steam and later electricity), and oil (for example in the motor and chemical industries). The trend in urbanisation increased throughout the twentieth century, especially in developing countries, and is likely to continue. There is increasing urbanisation in less developed countries, such as Africa and Asia. The global trend in increasing urbanisation is expected to continue, with UN population figures forecasting that 60 per cent of the world's citizens will be living in cities by 2030 (UN, 2005).

The problems associated with urbanisation include pollution, run-down urban areas contributing to high levels of crime and waste disposal (think about how often you see rubbish on the streets of the UK). In developing countries, the list includes poor sanitation and vast slum areas. The positive aspects of urbanisation include good access to health and education, which in developing countries could be a key factor in contributing to an improved quality of life.

Initially, there was great excitement about scientific discoveries and technological processes, viewed as problem solvers to all current and future challenges that people would face. Resources were considered to be infinite: waste issues were not considered a problem and science and technology could only march forward for the good of humankind. In 1969, when Neil Armstrong landed on the moon, we might suppose this was a point in time at the pinnacle of hopes that anything and everything could be achieved with science and technology.

However, there became a slow realisation that:

- the planet did not possess infinite resources
- there were consequences to waste generation of industrial processes and disposal of some products
- some chemicals used produced harmful side effects to people and animals
- population and economic growth, with the increased consumption that this entailed, could not be sustained by the planet
- human activity was a contributing factor to climate change – particularly, global warming.

Three major issues underpin and exacerbate the above: population growth, increasing consumption in the developed world and increasing consumption due to developing major economies such as those in India and China. These in turn lead to increasing pressure on the environment to sustain this growth.

To encapsulate the problem, reference is often made to the disparity between consumption and the Earth's resources. For example:

'If every country consumed natural resources at the rate the UK does, we would need three planets to live on.'

(Defra, 2007, p. 1)

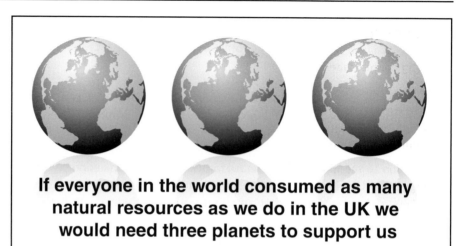

If everyone in the world consumed as many natural resources as we do in the UK we would need three planets to support us

Figure 14.3

The spark for the new emerging environmental movement

Rachel Carson's book *Silent Spring* (1962) has been widely attributed for sparking the environmental movement. A key theme of Carson's work was that humankind was but one part of nature, with a power to alter it (nature), irreversibly at times. A scientist by profession, Carson was concerned about the use of synthetic chemical pesticides and warned the public about their long-term misuse. Carson was active in calling on the US Government for new policies that would protect both human health and the environment (Lear, 1998).

From the 1960s onwards there has been a steady increase in calls to account for our treatment of the environment. The scales tipped at the beginning of the twenty-first century, with the view from most people that human activity contributes to climate change. There are now calls for individuals, organisations and governments to actively change their behaviour, to stem and reverse this tide of damage to the environment. A variety of methods are used to try and make people aware of the current environmental issues. Governments pass new laws and regulations, pressure groups use the media to keep incidents in the public domain, organisations either march forward and try and steal a competitive advantage or, wait and act only when they have to – that is, when legislation necessitates a response.

CASE STUDY

Getting the message across

What were you doing on 7th July 2007? You may have been listening to the musical performances from the Live Earth Concert – a 24/7 worldwide music event. It was billed as 'The Concert for a Climate in Crisis', and aimed to get the message across to two billion people and help start a worldwide movement to combat climate change.

In addition to the high-profile global music events to get the message about the issues of climate change across to us all, there have been films, such as *An Inconvenient Truth* made by Al Gore, former Vice President of the USA, and *The Age of Stupid* directed by Franny Armstrong. Made in 2006, *An Inconvenient Truth* is essentially a documentary film about Al Gore's own lifelong commitment to combating climate change and his attempts to get the message across to bring global warming high onto the public's agenda. Drawing on scientific evidence on climate change, and highlighting current and potential impacts of unchecked climate change, the film calls for action to be taken to reduce global warming. *The Age of Stupid* takes a different approach. The film has as its main character, a survivor of a devastated world living alone in 2055. The character watches archive footage from the year 2008 – a year where the effects of climate change were evident, such as the flash floods. The character sees this as a time when the world had a chance to prevent climate change disaster but did not (hence the title of the film).

To add to music and media events, there have been widely publicised campaigns such as the UK 10:10 campaign. Launched in September 2009, and formed by the director of *The Age of Stupid*, it has a target to cut the UK's carbon emissions by 10 per cent by the end of 2010. It calls on individuals, organisations and government bodies in the UK to sign up to the 10:10 campaign and pledge to reduce their carbon emissions by 10 per cent by the end of 2010. The campaign makes the point that you can make a difference. The campaign also hoped to demonstrate public support for taking action against global warming, and by doing so, exert pressure on the UK representatives at the crucial United Nations Climate Change Conference in Copenhagen in December 2009, to commit substantial cuts in carbon emissions.

(Sources: http://www.liveearth.org/en/liveearth/070707, n.d.; Carrington and Adam, 2009; http://www.1010uk.org/1010/what_is_1010, n.d.; Gray, 2009)

1 If you are not familiar with the above examples, go to their websites and find out more. Think about what they are trying to achieve. Do you think high-profile events, films and campaigns such as these lead to:
   ● increasing awareness of potential environmental impacts of organisations?
   ● the will to confront these challenges?
2 Think of ways that you think would be effective in informing people and organisations about climate change.
3 What might motivate you to take action?

Environmental issues and the law

There has been 'bottom up' pressure by diverse sets of people including environmental groups such as Friends of the Earth and Greenpeace, former vice-president of the USA, Al Gore, scientists, politicians and some in the business community. Over time, bottom up pressure forces changes. This occurs when public pressure from various groups forces issues to become mainstream and eventually these become codified into laws and regulations (see Chapter 13). The main environmental regulatory body in England and Wales is the Environment Agency.

There is usually a time lag between the accepted environmental issues of the day becoming codified into regulations and law. It is during this period that decisions by individuals and organisations are influenced by:

- the rate and quantity of reliable information about environmental issues becoming available
- the environmental response trends of individuals and organisations.

In time, environmental regulations and laws are passed. This may bring issues even more into the public domain and influence public perception and demands with regard to environmental issues, potentially leading to the creation of new environmental laws and/or regulations. These can affect organisations, and can be analysed under the legal element of the analysis (see Chapter 13) demonstrating the inter relationship of the PESTLED elements that can occur at times.

14.3 Key environmental influences

In order to analyse organisations' responses to environmental influences, it is useful to have some basic background knowledge and understanding of the causes and consequences of the key environmental issues currently facing us all; to be aware of the global attempts to date to tackle these issues; and to examine how these challenges currently or potentially could impact on organisations.

Causes and consequences of the key environmental issues

The environmental movement emerged in the middle of the twentieth century to challenge the assumption that the earth's resources were infinite and the belief that the way in which human beings exploited nature would not lead to any lasting harm. The main issues of concern include ozone depletion, depletion of essential forests, the **greenhouse effect** and pollution – of air, water and land.

KEY TERMS

The **greenhouse effect** is the term given to the trapping of the sun's energy by greenhouse gasses, such as carbon dioxide (CO_2).

Ozone depletion

Ozone is a gas that occurs naturally at two levels: ground level and in the upper atmosphere. At ground level ozone is considered to be a pollutant and a health hazard. In the upper atmosphere, however, the ozone gas forms what is termed the 'ozone layer'. The ozone layer plays a key role in absorbing some of the sun's harmful ultraviolet (UV) rays. However, the ozone layer was found to have been depleted in the 1980s, with notable holes over the Arctic and Antarctic, and this was found to be due to use of a specific group of chemicals, the most well known of which are the chlorofluorocarbons (CFCs), which used to be found in aerosols and old refrigerators.

	Key issues:	Action taken:
Ozone layer	• damage to ozone layer preventing UV absorption • increased exposure to UV rays leads to potential development of skin cancers and eye cataracts • increased exposure to UV rays may damage plant and young marine life.	• phasing out of CFCs by industrialised countries (UK stopped production in 2000) • if global protocols are followed, full recovery of ozone layer over the Antarctic may be achieved by 2100.
(Source: Adapted from http://www.environment-agency.gov.uk)		

Table 14. 1   A summary of the key issues

Depletion of essential forests

Tropical forests have a role to play in human life-support systems by:

• regulation of local climates
• water flows and nutrient cycles
• pools of biodiversity and
• habitats of a variety of species (Middleton, 2003).

There are two key reasons why forests have been cleared:

• the trees are used for wood or wood products
• the land is used for urban development, grazing cattle or crop growing for production of biofuels.

Throughout time, humans have cleared forests and this was the first step away from hunter-gathering to farming settlements. From then on, although deforestation occurred, its rate began to accelerate in the developing economies of the world.

The causes of deforestation include urbanisation, agricultural expansion and increasing population/migration pressures. The causes of tropical deforestation include animal grazing (e.g. cattle ranching), road building, increasing population pressures, logging and growing crops.

Although there are concerns about deforestation world wide, there are major concerns about tropical deforestation. Nature has its own way of altering the landscape of the forests as some trees catch fire, are struck by lightening or, as in the case of older trees, die naturally. Nature's cycle, however, means that these are replaced by growing trees, so overall the forest stays in dynamic equilibrium. Major disruptions take place when volcanoes or cyclones occur. However, it is human activity in deforestation that concerns us here.

Consequences of deforestation:

- concerns over possible impacts of large scale deforestation on climate change
- release of CO_2 into the atmosphere, contributing to global warming
- loss of plant and animal species, perhaps losing forever as yet undiscovered medicinal plants.

The greenhouse effect

Some greenhouse gases occur naturally in the atmosphere. The earth's temperature is kept warm by this mechanism. If the earth did not have these greenhouse gases, then the temperature would fall by 33°C, as heat would escape back out into space. This would leave the majority of earth's surface frozen. The concern is that the levels of one of the greenhouse gases, CO_2, are rising. The majority of scientists now believe that these increasing CO_2 levels have resulted in global warming. The issue here is the extent of man-made contributions to increasing CO_2 levels, and the mechanisms that will be needed to control and reduce these CO_2 emissions.

Fossil fuels are formed by natural processes that result from particular climate conditions, and take hundreds of thousands of years to form. A major debate of the early twenty-first century concerns the quantity of fossil fuel the planet has left, and whether the remaining stock is accessible and economically viable to extract: for example, the extent to which they are buried in places which make extraction prohibitively costly. Fossil fuels are referred to as **non-renewable resources**, a reference to the hundreds of thousands of years needed, under certain conditions, for them to be formed. It is useful to understand how

Figure 14.4 Coal-fired power station

the different fossil fuels contribute to global warming. Tables 14.2–14.4 give some indication of the sources and quantities of carbon released into the atmosphere.

KEY TERMS

A **non-renewable resource** is a term used to refer to a natural resource such as coal, forest and oil, which either does not replenish itself or does so at a significantly slower rate than it is consumed. We are consuming these resources at a much faster rate than they can be replaced.

Coal	Contains large amounts of carbon, which is released as CO_2 when burned.
Oil/gas	Both oil and gas contain carbon, which contribute to CO_2 emissions when burned, but produce fewer pollutant residues.

Table 14.2   Fossil fuel and carbon quantities

Carbon source	Million tones of carbon released into the atmosphere per annum
Volcanoes	circa 50
Weathering	circa 200
Burning fossil fuels	circa 5,400
(Source: Adapted from Peasgood and Goodwin, 2007)	

Table 14.3   Carbon released into the atmosphere

(Around) 20 per cent	Dissolves in the oceans.
(Around) 40 per cent	Exits the atmosphere – most likely to be taken up by additional growth of trees.
What happens to the rest?	Build-up of CO_2 in the atmosphere (most likely due to increasing human activity) that can no longer be absorbed by oceans and trees, (as they have absorbed CO_2 to capacity).
(Source: Adapted from Peasgood and Goodwin, 2007) (Please note that the information given here is represented in a simplistic format. For more detail, see the section on recommended reading at the end of the chapter.)	

Table 14.4   Excess CO_2 emissions in the atmosphere – what happens?

Organisations have been, and are likely to continue, responding to calls to lower CO_2 emissions – in product design and process, organisational processes including supply chains and in their own organisational operating systems.

Environmentalists and green groups have been urging people not to choose air travel, but to choose other methods that will result in reduced carbon emissions. The airline industry has been a target by environmentalists who are concerned at the level of CO_2 emitted by aircraft. Many argue that current levels of air travel are not sustainable, and that the level of predicted growth worldwide of air travel, which in its current form uses oil as a fuel, is totally unsustainable.

Pollution of air, water and land

Over the past two centuries, the planet has been subjected to an unprecedented increase in pollution, and this continues to increase (Markham, 1994).

The list of key concerns with regard to pollution is long, and the information given in Table 14.5 below is not exhaustive. The key problems include the exhaustion of raw materials needed to produce energy and make products; the energy required to facilitate our current lifestyles in the developed, and increasingly, developing economies; chemical processes and potential toxic

Air	• Ozone depletion. • Man-made carbon emissions from burning fossil fuels. • **Acid rain** – the affect may not be localized. For example, in the 1980s, there were concerns that power stations in the UK were emitting sulphur dioxide into the atmosphere, and acid rain was falling in the Black Forest in Germany, ruining the trees and soil. • Radioactivity – accidents such as the Chernobyl disaster, where there was an accident at a nuclear reactor at Chernobyl in the Ukraine in 1986, which released radioactive material into the atmosphere, found in countries as far away as the UK. • Other nuclear accidents.
Water	• Sewage pollution. • Agricultural pollution – pesticides, fertiliser. • Industrial pollution (e.g. from mines, chemical factories, tanneries, paper industry. Some waste is pumped into water, sometimes causing a build up of toxins (toxic chemicals). • Over-fishing, leading to depleted fish stocks. • Increasing tourism, leading sometimes to coastal development and pressure on coastal ecosystems. • Oil spillages in the sea. • Nuclear waste: old nuclear material is sometimes dumped at sea. Some of this material will take hundreds of years to lose its nuclear properties. • Carbon emissions, possibly leading to the seas becoming more acidic and less able to support plant and marine life. • Increasing droughts (some of which are attributed to climate change) leading to decreasing quantities of (usable) water.
Land	• Waste from consumption: – plastic packaging – aluminium tin cans – over packaging – leading to further resource and waste problems – batteries – white goods (e.g. washing machines, fridges, tumble dryers) – cars • over development of land – swallowing up agricultural land and eco systems (the long term effect of which is still unknown) • nuclear waste

Table 14.5   Current key concerns of air, water and land pollution

waste; and the problem of waste disposal. For example, oil, energy and chemical processes are used to make plastic. Plastic does not decompose readily, and therefore, is a big problem for waste disposal. There are also accidents that can contribute to pollution: e.g. oil spillages and nuclear accidents.

KEY TERMS

Acid rain occurs when gases such as sulphur dioxide and nitrous oxide are released into the atmosphere, react with water, and fall down to earth as acid rain or snow.

Attempts to address the environmental issues

Having grasped an understanding of the key environmental issues, it is useful to examine the attempts to address these issues. The following represent some milestones in the task to confront and minimise the impact of human activity on the planet.

The list below provides just some of the key developments over the past few decades in tackling environmental issues:

- **UN conference on the Human Environment, Stockholm, 1972**
  - First major international conference to address the world's environmental concerns, with over 100 nations taking part.
  - World Environment Day, June 5th.
- **World Commission on Environment and Development (1987) The Brundtland Report – Our Common Future**
  - Sustainable development defined.
- **United Nations Conference on Environment and Development (UNCED), Rio de Janeiro, 3–14 June 1992 (Known as 'The Earth Summit')**
  - Agenda 21 – the name given to a comprehensive plan of action to be taken at every level – locally, nationally and globally – on how to make development sustainable.
  - United Nations Framework Convention on Climate Change – an international treaty, with a key aim to reduce global warming.
- **United Nations Framework Convention on Climate Change (UNFCC) (1997)**
  - UNFCC led to the Kyoto Protocol – an international (and legally binding) agreement, with a key aim of the reduction in global greenhouse-gas emissions. The USA and Australia were not signatories to the Kyoto Protocol – the two notable absences from the developed economies.
- **United Nations Millennium Summit September 2000**
  - Eight Millennium Development Goals. World leaders adopted the UN Millennium Declaration with a commitment to combating the world's major problems. Measurable and time-bounded targets, known as the Millennium Development Goals, were set, including the reduction of extreme poverty, child mortality rates, hunger and environmental

degradation; and also including the promotion women's rights and gender equality.

- **World Summit on Sustainable Development, Johannesburg , 26 August – 4 September (2002)**
  - The Johannesburg Declaration on Sustainable Development.
  - The Johannesburg Plan of Implementation, which included reaffirmation of commitment to the Rio Principles and a commitment to the achievement of the internationally agreed development goals.
- **UN Climate Change Conference (2005) Montreal**
  - Under the Kyoto Protocol – the process for future commitments beyond 2012 got underway.
- **The Stern Review on the Economics of Climate Change (October, 2006)**
  - Significant in that the review was headed by economist Sir Nicholas Stern – a former chief economist of the World Bank. A widely cited comprehensive review, which forecast that if action was immediately taken to reduce global greenhouse gases, then the costs of action could be just 1 per cent of global GDP.
  - Using data from the **Intergovernmental Panel on Climate Change (IPCC)**, the Stern Review further forecast that if no action was taken, then the costs of unchecked climate change could be at least 5 per cent of global GDP per annum. If there was any dramatic increase in scope of risks and impacts of climate change, then this could increase costs to as much as 20 per cent of global GDP per annum.
  - The Review stressed that the costs that could help stabilise the climate, although significant, were manageable. However, any delay in tackling climate change would incur significant increasing costs and would be dangerous for the planet.
  - The Review recommended that future international frameworks should contain elements such as emissions trading, technology cooperation, action to reduce deforestation and commitments by rich countries to help poor countries with increased aid, as poor countries would be more vulnerable to climate change. (Stern, 2006)
- **The United Nations Climate Change Conference Copenhagen COP 15 (Dec 7–18 2009)**
  - Considered by many as a crucial conference, where strong global commitments to take action to tackle global warming were needed.
  - The conference was attended by representatives from countries all over the world, for what was hoped to be the agreement of a comprehensive, strong and fair global climate change deal – a truly ambitious legally binding global agreement. However, the conference ended with a bare minimum agreement that fell for short of the summits' original goals.

EU Emissions Trading Scheme (EU ETS)

An EU target of 8 per cent reduction of greenhouse gases on 1990 levels by the first Kyoto Protocol commitment period (2008–2012) was a key target for the EU. The EU Emissions Trading Scheme (EU ETS) was one of the policies introduced in order to enable the EU to meet its greenhouse gas emissions reduction target under the Kyoto Protocol.

The EU ETS began trading early in 2005. The scheme works by the allocation and trading of greenhouse gas emissions allowances throughout the EU, where one allowance represents one tonne of carbon dioxide equivalent. The scheme covers the energy intensive and heavy industrial sectors, which account for just under half of the EU's carbon dioxide emissions.

EU nations each developed a National Allocation Plan (NAP). The NAP, within the EU ETS process, establishes the amount of carbon dioxide the nation allows its organisations. Organisations in the scheme can then buy or sell emission allowances.

What this means for organisations

For organisations in the scheme, this means that at the end of the year they must make sure they have enough allowances to cover their emissions. If an organisation comes to the conclusion that it will not need all its allocated credits – because, it had reduced its energy requirements, for example, by the introduction of low carbon technologies into its operations – then there is flexibility in the scheme, in which organisations could sell any surplus allowances credits they may have generated from reducing their emissions. Alternatively, if they needed more, they could buy additional allowances credits (on top of their allocated amount).

Individual carbon offsetting is a process whereby an individual's greenhouse gas emissions are calculated, again measured in tons of carbon dioxide equivalent, and then *credits* from emission reduction projects are bought – so that an equivalent amount of carbon dioxide has either been removed from elsewhere in the world, or has been prevented from being produced. For example, if you fly to a destination (business or holiday) you can carbon offset, that is, compensate for the emissions produced with an equivalent carbon dioxide saving.

The effectiveness of schemes such as Emissions Trading Schemes and individual carbon offsetting is subject to much debate. It is widely acknowledged that it is not a cure for climate change. Strategies that actually reduce emissions and generally movements to a low carbon economy are considered to be the more effective in trying to reduce overall greenhouse gas emissions and combat climate change.

ACTIVITY

a) Think about individual and organisational responses to reducing carbon emissions (your carbon footprint).
b) Go onto the website: http://actonco2.direct.gov.uk/actonco2/home.html and identify measures individuals and organisations could use to reduce their carbon footprint.

KEY TERMS

The Intergovernmental Panel on Climate Change (IPCC) is a scientific intergovernmental body and is open to all member countries of both the UN and World Meteorological Organisation (WMO). In 1988, it was in recognition of the problem of possible global climate change, that the WMO and the United Nations Environment Programme established the IPCC. The IPCC does not conduct research into climate change and its impacts. Its role is to review and assess scientifically respected worldwide information – scientific, socio economic and technological – to help in the understanding of the risks of climate change due to human activity, and the potential socio-economic and environmental impacts.

Using the information in the section 'Attempts to address the environmental issues' as a guide

a) List four key environmental initiatives.
b) Research the key aims of each initiative listed.
c) Consider the success and limitations of each of these initiatives.

Challenges to organisations

Environmental challenges could result in opportunities or threats for organisations. Elkington et al. (1991, p. 30) suggest that environmental threats = business opportunities.

As far back as the early 1990s, Elkington et al. (1991) pointed to five benefits for businesses in 'greening' their business:

- cutting waste and saving money
- increasing energy costs will drive up fuel and therefore costs to a business (in June 2008 the price of oil rose to nearly $140 dollars a barrel – almost double that of the price in early 2007)

● corporate kudos can be gained
● staff moral can be boosted – by the encouragement to participate in positive action
● and finally, it just makes good environmental sense.

Al Gore, the former US vice-president, and a leading environmental campaigner, suggests that a responsible business can be a profitable business.

Organisations with products or processes with high carbon emissions may find their response to the environmental issues are pressing. Other industry sectors that produce items, or by products that are non bio degradable on disposal, polluting, energy intensive, land consuming, or water intensive, may find the need to act sooner rather than later. Changing weather patterns will contribute to changing consumption habits. It remains to be seen which organisations will view the environmental concerns as threats, or opportunities to be taken.

The environment – organisational opportunity or threat?

1 Think about the environmental issues shaping the world we live in.
2 List the industry sectors that you think may be threatened from changing views and consumption patterns because of issues such as global warming, deforestation and pollution concerns, giving reasons for your answers.

There is still some disagreement over the existence and causes of climate change and although the debate continues, there seems to be a growing consensus to the belief that the climate is changing and that human activity is a significant contributor to climate change – hence, all the global initiatives highlighted previously in this chapter. Sustainable development now features high on many governments' and organisations' agendas.

REFLECTIVE QUESTIONS

Do you think sustainable development is achievable?

14.4 ## Emerging ethical and international issues around the environment

Organisations are not the only bodies required to respond to environmental issues. It is a challenge that affects individuals, governments and organisations. There is at times an inter-relationship between the affected three parties. This relationship is complex, as the three groups have conflicting agendas at times.

Emerging ethical issues around the environment

These are shown in Table 14.6 below.

	Conflicting agendas
Individuals	• Normally desire full employment, economic growth. How does this tally with government aims for sustainability, or business survival as currently organised, which depends on ever increasing consumption?
Organisations	• Organisations that embark on environmentally friendly strategies, may find that it means they have to charge higher prices to the consumer, but will consumers be willing to pay the higher price? • Organisations that follow environmental laws and regulations in their own country may find that they are at a competitive disadvantage with organisations that do not have as stringent environmental controls.
Governments	• Across the world, most governments are judged on their ability to manage the economy, which up to now has been the level of economic growth achieved. How does this tally with any sustainable agenda the Government might have? • Governments are elected (in democratic countries) by the people. Sustainability may require asking *voters* to alter their lifestyle, for example, give up the car/flying. How does this tally with a government's aim to be re-elected?
(Source: Adapted from Crane and Matten, 2004; 2007)	

Table 14.6   Ethical issues around the environment

In some ways, it is the complex relationship that brings about some ethical questions.

For example, a local authority might be intent on regeneration, and see the building or expansion of a local airport as a way to secure jobs and boost the local economy. The local population might want the jobs and a boost to the local economy, but not the noise pollution associated with an airport in close proximity to where they might live. The government might welcome the increasing employment and economic growth, but how does that assist in their aim to reduce carbon emissions with a high-carbon intensive industry and more consumption being created?

REFLECTIVE QUESTIONS

What is more ethical:
1 To give a number of people employment at the cost of increasing carbon emissions?
2 Or, to stem the increase of carbon emissions, by blocking plans for development or expansion at a UK airport, but at the cost of unemployment, with all the social problems that entails?

As for organisations, their ethical approach to environmental issues can be seen as the extent to which they view CSR as a responsibility and thereby translate into organisational strategy. As we have seen throughout the chapter, many organisations have CSR policies and there is an increasing trend for their CSR activities to be audited and included in financial reporting. This is called the triple bottom-line, where not only financial data of the organisation is measured, but also social and environmental impact is reported. However problematic it is measuring non-quantifiable data (e.g. how do you accurately measure an organisation's social and environmental impact?) it can be seen as a step in the right direction.

Throughout the chapter we have given examples that highlight some of the positive organisational responses to climate change. Even with more and more organisations outlining their environmental policies, translating these into concrete action is not always achieved. Some global surveys found that not all organisations respond to challenges to combat global warming. *The Independent* (Davis, Lean and Mesure, 2008) pointed to a global survey that found revenues were still the key concern for many businesses, with many large businesses saying that environmental initiatives to combat climate change were low on their list of priorities.

The CSR approach to dealing with climate change relies on a voluntary approach, taking action above and beyond what is required by law. A key question – is this voluntary approach by individuals, organisations and government bodies enough to tackle the problem? Does the problem of global warming require faster, more coordinated worldwide action that could only be achieved by strong political commitment and legally binding targets to reduce global warming? And, if we do not manage to get these strong global commitments and agreements – what then?

The effects of the global recession from 2008 onwards have also featured on debates about combating climate change. Some have the view that organisations will move away from environmental concerns because of the recession, citing costs and competitive issues. Others, however, view green technologies and industries as opportunities for growth to help get us out of the recession.

Emerging international issues around the environment

The key issue here is that the environmental issue is a global phenomenon. As such, it requires not only individuals, organisations and governments to work together, but also individuals, organisations and governments across the world to unite on this major issue. The developing economies in India, China and transition economies in the Eastern Bloc, such as Russia, are increasing their consumption of non-renewable resources and are thereby contributing to increasing carbon emissions at a fast-growing (and some feel, very alarming) rate. In China alone, there are some estimates of 200 million more middle-class consumers that will be shortly created – buying washing machines, fridges, cars, air-conditioning units and using air travel. Their argument is that they cannot be asked to forgo increased standards of living that have been enjoyed by the developed economies for years, to resolve a problem that has been caused mainly by these same developed economies.

The importance of getting everyone committed to the environmental agenda is crucial. Some argue that the developed economies need to take action against climate change, because if they do not, then there will be no chance on getting others on board. The idea is then to assist other developing nations to join in. Climate change affects everyone in the world and, therefore, a common approach would be helpful.

The success or otherwise of this call remains to be seen. In light of all the complexities and evidence presented with regard to environmental influences on individuals, organisations and governments, you need to make your own mind up about these issues and how we should all play our part in tackling them.

14.5 Analysing the effect of current and future key environmental influences on organisations

In order to analyse the effect of the environmental influences on a particular organisation, we need to consider the environmental elements and identify which are the relevant factors that apply to that organisation.

After the key factors have been identified, the next step is to analyse how each one of them impacts on the organisation, and decide whether it represents a threat that needs to be minimised, or an opportunity that can be taken advantage of. When analysing environmental influences you will find that they have varying degrees of importance for different organisations. For some organisations it might be the level of current use of fossil fuels that is most important, while for others it might be the impact of climate changes.

It is important not only to describe factors, but also to think through what they mean and how they affect the organisation in the present and how their impact on the organisation might change in the future. Considering how and why the present is different from the past can be useful for your analysis.

ACTIVITY

Choose an organisation and, using the template in Table 14.7 below, analyse how the environment impacts on your chosen organisation.

Top tips:
- Make sure you systematically consider each of the elements.
- Carefully analyse how each in turn might affect the organisation now and in the future.
- Assess the likely impact as high, medium or low.
- In light of your assessment, consider what action might be appropriate. For example, for any future trends that seem likely, you might wish to monitor the trend and/or prepare action plans for the organisation, so it is ready to exploit opportunities or minimise any threats.

Macro environmental element	What is the current status?	What seems to be the trend? Why – give reason/s	Likely current impact on organisation: ● high ● medium ● low	Potential future impact on the organisation: ● high ● medium ● low	Suggested action:

Climate change:
  – temperature
  – rainfall
  – other.					

Energy supplies:
  – fuel
  – electricity
  – other.					

Air pollution:
  – ozone
  – carbon emissions
  – acid rain
  – gas emissions
  – other.					

Water pollution:
  – sewage pollution
  – pesticides
  – toxic chemical by products
  – oil pollution
  – over fishing
  – pressure on coastal region due to tourism
  – other.					

Access to water					

Land
  – waste, such as plastic, packaging, batteries, chemical
  – other types of land pollution
  – resource access					

▶

Macro environmental element	What is the current status?	What seems to be the trend? Why – give reason/s	Likely current impact on organisation: ● high ● medium ● low	Potential future impact on the organisation: ● high ● medium ● low	Suggested action:
Emerging ethical issues					
Emerging international issues					
Other relevant environmental issues					

Table 14.7 Template for analysing the effect of current and future key environmental influences on organisations

 ## Summary

The chapter began with an introduction to environmental issues and the concept of sustainable development. Key issues of global warming, pollution and dwindling stocks of non-renewable resources were introduced.

The term 'environment', as used in this chapter, was clarified. The chapter then considered the historical background and influences that led to the present-day environmental issues. It went on to provide key environmental issues shaping our world, and the need for organisations to respond to these influences. Finally, the chapter presented the complexity surrounding these issues.

KEY IDEAS

Some of the main points covered in this chapter are listed below. If you feel unsure about any of them, revisit the appropriate section. If you would like some additional reading on the topic, try out the books listed below in recommended reading.

What do we mean by the term 'environment'?
● The term 'environment', for the purpose of this chapter, refers to the physical environment of the planet, which includes land, sea, air and fresh water.
● Naturally occurring environmental changes can occur, however, there is concern that human activity is increasing the rate and pace of some environmental changes such as global warming.

continued . . .

◄ *. . . continued*

Historical perspectives on environmental issues

- As towns and cities developed over the decades, so did the problems in terms of water and air pollution; waste management; and population growth.
- From the industrial revolution in the UK onwards, pollution and urbanisation have increased.
- Science and technological achievements initially were seen as a 'cure-all' for humankind.
- There was a slow realisation that pollution, over-use of resources, and waste issues were affecting the planet's environment and ultimately affecting the climate.
- Population growth and increasing consumption in the developed and developing economies were exacerbating these environmental problems.
- The environmental movement as we now know it, began in the 1960s.
- Public and scientific pressure causes the enactment of environmental laws and regulations.
- The time lag between this happening is a crucial area where organisations need to decide how to respond to environmental influences.

Causes and consequences of the key environmental issues:

- Ozone depletion, essential deforestation, greenhouse effect and pollution – air, water and land were explained and their consequences examined.

Attempts to address the environmental issues:

- From the first major international conference to address the world's environmental concerns – the UN conference on the Human Environment, Stockholm, 1972, key initiatives to date include Agenda 21, the Kyoto Agreements and the Stern Report and The United Nations Climate Change Conference Copenhagen COP 15.

Challenges to organisations:

- The response of an organisation to these environmental issues could be an opportunity or a threat.
- Some industries and sectors will be winners as consumers change their habits in changing climatic conditions.
- Some industries and sectors will be losers as consumers change their habits in changing climatic conditions.

Some emerging issues

- Organisations are not the only bodies required to respond to environmental issues. It is a challenge that affects individuals, governments and organisations.
- It is the complex relationship that brings about some ethical questions when there are conflicting agendas, such as lower carbon emissions versus jobs, strong government leadership (maybe asking voters to do unpopular things like using the car less) versus re-election and keeping voters happy.
- Organisations' ethical approach to environmental issues can be seen by the extent to which they view CSR as a responsibility and thereby translate into organisational strategy and their operations throughout.
- The key international concern is that the environmental issue is a global phenomenon. As such, it requires individuals, organisations and governments across the world to unite on this major issue.
- The importance on getting everyone on board is crucial.
- Some argue that the developed economies need to take action against climate change, because if they do not, then there will be no chance on getting others on board. The idea is then to assist other developing nations to join in.

1 List the causes of key environmental concerns.

2 Outline some major global initiatives attempting to tackle these environmental concerns.

3 How are organisations beginning to respond to these environmental initiatives? Give some examples.

4 What do you the think is the role of consumers and governments in combating climate change should be?

RECOMMENDED READING

You might like to consider the following titles.

Brown, N.J. and Quiblier, P. (1994) *Ethics and Agenda 21: Moral Implications of a Global Consensus: Ethics & Agenda 21* United Nations (21 Oct).

Carson, R. (1962) *Silent Spring.* Boston, MA: Houghton Mifflin.

Crane, A. and Matten, D. (2007) *Business Ethics.* 2nd edn. Oxford: Oxford University Press.

Dresner, S. (2002) *Principles of Sustainability.* London: Earthscan Ltd.

Peasgood, A. and Goodwin, M. (2007) *Introducing Environment.* Oxford: Oxford University Press.

The World Commission on Environment and Development (1987) *Our Common Future.* Oxford: Oxford Paperbacks.

USEFUL WEBSITES

Business in the Community – **www.bitc.org.uk/**

Department for Environment, Food and Rural Affairs – **www.defra.gov.uk/**

Intergovernmental Panel on Climate Change – **www.ipcc.ch/**

'The Earth Summit' United Nations Conference on Environment and Development (UNCED), Rio de Janeiro, 3–14 June, 1992 **www.un.org/geninfo/bp/enviro.html**

United Nations Framework Convention on Climate Change – **unfccc.int**

United Nations Framework Convention on Climate Change Kyoto Protocol – **unfccc.int/kyoto_protocol/items/2830.php**

End Poverty 2015 Make it Happen. The 8 United Nations Millennium Goals – **www.un.org/millenniumgoals/bkgd.shtml**

REFERENCES

BBC News (2007) 'July Floods: At-a-Glance'. *BBC* News, (online) 30 July. Available at: http://news.bbc. co.uk/1/hi/uk/6911778.stm (Accessed 18 December 2009).

Bowers, S. (2007) 'M&S Promises Radical Change with £200million Environmental Action Plan'. *The Guardian*, (online) 15 January. Available at: http://www.guardian.co.uk/business/2007/jan/15/ marksspencer.retail (Accessed 10 November 2009).

Business in the Community (2007) *Barclays PLC – Environmental Leadership: Environment Impact Awards EDF Energy Environmental Leadership Award in association with Institute of Environmental*

Management and Assessment (online). Available at: http://www.bitc.org.uk/resources/case_studies/afe1597_barclays.html (Accessed 5 November 2009).

Carrington, D. and Adam, D. (2009) '10:10 Climate Campaign Gathers Momentum'. *The Observer*, (online) 27 September. Available at: http://www.guardian.co.uk/environment/2009/sep/27/10-10-climate-campaign-momentum (Accessed 14 November 2009).

Crane, A. and Matten, D. (2004) *Business Ethics*. Oxford: Oxford University Press.

Crane, A. and Matten, D. (2007) *Business Ethics*, 2nd edn. Oxford: Oxford University Press.

The Crown Estate (2007) *The Crown Estate Acquires 60,400sq.m. Warehouse at Gazely and Land Securities' Magna Park Milton Keyes* (online) 26 March. Available at: http://www.thecrownestate.co.uk/newscontent/92-magna-park-milton-keynes.htm (Accessed 29 October 2009).

Davis, H.T. Lean, G. and Mesure, S. (2008) 'Big business says addressing climate change "rates very low on agenda"'. *The Independent*, (online) 27 January. Available at: http://www.independent.co.uk/environment/climate-change/big-business-says-addressing-climate-change-rates-very-low-on-agenda-774648.html (Accessed 15 November 2009).

Defra (2007) *Waste Strategy for England 2007: Executive Summary* (online) Defra. Available at: http://www.defra.gov.uk/environment/waste/strategy/strategy07/documents/waste07-summary.pdf (Accessed 17 December 2009).

Elkington, J., Knight, P., and Hailes, J. (1991) *The Green Business Guide*. London: Victor Gollancz Ltd.

Gray, L. (2009) 'New Campaign to Cut UK's Carbon Emissions by 10 per cent'. *The Daily Telegraph*, (online) 1 September http://www.telegraph.co.uk/earth/earthnews/6122110/New-campaign-to-cut-UKs-carbon-emissions-by-10-per-cent.html (Accessed 14 November 2009).

John Lewis (2008) *John Lewis Corporate Social Responsibility Report 2008* (online). Available at: http://www.johnlewispartnership.co.uk/Display.aspx?MasterId=81f00253-1639-4749-a590-d2cd32540b62&NavigationId=613 (Accessed 10 November 2009).

Jones, P., Comfort, C., Hillier, D. and Eastwood, I. (2005) 'Retailers and Sustainable Development in the UK', *International Journal of Retail and Distribution Management*, vol. 33, no. 3, 207–214.

Lear, L. (1998) *The Life and Legacy of Rachel Carson: Rachel Carson's Biography* (online). Available at: http://www.rachelcarson.org/?v1=About (Accessed 2 July 2007).

Lynch, D.J. (2007) 'Brazil Hopes to Build on its Ethanol Success'. *USA Today*, (online) 28 March. Available at: http://www.usatoday.com/money/world/2006-03-28-brazil-ethanol-cover_x.htm (Accessed 19 July 2009).

Markham, A. (1994) *A Brief History of Pollution*. London: Earthscan Publications Ltd.

Middleton, N. (2003) *The Global Casino: An Introduction to Environmental Issues*. 3rd edn. New York: Oxford University Press.

Peasgood, A. and Goodwin, M. (2007) *Introducing Environment*. Oxford: Oxford University Press.

Smith, H., Burke, J. and Mckie, R. (2007) 'Over-Heated Med Stokes Tourism Fears'. *The Observer* 22 July 2007, p. 35.

Stern, N. (2006) *Stern Review: The Economics of Climate Change: Summary of Conclusions* (online) HM Treasury. Available at: http://www.hm-treasury.gov.uk/media/3/2/Summary_of_Conclusions.pdf (Accessed 23 June 2008).

Turton, S. (2007) 'Brazil's "Green" Fuel Miracle?'. *Channel Four News*, (online) 8 March. Available at: http://www.channel4.com/news/articles/society/environment/brazils+green+fuel+miracle/282947 (Accessed 19 July 2007).

UN (1987) *Report of the World Commission on Environment and Development* UNGA Res 42/187 (11 December 1987) UN Doc A/RES/42/187 (online). Available at: http://www.un.org/documents/ga/res/42/ares42-187.htm (Accessed 2 July 2007).

UN (2005) *DESA, Population Division, World Population Prospects: The 2005 Revision* (online). Available at: http://www.un.org/esa/population/publications/WUP2005/2005WUPHighlights_Exec_Sum.pdf (Accessed 5 November 2009).

http://www.1010uk.org/1010/what_is_1010 (n.d.) (Accessed 14 November 2009).

http://www.environment-agency.gov.uk/research/library/data/34413.aspx#stop (n.d.) (Accessed 10 November 2009).

http://www.liveearth.org/en/liveearth/070707 (n.d.) (Accessed 19 February 2010).

http://plana.marksandspencer.com/about (n.d.) (Accessed 10 November 2009).

15 The Macro Environment – Demographic Influences

'Basic human principles don't change, but demographics and other circumstances do, and so should our responses to them.'

(Jon Kyl, US Senator)

CHAPTER OUTLINE

15.1 Introduction
15.2 Key demographic influences
15.3 Current and emerging ethical and international issues in demographics
15.4 Analysing the effect of current and future demographic influences on organisations
15.5 Summary

CHAPTER OBJECTIVES

After carefully reading and engaging with the tasks and activities outlined in this chapter, you should have a better understanding of:
- the concept of demographics
- key factors and trends in demographics
- how demographics affect organisations
- the current and emerging ethical and international issues in demographics.

15.1 Introduction

Populations change over time. For example, the average age of the population may increase. It is important for organisations to follow, analyse, and as Jon Kyl suggests, respond accordingly to change, because demographic trends could influence what customers demand and value, and therefore impact the organisation's operations and markets.

Demographic trends could affect organisations in a number of ways (Palmer and Hartley, 2002):

- They determine the size of the potential market for the organisation's products or services. For example, the healthy ageing population in the UK has created a market for organisations such as Saga, which focuses exclusively on the provision of services, including holidays, insurance and financial products, for people aged 50 and over.
- They can have an impact on the availability of human resources. UK call centres, which rely on the availability of relatively cheap and young human resources, generally operate in some of Britain's most depressed areas. Controversially, many call centres have relocated to countries such as India, where there is an abundance of staff that can be well paid in local terms, but at a fraction of UK wages (Sabbagh, 2003).
- They have an impact on public sector services. The number of children in an area will determine the need for local schools and teachers. The decrease in student numbers in Lancashire and Liverpool has led the way to school mergers in an attempt to curb unfilled school places (BBC News, 2003).
- They can ultimately impact not only on organisations, but also the community as a whole as well as government and economic systems. As the numbers of older people escalate and the cost of state pensions gets bigger, cuts in these will be unavoidable, and governments might need to look at immigration policies to help stabilise the labour force (Duncan, 2007).

CASE STUDY

According to Hometrack, landlords with large property portfolios own 82 per cent of rental property. This type of investor can take advantage of the weak housing market by buying properties that have been for sale for a long time, at about 20 per cent below their market value, and then renting them out.

The credit crunch means there are fewer buyers in the market and more demand for rental property. According to Paragon Mortgages, rents are predicted to increase by 5.8 per cent in 2009.

In addition to this, demographics also play a role in the increase in the rental market. Net known immigration into Britain is 200,000 people a year. Families are getting smaller and more people are living alone. In 2003, there were 153,000 divorces, and the rate is rising by 3 per cent a year. According to the projections of The Association of Residential Letting Agents (ARLA) demand for rental property will grow between 20,000 and 30,000 a year for the next ten years.

(Sources: Emmet, 2008; Pereira Grey, P. and Pereira Grey, 2004)

What do we mean by demographic influences?

Demography is the study of populations in terms of their size and structure, including characteristics such as age structure, income, race, and geographic distribution. Frequently, the term demography is erroneously used interchangeably with the word demographics. The term 'demographics' refers to the characteristics of a given population. So, when we refer to demographic influences, we mean the way in which the size and structure of populations impact on organisations.

15.2 Key demographic influences

The key demographic influences that we will study in this chapter are:

- size of the population
- age of the population
- geographic distribution of the population
- income, and
- employment.

The above will provide the basis for studying changes in the size and structure of the British population.

The size of the population

The UK's population has been growing since 1971 to reach 61.4 million people in 2008, of which 51.4 million live in England. Although growth has been continuous, in recent times the pace of growth has accelerated (Office for National Statistics 2008b). Since 2001 the population has grown at an average yearly rate of 0.5 per cent, compared to an average 0.3 per cent between 1991 and 2004. If past trends continue, the UK's population would reach 71 million by 2031 (Office for National Statistics).

As of 2008 the UK's population is distributed as shown in Table 15.1.

	Population (thousands)	Percentage of total UK population
England	51,446	84
Wales	2,993	5
Scotland	5,169	8
Northern Ireland	1,775	3
Source: www.statistics.gov.uk/cci/nugget.asp?id=6. .		

Table 15.1   Distribution of UK population, by country (in 2008)

The main causes of population growth are **natural change** and **migration**.

KEY TERMS

Natural change is the difference between births and deaths.
Migration is the systematic movement of a group of people.

Since the beginning of the twentieth century births have outstripped deaths in the UK. However, in the new millennium natural change is only responsible for about one third of population growth, with migration accounting for almost two-thirds of growth (Population Change, Office for National Statistics) as shown in Figure 15.1 and Table 15.2.

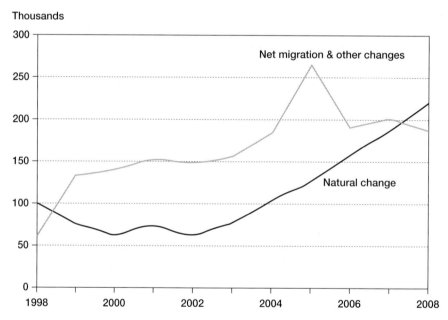

Figure 15.1 Components of population change in the UK, 1998 – 2008
Source: Office for National Statistics, 2008a

The rise in migration to the UK since 2004 reflects the enlargement of the European Union in May 2004, and removal of barriers to the people of the ten new member countries: Czech Republic, Cyprus, Hungary, Slovakia, Estonia, Latvia, Lithuania, Malta, Poland, and Slovenia.

Thousands	01–02	02–03	03–04	04–05	05–06	06–07	07–08
Population at start of period	59,113	59,323	59,557	59,846	60,238	60,587	60,975
Births	663	682	707	717	734	758	791
Deaths	601	605	603	591	575	571	570
Natural Change	**62**	**77**	**104**	**127**	**159**	**187**	**220**
In migration	487	514	539	601	576	605	561
Out migration	339	360	353	338	387	406	375
Net migration	**148**	**154**	**185**	**263**	**189**	**198**	**186**
Other changes	0	3	0	3	1	3	1
Net migration & other changes	**148**	**157**	**185**	**266**	**190**	**201**	**187**
Total change	210	234	289	393	349	388	408
Population at end of period	**59,323**	**59,557**	**59,846**	**60,238**	**60,587**	**60,975**	**61,383**
(Sources: Office for National Statistics, 2008a.)							

Table 15.2   Components of population change in the UK, mid-2001 to mid-2008

CASE STUDY

The Catholic Church has become an unexpected beneficiary of migration to the UK. After continuous decline in numbers in Catholic parishes, mass attendance could soar as there has been an increase in the number of Roman Catholics in the UK as a result of migration.

However, the influx of Catholic migrants also poses challenges to Catholic parishes, as many of the newcomers have limited knowledge of the English language or of life in the UK, no jobs, and nowhere to live. The Church is their first port of call when they need advice or help, and this poses an additional strain on the resources of the parishes, which in some cases find themselves acting as job and welfare centres. (Sources: Gledhill, 2007a and 2007b).

Age of the population

Although since the 1970s the UK's population has grown by approximately 8 per cent, growth has not occurred evenly across all age groups. The median age of the UK population rose from 34.1 years in mid-1971 to 38.8 in mid-2005. By 2008, 18 per cent of the population were under 16 years of age and

Percentages

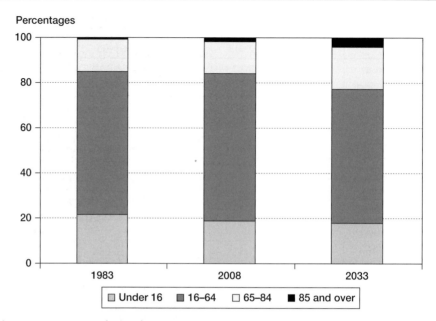

Figure 15.2 UK Population by age
(Source: Office for National Statistics, 2009a)

16 per cent over 65. This has been a consequence of the decline in fertility and mortality rates. As a result the UK has an ageing population, as shown in Figure 15.2, with the number of people aged 85 and over reaching 1.3 million in 2008 and the number of people over 65 projected to continue to increase (Office for National Statistics, 2009a).

As the population ages and medical progress makes older people healthier, it might be necessary to extend the working lives of older people so that they can continue to contribute to the economy and compensate for the smaller number of people of traditional working age. To make this possible there would be a need for essential changes in the workplace to accommodate an older workforce.

ACTIVITY

Discuss what changes might be necessary in the workplace, such as legislation, attitudes to elderly people, recruitment practices, workplace culture, to accommodate an older workforce.

Figure 15.3 B&Q staff member

CASE STUDY

The NHS is an organisation that has had to face increasing pressures from the UK's ageing population. Whereas originally there were five people of working age for every person over the pensionable age, it is expected that by 2050 the ratio will have changed to 2:1.

Despite health spending as a proportion of GDP increasing from 6.8 per cent to over 9 per cent (more in line with the European average), it will be increasingly difficult for the NHS to keep its current levels of coverage and treatment. A range of treatments may no longer be available under the NHS, as an ageing population makes them increasingly costly and unaffordable. For example, in 2007 the Government faced a public outcry when, due to cost limitations, the breakthrough cancer treatment Herceptin was made available to only some patients.

Patricia Hewitt, the Health Secretary, said that the traditional model of the NHS was no longer suitable and changes such as greater involvement by the private sector and moving care from hospitals into community-based settings and the home were necessary.

(Sources: Bhat, D. and P.A. 2006; Miles, 2006; Webster, Miles, and Rumbelow, 2007)

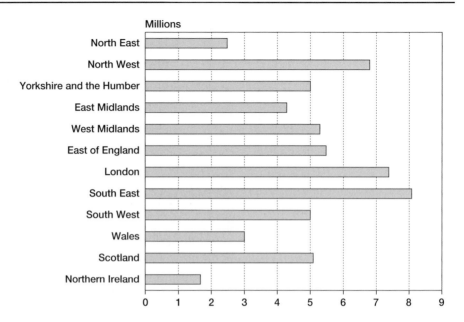

Figure 15.4 UK population size by country and government office region, 2004
(Source: Office for National Statistics, 2005c)

Geographic distribution of the population

The UK's **population density** is one of the highest in the world. However, the population is distributed unevenly between regions and countries and between urban and rural areas. The UK has pockets where the population is concentrated.

The UK regions with the largest populations are the South East of England (8.1 million), London (7.4 million) and the North West (6.8 million). At the other end of the scale, Northern Ireland has the smallest population with 1.7 million (see Figure 15.4). Twenty six per cent of the UK's population is concentrated in London and the South East despite the fact that these two regions combined only consist of less than a tenth of the UK's land area (Source: Office for National Statistics, 2005c).

 How does the geographic distribution of the UK's population impact on the NHS? Consider both supply and demand.

The highest population densities in the UK are found in London and the North West. However, there is a huge gap between the population densities of these two regions. London's population density (4,726 people per square kilometre) is almost ten times higher than that of the North West (484 per square kilometre). On the other hand, Scotland's 65 people per square kilometre makes it the region with the lowest population density in the UK (Source: Office for National Statistics, 2005c).

KEY TERMS

Population density is the number of inhabitants per unit area of land, i.e. how closely people live together.

A third of the UK's population lives in the ten largest urban areas, with 12 per cent of the population living in London, which remains the fastest growing and most densely populated British region (Office for National Statistics).

However, there is not a direct relationship between the number of people living somewhere and the population density. Although Greater Glasgow's population is the fifth largest in the UK, the city's population density is 24th in the UK. On the other hand, Brighton/Worthing/Littlehampton's population is only the 12th largest in the UK, but the area ranks second in terms of population density.

CASE STUDY

In locations with higher population density, congestion, limited and expensive parking, plus rising fuel prices have led more and more drivers to look for alternatives to owning a car or using public transport.

There is a new type of car club running around the UK, where members only pay for the actual time and distance they travel. Cars are booked for a fixed amount of time, collected from a designated spot, and returned to a designated parking space for the next member to collect them. This alternative still offers people access to a car when necessary, whether it is to do the daily school run, to do the weekly grocery shopping, or to go on weekend trips, without the hassle of owning it.

(Sources: City Car Club; Mulkerrins, 2004)

Income distribution

Income distribution patterns in the UK have changed dramatically since the 1970s, and income inequality in Britain remains high. In the 1980s, real disposable income grew by 38 per cent for the top 10 per cent of the population, but only by 7 per cent for the bottom 10 per cent (see Figure 15.5).

The gap between rich and poor has become wider with the wealthy becoming better-off, and an increase in the number of families on **low incomes**. In 2002/03, 17 per cent of households were classified as having a low income (Office for National Statistics, 2004).

KEY TERMS

Low income is where a household's income is below 60 per cent of median disposable income.

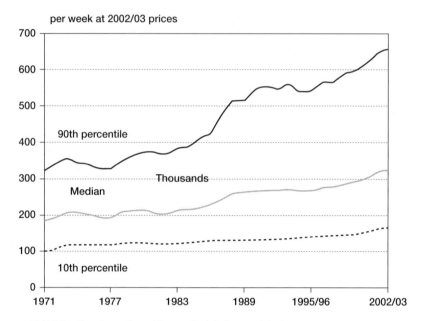

Figure 15.5 Distribution of real household disposable Income
(Source: Office for National Statistics, 2004)

The number of people in severe poverty in the UK peaked in 1997 at 8.8 per cent of households, and this trend has not reversed. The figure in 2008 is 8.7 per cent. While in 1979, 18 per cent of those on low incomes were classed as in severe poverty, in 2008 the proportion is two fifths. At the same time, the household income of the richest 10 per cent has reached peak levels not seen since the 1940s (Duncan, 2008).

The persistent high levels of income inequality could be explained by:

● a fall in male labour market participation in households where there is only one wage earner, whereas there has been an increase in female participation in the labour market, particularly in households with two wage earners.
● the increase in the gap between the wages for skilled and unskilled labour, which could be due to skills-biased technological change, and a decline in the role of trade unions.

A report from the House of Lords' Economic Affairs Committee points out that today 'millions of young people have missed vital chances to improve their skills and earnings, representing a serious loss to the country'. As the UK has moved from the manufacturing sector to the service sector, young people with no academic qualifications cannot rely on apprenticeships to learn the skills that would help them secure a job: with no qualifications and no skills they then become unemployable. Therefore, in the last few decades we have seen a gap emerge between the incomes of those people who are prepared and have the necessary skills to participate in the global economy and those who lack skills (Smith, 2007).

CASE STUDY

Ever more people, particularly those who are less affluent, use credit cards to bridge the gap between income and spending. About a third of adults in general and more than half of 25- to 34-year-olds do not pay their **unsecured debt** in full by the end of each month. The average debt is £3,500; however, a significant 13 per cent of people owe more than £10,000. Those trapped in debt are more likely to face financial difficulties if interest rates fluctuate upwards.

The debt culture has also generated debate about the lending practices of card issuers, amid fears of an exacerbating crisis in credit card borrowing.

Some credit cards have dropped the minimum payment customers have to make each month. In most cases the interest rate has only gone down by a quarter of a percentage point, but although this seems insignificant it could have a huge impact on the amount of time it takes someone to clear a credit card loan.

(Sources: Francis, 2007; Lewis, 2007)

KEY TERMS

Unsecured debt includes personal loans, overdrafts and credit cards, which are not secured against an asset, i.e. property.

Employment

The levels of employment and unemployment are also key demographic indicators which are affected by the business cycle or trade cycle. For information on employment and the business/trade cycle please refer to Chapter 10.

Figure 15.6 Shopping with a credit card

 15.3 Current and emerging ethical and international issues in demographics

Ethical issues

As people become more aware and concerned about the urgent challenge of climate change and other environmental issues (as discussed in Chapter 14), **entrepreneurs** have taken advantage of this by offering individuals and organisations the chance to reduce their **carbon footprint** for a fee.

KEY TERMS

An **entrepreneur** is someone who undertakes and operates a new business enterprise and takes some responsibility for the financial risks involved.
Carbon footprint is the amount of carbon dioxide emitted by an organisation or individual as part of their everyday operations and/or activities.

CASE STUDY

Schemes that help offset our carbon footprint are increasingly popular. However, a study conducted by the Tyndall Centre at the University of East Anglia and the Lund University in Sweden suggest that schemes that include forestry to reduce our 'carbon footprint' could take up to a 100 years to offset the emissions from one single flight.

If it takes up to a century to see results, then these schemes could be flawed. For Dieter Helm, professor of energy policy at Oxford University, they are aimed at making us feel better about ourselves without sacrificing our luxury lifestyles. He says, 'If we really want to live sustainably we are going to have to accept the knocks and give up things like flying. In the end they are unsustainable.'

The renowned economist, Jeffrey Sachs, director of the Earth Institute at Columbia University and the United Nations Millennium Project believes that the problem is 'the world's going to get a lot more crowded and it's going to get a lot more crowded in its effect on the environment'.

The Optimum Population Trust, a population control lobby group, has made a call for no more than two children per family in the UK. Professor John Guillebaud, author of its report, says, 'Each new UK birth, through the inevitable resource consumption and pollution that UK affluence generates, is responsible for about 160 times as much climate-related environmental damage as a new birth in Ethiopia'.

(Sources: Leake, 2007; McDonagh, 2007; Smith, 2007)

 Consider what are the ethical issues raised by the above case study.

International issues

In the last decade there has been an upward trend for migration to and from the UK (see Figure 15.7). In 2008 a record 427,000 left the UK to settle abroad and 590,000 people came to settle in the UK. **Net migration** was therefore 163,000. This means that 163,000 more people came to the UK than emigrated (Office of National Statistics, 2005b).

KEY TERMS

Net migration is the difference between immigration and emigration.

One of the reasons for this increase in migration relates to movement of people from the ten accession countries that joined the European Union in May 2004 (see also Section 15.2). They account for a significant percentage of people

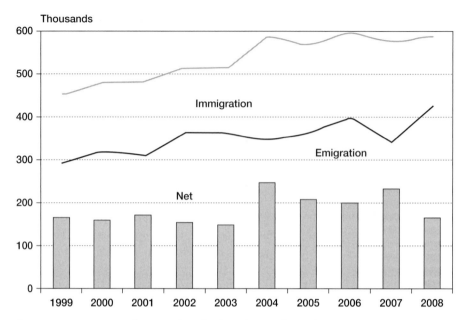

Figure 15.7 Long-term international migration to/from the UK, 1999 – 2008
(Source: Office for National Statistics, 2009b)

coming to the UK, but as they return to their home countries they also account for more than 50 per cent of non-British citizens emigrating from the UK. In the main, migration is more frequent among younger adults, with most immigrants coming either to study in the UK or to work in a specific job, and most emigrants leaving to take jobs abroad (Office for National Statistics, 2005b).

This migratory movement is changing the composition of the UK population. In 2006, 25 per cent of children born in the UK had a foreign mother or father, compared to 20 per cent in 2001. The trend is expected to continue for the next three to five years and reflects the cumulative effect of migration in the last 40 years (Ford, 2007a).

In the 50 years between 2001 and 1951, the percentage of the UK population born overseas almost doubled from 4.2 per cent to 8.3 per cent, and by 2001 one in every 12 people living in the UK had been born overseas. Whereas almost all of the UK born population is ethnically white, the overseas born population comes from a wide range of ethnic backgrounds (see Figure 15.8). Only over half of the foreign-born population is white. Other large ethnic groups settled in the UK are Indian, Pakistani, Black African, Black Caribbean, Chinese and Bangladeshi (Office for National Statistics, 2005b).

The overseas born population is also younger than the UK-born population: 75 per cent are of working age compared to only 60 per cent of the UK-born population (Office for National Statistics).

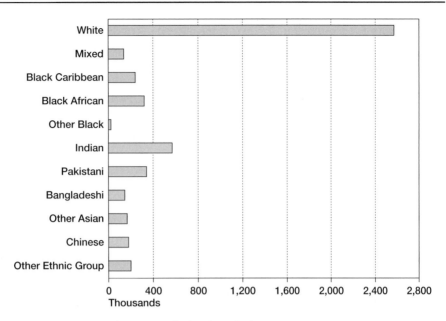

Figure 15.8 Overseas-born population by ethnic group, 2001
(Source: Office for National Statistics, 2005a.)

The above figures support the argument for opening national borders further
to foreign migrant workers as one of the necessary measures to cope with the
UK's rapidly ageing population. In any case, immigration can only be one of
the solutions to the UK's ageing population issue, since for the labour force
to become stable, migrants would be needed in such a large scale that the
process would not be viable (Duncan, 2007).

However, there is still hostility towards migration and some consider that
although migration has made Britain richer, it puts too much pressure on the
nation's resources, especially in the poorest communities.

REFLECTIVE QUESTIONS

Consider the pressures that increased migration to Britain puts on the nation's
resources.

 (15.4) # Analysing the effect of current and future demographic influences on organisations

In order to analyse the effect of demographic influences on a particular
organisation, the first step is to consider the elements of the demographic
environment and identify the relevant factors that apply to that organisation.

After the key factors have been identified, the next step is to analyse how each one of them impacts on the organisation, and decide whether it represents a threat that needs to be minimised or an opportunity that can be taken advantage of. When analysing demographic factors you will find that they have varying degrees of importance for different organisations. For some it might be the age and geographic distribution of the population that are the most important, while for others it might be income distribution.

It is important not only to describe factors, but also to think through what they mean and how they affect the organisation in the present and how their impact might change in the future. Considering how and why the present is different from the past can be useful for your analysis.

ACTIVITY

Complete the template in Table 15.2 to help you in your analysis.

Top tips:
- Make sure you systematically consider each of the elements.
- Then, carefully analyse how each in turn might affect the organisation now and in the future.
- Assess the likely impact as high, medium or low.
- In the light of your assessment, consider what action might be appropriate, for example, for any future trends that seem likely, you might wish to monitor events and/or prepare action plans for the organisation so it is ready to be able to exploit opportunities or minimise any threats.

(15.5) Summary

The word demographics refer to the characteristics of a given population. Demographic trends impact on organisations in a number of different ways. They determine the size of the potential market for organisations; they have an impact on the availability of human resources; they have an effect on public sector services; and can also influence communities, governments, and economic systems.

They key demographic trends we have studied in this chapter are the size and age of the population, geographic distribution of the population, income, and employment.

Factor	What is the current position?	What seems to be the current trend and why – give reason/s	Likely current impact on organisation: ● high ● medium ● low	Potential future impact on the organisation: ● high ● medium ● low	Suggested action:
Size of the population					
Age of the population					
Geographic distribution of the population					
Income					
Employment					
Any other relevant issues					

Table 15.2   Template for analysing the effect of current and future key demographic influences on organisations

KEY IDEAS

Some of the main points covered in this chapter are listed below. If you feel unsure about any of them revisit the appropriate section. If you would like some additional reading on the topic try out the books listed below in recommended reading.

What do we mean by demographic influences?
● When we refer to demographic influences we mean the way in which the size and structure of populations impact on organisations.

Key demographic influences
● The United Kingdom has a growing population. This is mainly due to natural change and migration.
● Although the rate of population growth has accelerated in recent years, growth has not been even across different age groups.
● The decline in fertility and mortality rates has translated into a decline in the population aged under 16 and the opposite effect for the population over the age of 65. As a result the UK has an ageing population.
● The population density of the United Kingdom is one of the highest in the world, but the population is distributed unevenly with pockets where the population is concentrated.

continued . . .

◀ | *. . . continued*

- Despite the fact that London and the South East take up less than one tenth of the UK's land area, more than 25 per cent of the UK's population lives in these regions. Scotland has the lowest population density in the UK.
- The level of inequality in income distribution in British society has increased in the last three decades.
- The persistent gap between the rich and the poor could be explained by the fact that male participation in the workplace has fallen in households where there is only one wage earner; whereas female participation in the workplace has increased, particularly in households with two wage earners.

- There has been an increase in the gap between the wages for skilled and unskilled labour.

Current and emerging ethical and international issues
- Demographic trends also raise some ethical and international issues.
- Entrepreneurs have taken advantage of the increasing awareness and concern regarding environmental issues, and now offer individuals and organisations the chance to reduce their carbon footprint.
- Some studies suggest that these schemes could take up to a century to produce results, thus questioning their credibility.
- The increased migratory movement experienced by the UK in recent years is changing the composition of the country's population.
- Some consider opening national borders to foreign migrant workers is one of the possible solutions to cope with the UK's ageing population.
- There is still hostility towards migration and concerns regarding the pressure it puts on the nation's resources.

REFLECTIVE QUESTIONS

1 Consider the impact of the increase in the size of the UK's population on an organisation of your choice.
2 Consider what organisations could be affected by the UK's ageing population. Does this trend pose an opportunity or threat for the organisations? Use the table below to record your answer.

Organisation	Opportunity/Threat	Explain

continued . . . ▶

◀ *. . . continued*

3 Consider the external macro environment. How have different factors in the macro environment contributed to increased migration to and from the UK? Use the table below to record your answers.

The external macro environment	Factors	Impact
Political		
Economic		
Social		
Technological		
Legal		
Environmental		
Demographic		

4 The income gap in the UK has become wider. Conduct research and analyse how the UK's income gap compares to that of other developed nations in the European Union and outside the European Union.

USEFUL WEBSITES

BBC – **www.bbc.co.uk**
Directgov – **www.direct.gov.uk**
Eurostat – **http://epp.eurostat.ec.europa.eu**
EU Statistics UK – **www.eustatistics.gov.uk**
General Register Office for Scotland – **www.gro-scotland.gov.uk**
The Guardian – **www.guardian.co.uk**
Northern Ireland Statistics and Research Agency (NISRA) – **www.nisra.gov.uk**
Office of National Statistics – **www.statistics.gov.uk**
The Times – **www.thetimesonline.co.uk**
Welsh Assembly Government, Statistics for Wales – **http://new.wales.gov.uk/topics/statistics/**

REFERENCES

BBC News (2003) 'Parents Angry at School Mergers'. *BBC News*, (online) 25 September. Available at: http://news.bbc.co.uk/1/hi/england/lancashire/3138954.stm (Accessed 1 July 2007).

Bhat, D. and PA (2006) 'Reforms in NHS Must Continue, Says Hewitt'. *Times Online*, (online) 19 September. Available at: http://www.timesonline.co.uk/tol/news/politics/article643906.ece (Accessed 1 July 2007).

City Car Club (online) http://www.citycarclub.co.uk (Accessed 12 November 2009).

Duncan, G (2007) 'Ageing Population Brings Grave Problems'. *Times Online*, (online) 25 June. Available at: http://business.timesonline.co.uk/tol/business/columnists/article1980413.ece.

Duncan, G. (2008) 'Divided Britain Needs New Ladder of Opportunity'. *Times Online*, (online) 28 April. Available at: http://business.timesonline.co.uk/tol/business/columnists/article3828343.ece (Accessed 25 June 2008).

Emmet, S. (2008) 'Change to Buy-to-let: Professional Investors Cash in on the Credit Crunch'. *Times Online*, (online) 9 May. Available at: http://property.timesonline.co.uk/tol/life_and_style/property/investment/article3893176.ece (Accessed 25 June 2008).

Ford, R. (2007) '1 in 4 Children Born to a Foreign Parent as Immigration Grows'. *Times Online*, (online) 23 August. Available at: http://www.timesonline.co.uk/tol/news/uk/health/article2310435.ece (Accessed 25 June 2008).

Francis, C. (2007) 'Poverty Gap "Widest in 40 Years"'. *Times Online*, (online) 17 July. Available at: http://business.timesonline.co.uk/tol/business/money/consumer_affairs/article2090632.ece (Accessed 25 July 2007).

Gledhill, R. (2007a) 'Catholics Set to Pass Anglicans as Leading Church in the UK'. *Times Online*, (online) 15 February. Available at: http://www.timesonline.co.uk/tol/news/article1386939.ece (Accessed 1 July 2007).

Gledhill, R. (2007b) 'The Polish Pastor Whose Flock Has Doubled in Just Two Years'. *Times Online*, (online) 15 February. Available at: http://www.timesonline.co.uk/tol/news/article1386945.ece (Accessed 12 November 2009).

Leake, J. (2007) 'Offsetting your Carbon Footprint Takes Decades'. *Times Online*, (online) 11 March. Available at: http://www.timesonline.co.uk/tol/news/uk/article1496888.ece (Accessed 1 July 2007).

Lewis, M. (2007) 'Why Your Credit Card Debt Could Last 40 Years'. *Times Online*, (online) 27 June. Available at: http://business.timesonline.co.uk/tol/business/money/borrowing/article1976831.ece (Accessed 1 July 2007).

McDonagh, M. (2007) 'The Cry should go Up in Europe: More Babies, Please'. *Times Online*, (online) 13 July. Available at: http://www.timesonline.co.uk/tol/comment/columnists/guest_contributors/article2067023.ece (Accessed 30 July 2007).

Miles, A. (2006) 'The NHS: Who's Going to Pay?' *Times Online*, (online) 5 April. Available at: http://www.timesonline.co.uk/tol/comment/columnists/alice_miles/article702065.ece (Accessed 1 July 2007).

Mulkerrins, J. (2004) 'Don't Want to Buy a Car? Join the Club'. *Times Online*, (online) 28 November. Available at: http://driving.timesonline.co.uk/tol/life_and_style/driving/article395888.ece (Accessed 1 July 2007).

Office for National Statistics (2004) *Income* (online) (7 December 2004). Available at: http://www.statistics.gov.uk/CCI/nugget.asp?ID=1005&Pos=1&ColRank=2&Rank=672 (Accessed 12 November 2009).

Office for National Statistics (2005a) *Foreign Born* (online) (15 December 2005). Available at: http://www.statistics.gov.uk/cci/nugget.asp?id=1312 (Accessed 12 November 2009).

Office for National Statistics (2005b) *International Migration* (online) (15 December 2005). Available at: http://www.statistics.gov.uk/cci/nugget.asp?id=1311 (Accessed 24 June 2008).

Office for National Statistics (2005c) *Where People Live* (online). Available at: http://www.statistics.gov.uk/cci/nugget.asp?id=1306 (Accessed 25 June 2008).

Office for National Statistics (2008a) *Population Change. Mid- year population estimates* (online). Available at: http://www.statistics.gov.uk/cci/nugget.asp?id=950 (Accessed 25 June 2008).

Office for National Statistics (2008b) *Population Estimates* (online). Available at: http://www.statistics.gov.uk/cci/nugget.asp?id=6 (Accessed 25 June 2008).

Office for National Statistics (2009a) *Ageing* (online) (27 August 2009). Available at: http://www.statistics.gov.uk/cci/nugget_print.asp?ID=949 (Accessed 12 November 2009).

Office for National Statistics (2009b) *Migration* (online). Available at: http://www.statistics.gov.uk/cci/nugget.asp?id=26 (Accessed 12 November 2009).

Office for National Statistics (2009c) *Population Change* (online). Available at: http://www.statistics.gov.uk/cci/nugget.asp?id=950 (Accessed 12 November 2009).

Palmer, A. and Hartley, B. (2002) *The Business Environment*. 4th ed. Maidenhead: McGraw- Hill.

Pereira Grey, P. and Pereira Grey, D. (2004) 'Housing Foundations Remain Rock Solid: Demographic and Financial Forces Still Support Property'. *Times Online*, (online) 23 November. Available at: http://property.timesonline.co.uk/tol/life_and_style/property/article394481.ece (Accessed 1 July 2007).

Sabbagh, D. (2003) 'BT Defends Transfer of Call Centres to India'. *Time Online*, (online) 17 July. Available at: http://business.timesonline.co.uk/tol/business/article1151732.ece (Accessed 1 July 2007).

Smith, D. (2007) 'Our Real Poverty is in Lack of Skills'. *Times* Online, (online) 22 July. Available at: http://business.timesonline.co.uk/tol/business/columnists/article2115125.ece (Accessed 25 July 2007).

Smith, D. (2007) 'We Have to Know when to Stop'. *Times Online*, (online) 15 April. Available at: http://women.timesonline.co.uk/tol/life_and_style/women/the_way_we_live/article1654452.ece (Accessed 1 July 2007).

Webster, P., Miles, A. and Rumbelow, H. (2007) 'NHS will 'Run Out of Funds for Best Drugs': Health Chief Warns of Treatment Rationing'. *Times Online*, (online) 13 January. Available at: http://www.timesonline.co.uk/tol/news/article1292482.exe (Accessed 1 July 2007).

INDEX